HIT THE DRUM

AN INSIDER'S ACCOUNT OF HOW THE
CHARTER SCHOOL IDEA BECAME A
NATIONAL MOVEMENT

SARAH TANTILLO

TABLE OF CONTENTS

PART III
ROOTS TAKING HOLD

INTRODUCTION

Whether you know much about charter schools or not, you have prob-
ably—at some point in your life—wondered: *Why is K-12 education the
way it is? Why isn't it more the way I want it to be?* People have asked
themselves these questions for decades and have made countless attempts
to reform "school" as we know it.

To understand how we got to where we are and how charter schools
came about, it may help to recall some highlights of American education
in the 20th century:

In the early 1900s, while African-Americans in the South struggled
with discriminatory Jim Crow laws, a flood of immigrants poured into the
country and typically found blue-collar jobs in factories, coalmines, and
mills, and on farms—jobs that did not require much education. During
the Great Depression in the 1930s, putting food on the table continued to
be more of a priority than education (My own grandparents—children of
immigrants—were fairly typical in that regard: none of them made it past
the 8th grade).

In the 1940s and 1950s, as the economy improved, occupational
and educational opportunities expanded—for some. For women, limitations persisted: the general expectation was that you could be a secretary,
a nurse, or a teacher, or you could get married. Many highly intelligent
women went into classrooms, and for various reasons, were poorly paid

(e.g., they were not viewed as the primary breadwinner), a problem that would have long-term consequences for the field. As opportunities for women in the workforce increased, it would become increasingly difficult to recruit top college graduates to these low-paying teaching positions.

In the 1960s, racial conflicts and riots in major cities caused teaching shortages. Anyone with means—families with enough money and teachers who wanted to avoid the violence—fled to the suburbs. To fill the gaps, districts often resorted to hiring staff with emergency certificates—individuals who were not fully qualified and who might not have passed the National Teacher Examination. These under-qualified, under-trained teachers were "grandfathered in," receiving certification and then tenure, and they became impossible to fire, no matter how ineffective they were.

Over the next few decades, many inner-city schools fell prey to this pattern: bring in children who can't read, don't teach them how to read—year after year—and socially promote them through 8th grade. In high school, many students became frustrated, realized they would never pass their classes, and dropped out.

In 1983, the Reagan Administration released *A Nation at Risk*, a report that made clear that many American public schools were failing.

Eight years later, in 1991, the first charter school law was passed, and a year after that, the first independently governed public school of choice was opened. The idea of chartering spread rapidly across the country. Within two decades, many charter schools had long waiting lists and parents willing to march on their behalf. By 2017, more than 6,900 charter schools were operating in 44 states plus DC, serving 3.2 million children.[1] Today, in spite of the controversy that often swirls around them, these schools have dropped strong roots into the field of education.

How and why did this happen? Who made the idea of charter schools spread, and why? How important are charter schools? How have they affected the field of education and how parents view schools? What's next?

As a high school teacher who jumped into the charter school movement in 1996 and led state-level efforts in New Jersey, I knew parts of the story, but no one had answered these questions to my satisfaction. One day I thought: *Now that it's clear that charters are not going away, someone ought to explain how this happened and what it might mean for education more broadly. Also: people need to see how individuals can change the world and how an idea can become a social movement.*

This book traces the work of several dozen key players. Although I've included some of my own experiences in this narrative as a way to connect a few dots, I don't think for a second that I have played anything more than a bit part.

The charter school movement is the result of contributions of *thousands* of hard-working, committed citizens, and it would be impossible to tell all of their stories. My sincere apologies to everyone I was unable to include (PS, I am hoping to write a sequel!). I hope that the individuals I've highlighted will capture the spirit of this remarkable collective effort. With great humility and respect for everyone in the field, I hope this narrative will be of some use.

PART I

FIRST STEPS

CHAPTER 1

SEEING WHAT'S POSSIBLE: DAY ONE AT NORTH STAR ACADEMY

In September 1997, the first thirteen charter schools in New Jersey opened their doors.

As the Coordinator of the New Jersey Charter School Resource Center, I had spent the past year helping the schools' founders. They had countless questions: *How do we reach out to parents? Who should be on our board? Can we turn an old factory into classrooms? How can we convince students to come? How will we bus them? What do we feed them? How can we order desks and chairs and books and pay teachers without any money up front? Can someone please give us a grant?* We had all been running at a full sprint for months.

So it was with great eagerness and curiosity that I drove to Newark to visit North Star Academy Charter School on the day it opened.

At first it didn't seem like much. I arrived shortly before noon, and co-founder Norman Atkins—in a shirt and tie with his sleeves rolled up—stood surveying the large multi-purpose room, where 72 fifth- and sixth-graders, a sea of green polo shirts and khaki pants, sat at long fold-down tables in half of the room, eating lunch. "We gave them cake," Norman said with a sheepish grin, "to celebrate the birth of the school."

He shrugged, probably sharing my thought that giving the kids so much sugar might have been a mistake. But as we looked around, no one seemed too hyped up. Several teachers, along with co-founder Jamey Verrilli, were circulating and giving students quiet directions about how to clean their tables. Each table had its own bucket and sponge.

All morning, Norman informed me, students had been in classrooms learning about the four Core Values: Caring, Respect, Responsibility, and Justice. He showed me the one-page document that each student had received, the Core Values pledge.

Now they were going to have their first Community Circle.

Jamey strode into the middle of the tables and raised one hand with two fingers together. He pivoted to show the sign. Within a moment, the cafeteria became hushed, then silent. Jamey praised their effort for following the signal, then directed students to finish cleaning up and return to their seats. In a minute, they would have a special Circle.

Moments later, the students formed a giant circle in the open half of the multi-purpose room. Then, for the next 20 minutes, while the students stood as still as they humanly could, Jamey and Norman began to lead a discussion—a discussion with lots of questions and interaction, not a lecture—with these 72 fifth- and sixth-graders about the school's Core Values. They talked about what it means to be caring ("What does it look like? Can someone give us an example?"), to show respect ("How can you tell when someone respects you? How can you tell when they don't? What do they do?"), and to be responsible ("What kinds of things do you do at home that show you're responsible? What kinds of things can you do—*should* you do—here in school to show responsibility?"). They considered the meaning of "justice"—what it looks like, what it doesn't look like, and what it would look like at North Star ("You have a right to get a great education, and we're not going to let anyone interfere with that. And that also means that you cannot prevent any of your peers from learning. For example, if you disrupt class, if you take away from someone else's opportunity to learn, if you try to prevent their star from shining, there will be consequences for that."). They also talked about what it means to be part of a community, how "we can all help one another so that *all* of our stars can shine."

In the middle of the circle was a small folding table, and next to it was a tall djembe drum. The name of this African drum derives from a saying that translates to "everyone gather together in peace," and the drum is used to call people together for important ceremonies. On this first day at North Star, no one had touched the drum yet, but from this day forward, every morning, several students would be given the honor of playing the djembe to welcome the community to join the Morning Circle.

Now Jamey, satisfied that students had a clearer idea of what was written on the Core Values pledge, intoned the following: "We've talked about the Core Values; we've talked about what it means to be part of a community. If you choose to accept and respect these values, if you would like to be part of *THIS* community, here is what I would like you to do. One by one, I want you to come up to the table, sign this pledge which we have just talked about, put it under this drum, then hit the drum—*HARD*, like this." He hit it hard. Amidst his commanding silence, the *PWOWW* reverberated for us all to contemplate. Then he said, "After you hit the drum, come and join the circle with the rest of us, the teachers and the other students who have chosen to be part of this community."

Then, one by one, each student walked up, signed the pledge, hit the drum, and returned to the circle. As we all stood there, the only sound was the loud slam of each child's fist on the drum. *PWOWW. PWOWW. PWOWW....*

I felt my heart being pulled in. As I watched and listened and fought back tears, all I could think was, *If this is the FIRST day of school, what is TOMORROW going to be like? And the day after that? And the day after that? Where will these children be in 5 years? In ten? In 15? In 20? And where will Norman and Jamey be?*

On the drive home, I began to wonder: *How had Norman and Jamey accomplished this—so much, even on the first day? What did it take to build such a strong school culture? Could others do it? Would they? The charter school law offered a compelling opportunity: to create new*

Sarah Tantillo

schools from scratch. What other great schools would emerge, all across the country? And how might they affect other educators in the field? How might they change *the field?*

For me, Jamey Verrilli's invitation to "hit the drum" became a metaphor: a call to action, an invitation to join a small but growing community of educational activists—risk-takers, hard workers, committed citizens—who wanted to improve the quality of public education in cities and towns across the country. That night, I wrote in my journal: *It was a beautiful expression of hope and wisdom. These children can succeed. They will. The community they themselves are creating will hold them up. Those 72 hands that hit the drum will protect them. I hope, I hope, I hope.*

North Star became one of many schools contributing to the relentless drumbeat of reform. In its first three years of operation from 1997 to 1999, more than 900 people visited the school.[2] And in the years that followed, thousands more.

Many, like me, suddenly saw what was possible.

CHAPTER 2

A NATION AT RISK AND TIME FOR RESULTS

Where did the charter school movement come from?

One could argue that it started with *A Nation at Risk,* an alarming government report that set off ripple effects for years. Released in 1983, this report confirmed what many suspected and feared:

> The educational foundations of our society are presently being eroded by a rising tide of mediocrity that threatens our very future as a Nation and a people.... If an unfriendly foreign power had attempted to impose on America the mediocre educational performance that exists today, we might well have viewed it as an act of war.[3]

The report further asserted: "We must demand the best effort and performance from all students, whether they are gifted or less able, affluent or disadvantaged, whether destined for college, the farm, or industry."[4] Whereas previous research and reports might have blamed poverty for this lack of student achievement, *A Nation at Risk* made it clear that the problems with education affected *all* children.

Probably the most amazing thing about this report was that, unlike countless others which preceded it, it didn't get dismissed or ignored.[5]

As soon as the report came out, Al Shanker, the head of the AFT (American Federation of Teachers), sat down with other union leaders to eagerly examine its contents. Then, as Sandra Feldman (president of New York's United Federation of Teachers) recalled, "he closed the book and looked up at all of us and said, 'The report is right, and not only that, we should say that before our members.'"[6]

Al Shanker's willingness to accept the findings opened the door and made it politically safe for others to admit that the country had problems in education and needed to deal with them. Other union leaders would soon follow suit. Bob Chase, then the leader of the NEA (National Education Association) said that Shanker's "bold" decision "changed everything" and added: "Without Al's unwavering support, the report's call for educational reform and renewal would have languished."[7] Not even President Reagan, whose own Secretary of Education, Terrel Bell, had called for the report in the hope that it would improve the public perception of American education, was inclined to listen to it. None of Reagan's educational policies—abolishing the Department of Education, promoting tuition tax credits and vouchers, and restoring voluntary prayer in the schools—were mentioned. In fact, initially Reagan's aides threatened to cancel the ceremony in which he was to receive the first copy. (They later compromised, and Reagan used the White House reception as an opportunity to reaffirm his own objectives.)[8]

Union support opened a huge door for education reform, and one immediate consequence was that politicians and political candidates began to parade right through. Governors such as Bill Clinton of Arkansas and two future Secretaries of Education, Lamar Alexander of Tennessee and Dick Riley of South Carolina, began referring to themselves as "education governors," and various education reform initiatives started to emerge.[9] The National Governors' Association (NGA) created seven task forces to study key problems in education and in 1986 produced a report, *Time for Results: The Governors' 1991 Report on Education.*[10] As NGA Chairman Lamar Alexander explained, the report addressed "seven of the toughest questions that can be asked about education in the U.S.A.":

- Why not pay teachers more for teaching well?

- What can be done to attract, train, and reward excellent school leaders?

- Why not let parents choose the schools their children attend?

- Aren't there ways to help poor children with weak preparation succeed in school?

- Why are expensive school buildings closed half the year when children are behind in their studies and many classrooms are overcrowded?

- Why shouldn't schools use the newest technologies for learning?

- How much are college students really learning?

The governors explored these questions, Alexander noted, to ensure that Americans could "keep our high standard of living. To meet stiff competition from workers in the rest of the world, we must educate ourselves and our children as we never have before."[11]

Although no one knew it at the time, at least one of the reform initiatives laid the foundation for the later emergence of charter schools. Beginning in the mid-1980s,[12] New Jersey, Texas, and California created alternative paths to certification, which brought dozens, then hundreds, then thousands of new, often highly-educated candidates into teaching.

How did this happen?

The first alternate teaching certification program in the nation was created in 1984. New Jersey Governor Thomas Kean and his Commissioner of Education, Saul Cooperman, enlisted former Princeton University admissions director Jack Osander to design a Provisional Teacher Program to enhance both the quantity and quality of teaching candidates in public schools.[13] At Princeton from 1966 to 1971, Osander had played an instrumental role in admitting women and increasing African-American enrollment from less than 1 percent to 10 percent.[14] He quickly established the

Alternate Route Recruitment and Placement Office and began visiting selective colleges up and down the East Coast to recruit potential teaching candidates.

These new candidates—many from the top quarter of their graduating classes—might not have entered the field without this new option, and they arrived with a different set of expectations. While most came directly out of college, some were drawn to education after years of experience in other fields. Lacking formal pedagogical training (aside from the Alternate Route training and the support of mentors), they were not accustomed to the norms of the field and were, perhaps, more likely to challenge those norms.

In the first few years, the numbers were low—in the dozens, then hundreds. I know this for a fact because in 1987, near the end of my senior year in college, I'd seen their resumes firsthand.

I'd taken an internship with Jack Osander to help people like myself find teaching jobs.

On my first day, as Jack explained my responsibilities, he gave me a quick tour. Although the work sounded exciting, the office, located in a former carpet warehouse several miles from Trenton, was not. Aside from sectioning it off with drab cork-board cubicles, the State had done very little to change the impression that you were standing in poorly-lit warehouse. Jack had brought in some yard-sale lamps to brighten his workspace, and as a practical form of decoration, he had pinned promising resumes neatly to the walls. "Here are the math candidates," he said, pointing to a column of five resumes. "We're a little short on science candidates," he joked, pointing to the next column, where there were only two. "We've got our work cut out for us. I'd like to use more thumbtacks."

In the beginning, the Alternate Route faced three major challenges: 1) the program was new, and it was hard to market something that didn't have much of a track record; 2) district superintendents were reluctant to spend the extra money on the mentors that these provisional teachers required; and 3) launching and growing the program required a lot of legwork. For a while, the office consisted of him, a secretary, and the occasional intern. This was in the late 1980s, before the Internet or cell phones. You couldn't sit in your office and video chat to interview someone. You had to drive four, five, six hours to see the people whose attention you were trying to attract. And even though the governor had raised the minimum starting teaching salary to $18,500,[15] it was still relatively unattractive compared to what recruiters from other fields could offer.

However, mirroring a pattern that would be repeated year after year to accelerate the pace of education reform across the country, philanthropists stepped in to help. (We'll discuss this more in Part III.)

The ball began rolling when Scott McVay, the executive director of the Geraldine R. Dodge Foundation, and Ernest Boyer, the president of the Carnegie Foundation for the Advancement of Teaching, met one morning for breakfast at the Nassau Inn. McVay had brought along his copy of Boyer's report on high schools in America.[16] Not long into the conversation, he pointed to a page and said bluntly, "Look, it seems to me that a critical thought here is to get behind good teachers and give them a boost."

Boyer replied, "Yes, that's where the multiplier is."

As McVay recalled nearly 30 years later, "That became the touchstone for everything we did at the foundation." When the Alternate Route was launched, he thought, *Why not get behind the top? They have a bigger ripple. One person can affect hundreds, if not thousands.*[17] For decades, he would apply this principle to great effect in programs dealing with education, the welfare of animals, and the environment. That year, the Dodge Foundation launched a program to offer $5,000 fellowships to "the top 25 Alternate Route teaching candidates." The Foundation's cachet and incentives enabled Osander to entice more top-level college graduates to consider teaching. And it turned out there was another benefit to those fellowships. You became connected with Scott McVay. That connection, I discovered later, could change your life.

While the results of New Jersey's Alternate Route Recruitment and Placement Office were initially modest, that number continued to grow. By 1992, *nearly half* of the new teachers (43 percent) hired in the state went through the Alternate Route.[18]

Following New Jersey's lead, other states launched their own alternate routes to certification, and the floodgates were opened. Nationally, the number of teachers entering through alternate routes annually jumped from 275 in 1985 to *59,000* in 2009.[19] By 2009, about one-third of new teachers hired across the country were coming through alternate routes.[20] By 2010, 48 states plus the District of Columbia had alternate routes. At least 500,000 teachers had entered the profession through these routes since the mid-1980s.[21] Many of these teachers might not have joined the field otherwise, and they provided a vital source of out-of-the-box thinkers when charter school laws emerged.

The appearance of these alternative certification paths also paved the way for the creation of Teach For America (TFA). A few years after Jack Osander had laid the groundwork, Princeton undergrad Wendy Kopp wrote her senior thesis on a plan to start this national teaching corps to serve students in urban and rural communities. In retrospect, three key factors contributed to the launching of TFA: 1) the existence of Alternate Route programs in more than a dozen states,[22] where recent college graduates could jump into teaching without having acquired traditional certificates, 2) the organization's patriotic mission, and 3) Kopp's sheer will to make it happen. Without Alternate Route programs, Kopp would not have been able to place teachers in public schools, and without her fierce determination, she wouldn't have been able to raise the funds needed to recruit them. Her thesis advisor, Marvin Bressler, wondered how she would be able to raise $2,500, much less the $2.5 million she needed.

Kopp was incredibly sure of herself. She later wrote, "I wasn't feigning confidence; I really was confident.... Looking back, it seems somewhat astounding that anyone would take me seriously. But at the time I didn't see any reason for these funders to doubt me."[23] She was convinced that she had a good idea. From the beginning, as Jack Schneider observed in *Excellence for All*, Kopp framed TFA as "a big-tent reform movement." It would "promote excellence for all, and in so doing would serve both the nation and the underprivileged."[24]

Coupling confidence with hard work, she was able to convince enough people to support her plans, and in 1990—the year before the country's first charter school law passed—TFA sent its first cohort of 500 recent college graduates into urban and rural districts, to begin "fueling the movement to eliminate educational inequity."[25]

Approaching 30 years later, by 2019, nearly 60,000 participants had joined the TFA Corps.[26] And quite a few found themselves launching, leading, or teaching in charter schools.

CHAPTER 3

WHERE DID THE IDEA
OF CHARTERING COME FROM?

Al Shanker, the AFT leader who was probably best known for helping American teachers win the right to bargain collectively, was one of the earliest proponents of chartering.[27] (To be clear, I would add: "to a point."[28] Shanker's notion of chartering was in fact somewhat different from that of others who stepped up to carry the concept forward.)

Shanker was relentless about the need for teachers to be treated as professionals, and he saw school restructuring as a way to achieve "differentiated staffing, in which certain highly talented teachers took on greater responsibilities and were paid more, accordingly."[29] He became captivated by the idea of chartering when he read Ray Budde's 1988 book *Education by Charter: Restructuring School Districts*,[30] which suggested that "districts [should] be reorganized and innovative teachers should be given explicit permission by the school board to create innovative new programs, and like explorers hundreds of years earlier, report back about their discoveries."[31] In fact, Shanker thought this idea should be extended even further, to include *entire new schools*.[32]

It should be noted that around the same time, a policy researcher named Joseph Loftus was also pushing the idea of chartering in Chicago. In 1987, not long after the Chicago Teachers Union had struck for the *ninth* time since 1969,[33] US Secretary of Education William Bennett called Chicago's public schools "the worst in the nation." He pointed to the 43 percent dropout rate and abysmal ACT (American College Test) scores, adding, "How can anyone who feels about children not feel terrible about Chicago schools? You have an educational meltdown."[34] Mayor Harold Washington appointed a 50-member citizens group to hear proposals for reform and develop a strategy to tackle the problem(s). Joe Loftus's paper "Charter Schools: A Potential Solution to the Riddle of Reform," emerged in 1989 as part of that work.[35] But in the debate about what to do, the winner was "parent-run schools." So Loftus put his paper away.

Unaware of the work that Loftus was doing in Chicago, Al Shanker became intrigued by Ray Budde's ideas and began to pitch them publicly.

On March 31, 1988, Shanker gave a speech at the National Press Club in which he reflected on the reforms that had taken hold in the five years since the release of *A Nation at Risk*. The way he saw it, "so many things have happened as a result of reform that we are at a point where there is now more than one reform movement in this country. There are really two."[36]

The first was a push for a higher standards. He noted:

These reforms are very good for kids who are able to learn in a traditional system, who are able to sit still, who are able to keep quiet, who are able to remember after they listen to someone else talk for five hours, who are able to pick up a book and learn from it – who've got all these things going for them.[37]

But this reform movement, he lamented, "is bypassing about 80 percent of the students in this country."[38] He compared it to a doctor who prescribes a pill that doesn't work, who says when the patient returns uncured, "You've got a hell of a lot of nerve not responding to my pill. What's wrong with you?"[39]

He explained that there was a second movement, "a radical and tiny movement,"[40] which needed to be nurtured because it was composed of a small number of people who were trying to build something different that would meet the needs of the remaining 80 percent. Frustrated with the slowness of the first reform movement, he exhorted:

> We can't wait until all the districts throughout the country have the strongest and the best bargaining relationships. We can't wait until there are more districts that have both charismatic union leaders and superintendents. We can't wait to find places where everyone feels free to risk things. The question is, can we come up with a proposal which will move us from five or six or seven or ten districts that are doing these very exciting things to reach many, many more students? Can we expand that number very rapidly; not from 10 to 20, but from 10 to 1,000 or 2,000 or 3,000? Can we put in a new policy mechanism that will give teachers and parents the right to "opt for" a new type of school, to "opt for" the second type of reform?

> I believe that we do not have to wait for the impossible to create the possible. I do not believe that all the conditions have to be right throughout the system in order to do the possible.[41]

He proposed that school districts and the teachers union could develop a procedure that would encourage any group of six or more teachers to submit a proposal to create a new school. Ultimately, that school-within-a-school could become a totally autonomous school within the district.[42]

A few months later, he reported in his Sunday *New York Times* column (the AFT's paid weekly advertisement called "Where We Stand") that at the 70th convention of the American Federation of Teachers, 3,000 delegates from across the country had "proposed that local school boards and unions jointly develop a procedure that would enable teams of teachers and others to submit and implement proposals to set up their own autonomous public schools within their schools' buildings."[43]

In October, Shanker was invited to speak at the Itasca Seminar, a three-day annual gathering sponsored by the Minneapolis Foundation at a resort on Gull Lake in northern Minnesota. For years, the seminar had mostly been an effort to connect civic and community group leaders, but in 1988 it focused on policy in the field of education. John Merrow, education correspondent for the *MacNeil/Lehrer Newshour*,[44] was brought in to moderate.[45]

Though Minnesota's charter law would not emerge for three more years, something definitely began to take root in that setting. First, Shanker spoke about the need to give teachers more opportunities to create innovative programs.[46] Then, Joe Nathan, a longtime educator and the founder of the Center for School Change at the University of Minnesota (and later the author of one of the first books about charter schools[47]), shared some key findings from the National Governors' Association's *Time for Results* report, which he'd helped to coordinate.[48] In particular, he stressed two themes that the governors supported: 1) more public school choice and 2) less regulation in exchange for better results.[49] Governor Lamar Alexander had noted in his "Chairman's Summary":

> We're ready to give up a lot of state regulatory control—even to fight for changes in the law to make that happen—*if* schools and school districts will be accountable for the results. We invite educators to show us where less regulation makes the most sense. These changes will require more rewards for success and consequences for failure for teachers, school leaders, schools, and school districts. *It will mean giving parents more choice of the public schools their children attend as one way of assuring higher quality without heavy-handed state control.*[50]

Nathan's focus on state policy caught the attention of Ember Reichgott Junge, the Democratic state senator who ultimately co-sponsored Minnesota's charter legislation.[51] These ideas also intrigued the president of the Minnesota PTA, Barbara Zohn, and a civil rights activist, Elaine Salinas.[52]

Then longtime educator Sy Fliegel stood up to speak. He and his colleagues in East Harlem District 4 were famous for having created a public school choice system of more than two dozen small schools. What had enabled them to do this? As Fliegel liked to joke, "We had the big advantage of being the worst district in the city of New York. It was always 32 out of 32."[53] In 1973, only 16 percent of the students were reading at grade level, and dropout rates were high.[54] The only place to go was up.

As he explained in his book, *Miracle in East Harlem*,

Nobody really wanted these kids, and because nobody at the central Board of Education cared enough about the worst school district in the city to keep them from trying something new, and because the local district authorities were desperate to try anything that might work, [one unusually dedicated teacher] was allowed, even encouraged, to start a small, experimental school.[55]

In 1976, Superintendent Tony Alvarado had named him the director of the Office of Alternative Schools, and from that point on, Fliegel had supported teacher after teacher in developing new small schools that offered parents, students, and teachers an array of new choices. Probably the best-known school leader he worked with was Deborah Meier, who founded three successful Central Park East elementary schools and the acclaimed Central Park East Secondary School.[56] By 1987, 63 percent of the students in East Harlem District 4 were reading at grade level, and the district was ranked 15th in the city.[57]

Not surprisingly, Fliegel viewed the idea of chartering schools as a natural extension of the work he had already begun. As members of the audience at the Itasca Seminar listened, they saw the possibilities. In fact, Reichgott Junge and others were so inspired by his presentation that after dessert they immediately began brainstorming about what chartering legislation would look like. Four of them took notes on a dinner napkin.[58]

Reichgott Junge soon had a lot more. The Citizens League Committee had spent several months preparing a report about the chartering concept, and on December 15, 1988, the group presented its recommendations, laying out a template for what would become the first charter school law in the country.[59] Many ideas proposed in the report eventually made it into that law.

But in spite of all of this enthusiasm, it still took *three more years* for the law to pass.

Why did it take so long?

There are many answers to this question. In Minnesota, as Ted Kolderie later recalled, "The original bill wasn't in very good shape when it went right straight into the Legislature, and the House wouldn't hear of it." For a couple of years, although the bill kept passing in the Senate, the House ignored it. Finally Becky Kelso, a House Democrat, approached Ember Reichgott Junge and said, "If you'd like to try that charter again next year, I'd like to help you."[60] That broke the logjam, and with the support of Kelso and Ken Nelson, after a series of compromises, Reichgott Junge managed to get it passed in 1991.[61]

Much of the initial resistance was probably predictable because chartering was such a radical departure from the norm. While charters are defined as "public" schools, they are not always under local district control. They have their own independent boards, they don't necessarily have to be unionized, and a certain percentage of per-pupil funding follows the students who leave district schools to attend charters.

Those in control—namely, school boards and teachers' unions— did not want to cede any of their power or "their" money. As Sy Fliegel remarked one day when a group of charter school leaders complained about how their local superintendent was not treating them well:

> "Wait a minute. Let's remember something. We started the fight. We basically said, 'We don't want to be under you or your board.' What did you think a superintendent was going to do? Or a chancellor? Or a board, a central board? What are they going to say, 'We love you anyway even though you don't want to be with us'?"[62]

One thing that pushed the chartering idea forward in Minnesota—and this was true in many other states, as well—was the threat of an alternative that, to some, seemed worse: publicly-funded private school vouchers. In 1990, vouchers appeared to be gaining momentum. John Chubb and Terry Moe, researchers from the Washington, DC-based Brookings Institution published *Politics, Markets, and America's Schools*, a pro-voucher book that received wide attention,[63] and in that same year, Wisconsin Democratic representative Polly Williams helped to pass legislation that gave a thousand low-income children in Milwaukee access to $2,500 per year in tuition assistance so that they could attend private schools.[64]

While some charter supporters also advocated for vouchers, many, including Ember Reichgott Junge and Joe Nathan,[65] did not. Reichgott Junge later wrote that she (like other voucher opponents) "resisted the diversion of public monies to private and religious schools for at least two reasons: 1) public funding to religious schools was a violation of the constitutional separation of church and state; and 2) private schools were not held to the same standards of accountability as public schools."[66]

This tension between charter and voucher proponents would percolate for decades.

CHAPTER 4

PREPARING THE FIELD AND PLANTING THE SEEDS

In 1991, Minnesota passed the first charter school legislation in the country. By 1996, when New Jersey's law was signed, nearly two dozen other states had joined the fray. *How did that happen?*

Joe Nathan explained it, in part, with a farming analogy. The National Governors' Association (NGA) had done substantial work to prepare a supportive policy environment:

> Key state governors like [Republican] Lamar Alexander and [Democrat] Bill Clinton had decided this was a great idea. The NGA and I had worked hard to get the *Time For Results* out all over the country, and Alexander arranged for follow-up after he left the chairmanship of NGA. It's a little like growing crops. You need both a field that is well-prepared and good seeds, and then nurturing. Good seeds (ideas) won't grow well if the field isn't ready. There was an enormous amount of work to get the field ready.[67]

Following this analogy, then, Ted Kolderie planted some of the most important seeds.[68] In July 1990, he drafted a policy paper suggesting that chartering could "withdraw the exclusive franchise" that our educational system had perpetuated.[69] For the chartering movement, this became a fundamental belief: that *the monopoly of the American public educational system needed to be broken up.*[70] "We are not serious about improvement if we do not withdraw the exclusive franchise," Kolderie concluded.[71]

In 1990 at a meeting in Washington, Kolderie explained his ideas to Will Marshall, the president of the Progressive Policy Institute (PPI), a project of the DLC. Marshall was intrigued.[72] He invited Kolderie to expand upon these ideas, and in November 1990, PPI published "Beyond Choice to New Public Schools: Withdrawing the Exclusive Franchise in Public Education."[73]

Looking back, it should be no surprise that one of the first people to see this paper and seize upon it for inspiration—nine months before Minnesota even had a charter school law—was Governor Bill Clinton, who took it with him on the presidential campaign trail and began to promote chartering as a "New Democratic Idea."[74] In 1986, Clinton had co-chaired the *Time for Results* report and also chaired the Task Force on Leadership and Management. He'd subsequently invited Joe Nathan to testify in Arkansas on behalf of cross-district public school choice. As Nathan recalled, "He was very intrigued by the idea of greater flexibility in exchange for more accountability."[75]

When Clinton became president, his support was vital to the growth of the charter school movement—both for his use of the bully pulpit to champion charters and for his practical support of federal charter school start-up funding. Not long after his election, he brought in South Carolina Governor Richard W. Riley, who'd chaired the *Time for Results* Task Force on Readiness, as his Secretary of Education. "One of the first things they did," Joe Nathan recalled, "was ask Jon Schnur [Special Assistant to the Deputy Secretary of Education] to call Ember Reichgott Junge and me to see what they could do to help the charter movement."[76]

As the years rolled on, Ted Kolderie's "Withdrawing the Exclusive Franchise" paper became required reading for anyone contemplating education reform. And for many years, Kolderie was a key leader (along with Joe Nathan and others) in spreading the idea of chartering. From 1992 through 1996, he shared the idea, either in person or on the phone, to somewhere between 25 and 30 states.[77]

Decades later, Kolderie noted that one of the striking things about chartering legislation was that "in Minnesota and everywhere, it was just automatically, instinctively opposed by all of the associations representing the organized elements of K-12."[78] From that standpoint, "The chartering idea simply sold itself. That's the only way you can explain how, in state after state after state, it was enacted as simply a state capitol initiative with no grassroots support, no basic media support, no big-name support, none of the things you usually associate with successful legislative initiatives."[79] He added, "How else could you explain the passage of something that violates all of state capitol conventional political reality?"[80]

Of course, the idea needed legislative champions, and they stepped up—from both sides of the aisle. *Why did they do it?*

Here is how Kolderie described his encounters with governors and state legislators:

> You found people, particularly Democratic elected officials, who were very disappointed and dissatisfied with what the state was getting from the districts. They knew there was the voucher option to go around the districts, but if they didn't want to do that—and most of them didn't—then they had concluded that there was no alternative but to accept the district structure and do the best you could with it.
>
> And all you had to do was look at them and say, "No, the legislature is God here. If the districts are not giving you what you want in the way of change and improvement and performance, it's fully within your power to get somebody else who will and to do that within the principles of public education."
>
> And they would look at you for about thirty seconds, and then this big smile would come over their face as they got it. And once they got it, it never left them. But it's amazing: it was really just that simple. And I think that's essentially what motivated folks in state after state after state.[81]

Governors and legislators across the country knew that something needed to be done to improve public education, and they realized that charters—being more palatable than publicly funded private-school vouchers—could be a valuable part of the solution. Because charters had bi-partisan support from the beginning, they spread more rapidly than some other reforms.

From his perch in the nonprofit Center for Policy Studies, Kolderie periodically sent out photocopied "little memos" to an informal network of several hundred education policy leaders across the country. These memos "went viral" in a pre-Internet way. From time to time, Kolderie received requests from people who said, "Can I get a clean copy? The one I have has been copied so many times that it won't copy anymore."[82] These updates, which included names and contact information for key players in each state where charter legislation had been approved or was pending, had more impact than he realized, as we shall see.

Along with Kolderie, five other Minnesotans also made vital contributions in spreading the charter idea: Joe Nathan, State Senator Ember Reichgott Junge, Eric Premack, Jon Schroeder, and Senator David Durenberger.[83]

Nathan, who led the Center for School Change at the University of Minnesota, became a prominent supporter of early charter developers and lawmakers. After the influential *Time for Results* report[84] came out in 1986, both Lamar Alexander and Bill Clinton asked him to talk with legislators about it, and in the five years that followed, he testified in front of more than 20 state legislatures, particularly emphasizing the recommendations regarding public school choice.[85] After 1991, as the charter school movement began to spread, he traveled to 37 states to share his insights and expertise.[86] In 1996, he published a seminal text, *Charter Schools: Creating Hope and Opportunity for American Education.*[87] In 2008 (and for the next six years), he found himself again on the road, working with governors in 18 more states as part of a collaboration with the National Governors Association.[88]

Reichgott Junge, whose efforts had led to the passage of the Minnesota law, also began to reach out to policy makers in other states, particularly Democrats who faced union pressure.[89]

Premack, who'd had a front-row seat as an intern at the Citizens League, played a major role in California, both before and after the legislation passed there. We'll hear his story in the next chapter.

Schroeder, who had worked with Kolderie at the Citizens League from 1972-1977, quietly facilitated the growth of the movement, beginning in 1991 with a much-needed piece of the puzzle. As director of policy development for Senator David Durenberger (R-MN), it was his job to find "good Minnesota ideas to take to Washington,"[90] and he kept a close eye on the progress of the charter legislation. Even before the law passed, he spoke with Joe Nathan and others who were thinking about starting schools. The first question he asked was, "What do you need?" and one thing clearly missing was start-up aid.[91] While a charter would receive some percentage of per-pupil funding from the district once the school opened, the founders had nothing to start with. And how could you create a school without money?

Schroeder and Durenberger realized that federal start-up funding could do more than just help charter school founders in Minnesota: *it could also raise visibility of the charter idea in Congress and in other states.* And it could build support for charter laws in states that were considering legislation, but needed an extra incentive to pass laws and help grow the charter movement nationally.

With this rationale, Schroeder drafted the "Public School Redefinition Act"–introduced by Durenberger in the early fall of 1991–to create a new federal start-up grant program for charter schools. The legislation proposed authorizing $50 million per year. The following year, Durenberger reintroduced this legislation with a Democratic co-sponsor, Senator Joseph Lieberman of Connecticut. The bill had bi-partisan co-sponsorship in the House, as well.[92]

When President Clinton was elected, his Administration made Durenberger's bill part of its comprehensive legislation reauthorizing the

Elementary and Secondary Education Act (ESEA). This was a huge political advantage. And, with Durenberger's continued vigilance and strong support from Mike Smith, Undersecretary of Education, and others in the Administration, the charter grant legislation passed with the overall ESEA legislation in the fall of 1994.[93]

Although the legislation included just $6 million for the program's first year, it recognized and addressed a key barrier to charter school development and helped expand awareness and support for the charter movement nationally. And the program continued to grow. By 2018, more than $4 billion had been allocated to states and charter schools across the country under the federal charter school program.[94]

While the federal charter program started small, it forced some early charter founders to seek creative solutions to obtaining start-up funding, as we shall see. In the meantime, the chartering wheels continued to turn, with laws passing in a dozen or so states by the mid-1990's. Even before his bill passed, Durenberger wrote a letter to his friend and former colleague in the Senate, Republican Governor Pete Wilson, encouraging him to support charter legislation in California.[95] Which he did.

How that law passed is kind of a funny story.

CHAPTER 5

CALIFORNIA AND MICHIGAN
AND THE EARLY CHALLENGES

When I first met Eric Premack in person at the Minneapolis charter school conference in July 1996, I was startled to find that he was short and slight, with the build of a cross-country runner. I'd called him a few weeks earlier for advice about how to launch a charter school resource center in New Jersey. On the phone, I'd pictured a burly linebacker engaged in trench warfare. He spoke in a rapid, urgent tone and said things like "when the shit hits the fan" and "you need to have a strong tactical sense." I'd scrawled four pages of notes about the stages of starting a charter school and the array of needs that founders would have. I also wrote, "MAKE SURE FOLKS UNDERSTAND HOW DIFFICULT THIS PROCESS IS!!!"[96] in two different places. Talking with him made me feel like I was preparing for battle—which, in retrospect, I was.

Years later, when I interviewed Eric for this book, I began to understand where his toughness and urgency came from and what he had gone through in the early days in California.

He actually grew up in Minneapolis, and in high school, he'd written some pointed pieces for his school newspaper, including one titled "Geriatric High," which described the disastrous effects that budget cuts were having. The good younger teachers were getting fired, and the remaining older teachers were being forced to teach subjects they hadn't taught for years in order to save their jobs.[97] Eric's father, Frank Premack, had been an award-winning city editor of the *Minneapolis Tribune,* where Ted Kolderie had also worked. In 1975, at the age of 42, Frank Premack died of a heart attack,[98] and Ted had stayed close to Eric, from time to time inviting him over for dinner to keep an eye on him and pick his brain about what was going on in the Minneapolis school system. It was clear that the district was faltering, and as Ted and his friends at the Citizens League explored various policy options, he wanted to know what things really looked like in the schools.

On one strange and memorable evening, Ted invited Eric along with some superintendents, principals, and teachers to a meeting at a local law firm. A dozen people sat around a long, elegant wooden table with three special guests: a managing partner at the law firm, another from an architectural firm, and a third from an engineering firm. Although the educators were aware of Ted's habit of bringing different folks together to discuss ways to shake up the status quo, none of them on this particular occasion knew what he had in mind, and Eric was awkwardly aware that he was 25 years younger than anybody else in the room.

After a quick round of introductions, Ted asked the guests, one by one, to explain how they ran their organizations. The partners described how they worked together to solve problems and get things done. Their firms weren't top-down bureaucracies; they were collections of professionals. The audience listened patiently, trying to figure out what it meant for them.

After the presentations, the room fell silent. Eric wondered, *What's the connection? What do these partners have to do with everyone else here?*

Finally one of the teachers blurted, "Oh, I get it! This is like I get to hire the principal and the superintendent, and they work for me!" It was like a flashbulb suddenly went off. Eric wasn't sure about the implications, but he knew that teachers worked for principals and this was something different. Looking around at the adults who were slowly nodding, he thought, *Well, what if that were the case, would my school be run differently?*

He continued to chew on this idea, and the next fall, when he arrived at the University of Chicago, he thought of it again when he realized just how poorly his high school had prepared him. Years later, he described what happened rather bluntly: "I got my clock cleaned by all these kids who went to high-end private and suburban schools. Academically it felt like scaling a concrete wall by your fingernails. That really gave me a sense for thinking, *I actually went to a pretty decent high school as urban high schools go in this country. Just how fucked are the other 80% of the kids out there?*" His own experience made him increasingly concerned about how policies, laws, and budget decisions affect what happens to actual human beings.

After graduating, he took a summer internship at the Citizens League, which enabled him to see how the Minnesota charter school law was being developed. Then he returned to Chicago for a Master's in Public Policy.

When he came back to Minneapolis again to look for work, he interviewed for a position as a California legislative analyst, as he put it, "mainly to get more practice in interviewing." Even though he argued with the interviewer (or possibly *because* he did: he discovered a problem with a bond financing question that none of the other prospective analysts had caught), he got the job. At first, he was stuck in the transportation section ("and I was *really* not interested in concrete"), so he did everything he could to wangle his way into the education finance position. Because he was so young and green, they didn't want to give it to him, but as he put it, "it was such a bear of an assignment that none of the experienced folks wanted it. They called it 'The Electric Chair.'" Eventually they gave him a chance, and he found it was a great way to learn the entire education funding system in a very short period of time and also get to know legislative staff quickly. And so, with his foot in the door, he began walking around the halls of the legislature to share his notes about the chartering idea.

For a while, no one took him seriously.

Then, one day not long after the Minnesota charter school law passed, the phone rang.

"Hey, Eric." It was Ted Kolderie. "Looks like I'm coming to Sacramento." While meeting with a group of businessmen in DC, he'd been invited by Jerry Hume, the CEO of Basic American Foods, to speak to the California Business Roundtable Education Committee.[99] "So I was wondering if you could help me set up some meetings with legislators who might be interested."

Of course he could. *Finally, some action.*

Not long after Ted's visit, State Senator Gary Hart (no relation to the U.S. Senator from Colorado who ended up as a disgraced presidential candidate[100]) and Assemblywoman Delaine Eastin, both Democrats, introduced competing chartering bills.[101] Charter supporters, including the Republican Governor, preferred Hart's bill, but Eastin's (which was more restrictive) had more support from the teachers' union. Rather than haggle from the beginning, Eric got both sides to agree to an unusual "handshake deal" that would move both bills forward through the legislative process and then let the conference committee work out the differences.[102]

On the day of the conference committee meeting, however, that handshake deal flew out the window. In the middle of the meeting, the education aide to Speaker of the Assembly Willie Brown (a supporter of the California Teachers' Association) entered the room and one by one, whispered into the ears of Eastin and all of the other Assembly Democrats on the conference committee. They all stood up and left the room. When they returned, they voted their bill out of committee and passed it on the assembly floor, as well.[103]

It looked like the weaker bill was going to win.

Eric and others felt deflated and assumed the fight was over, but when a senator who was known as an expert on parliamentary procedure overheard complaints that Eastin had reneged,[104] he said, "Why don't you just call the bill back if you haven't really amended it much?"[105]

That is exactly what Senator Hart did. Quietly, when no one was paying attention, he moved for his chartering bill to be brought back from conference committee, then for it to be approved "for immediate transmittal to the governor's desk." Just like that, he'd made his bill as ready for the governor to sign as Eastin's bill.

Watching a television screen from outside the senate chamber, Eric was baffled. No one had told him about this plan. And as he watched on the monitor, it suddenly looked like it was snowing in the chamber. Later he would learn that some education lobbyists up in the gallery had written "no" on their business cards and were tossing them down. But it was too late. Hart's bill passed, and the governor signed it.[106]

California's charter law, the second in the country, magnetized the attention of legislators in other states. Some might have looked at Minnesota's law and shrugged because, as Eric remarked, that state is known as somewhat of a "'policy hothouse,' where they grow interesting things that won't grow anywhere else or that are very difficult to transplant."[107] But when the most populous state in the country passed a law that was introduced by a Democratic legislator and signed by a Republican governor—well, people took notice.

Still, charter supporters couldn't take anything for granted. Because of the way the law had been passed, as Eric put it, "They had a real concern early on of just getting nuked."

California's was not the only law put in under controversial circumstances.

In Michigan in 1993, Republican Governor John Engler completely dismantled the school funding mechanism in his state. It started with a bluff: in an effort to score political points, Democratic State Senator Debbie Stabenow proposed the radical idea of eliminating the use of property taxes for school funding, and Engler decided to call her bluff. He signed the bill *without having any replacement plan in place*.[108] This stunning action prompted the *Washington Post* to run an editorial titled "Honey, I Blew Up the Kids!"[109]

Engler genuinely wanted to end the haves-versus-have-nots situation that resulted from property-tax-based school funding. Students whose families could afford to live near good schools had choice; those who couldn't, did not: their local schools were failing. This situation had persisted for decades, and Engler believed that the only way to get *everyone's* undivided attention to solve this problem was to take *all* of the money off the table. His plan was to use this crisis as an opportunity to improve public education by expanding public school choice. In a passionate address to a Joint Session of the Michigan Legislature, he made his case by lamenting the consequences of failing schools:

> I know there are many success stories…there are many good schools. But everyone knows a school that's not very good. Maybe your children don't go there—but someone's children do, and they're Michigan children. And they are children who will enter our economy and in turn have kids of their own. We have to reach them and help them. Otherwise, when these children fail, we all fail. Their failure will haunt us for years— in our jails, in our prisons, in welfare lines, in unemployment lines.[110]

Engler had read *Time for Results*, had spoken with Lamar Alexander about potential next steps,[111] and had been following Ted Kolderie's work. He agreed with Kolderie's argument that districts' "exclusive franchises" were the problem. In his speech to the Legislature, Governor Engler stated that directly: "No longer will there be exclusive franchises over education. No longer will there be a monopoly of mediocrity in the state. No longer will there be a company store holding our families hostage."[112] He declared that he was opposed to the "public education monopoly" and supported parents who wanted their children to have access to good schools no matter where they lived.[113] His staff called Joe Nathan and asked for help in drafting a charter bill.[114] Engler then proceeded to push for charter school legislation and a two-cent increase in sales tax to support a system of per-pupil funding for public schools. In 1994, Michigan became the ninth state to enact a charter law.[115]

Because the earliest charter laws were ripe targets for repeal and retribution, they felt tenuous at best. Most states had no actual constituents yet. There were no schools in existence, and no one would be affected (or organize and protest) if the laws were changed or revoked altogether. For charter advocates, it was a very risky time. Indeed, in Minnesota, less than a year after that first law was signed—and before the first school even opened—an attempt to repeal it narrowly failed.[116] In Michigan, the original charter law was challenged and ruled unconstitutional by a Circuit Court judge within months of its passing; the legislature was forced to pass another law to deal with those constitutional issues.[117] In Massachusetts (where a charter law passed in 1993), Linda Brown described the early days this way: "The urgency was so palpable then; sometimes it's really hard to tell people how urgent and nimble we were: we had to move quickly, we had to defend ourselves, we had to keep our land as it were because every day we were threatened by losing it."[118]

From his vantage point in California, Eric Premack said:

It became real clear that getting a law passed was only ten percent of the battle. The remaining ninety percent of the battle was dealing with the districts who were granting the charters and especially the bureaucrats. Everywhere you went, whether it was a school district or a state department of education or some other state agency, everybody said they loved charter schools as long as nothing that they did had to change.

Of course, not everyone was resistant: some educators were clamoring for change, and they viewed the new law as an exciting opportunity. Don Shalvey, who was then the superintendent of the San Carlos School District (in Silicon Valley), and Yvonne Chan, principal of the Vaughn Elementary School in Pacoima (one of the poorest sections of South Los Angeles), were first out of the gate. Their stories would reverberate across the country (as we shall see in later chapters).

Eric quickly became engrossed in responding to calls for help, many from Senator Hart's office. No one really knew how to implement the law, and as he described it,

The law was like six pages long and in California, a page of legislation is really like a half-page because they print it on 8.5 by 11 folded in half. There was almost nothing there. There was also no money at all and no resources at all for school planning or school launch, and we had clearly underestimated the difficulty of doing that work.

There was no infrastructure in place to support the creation (or conversion) of charter schools. Someone would have to step up, and Eric did, in a big way.

In those early days, he had no idea how much or for how long his life would be completely overtaken by charter school support work. Still at it more than two decades later, he said, "At first I thought, *I'm just going to do this for a little while. I figured, you know, folks will figure out how to do this stuff within six months to a year, and I'll just help make that happen.*" The lobbying firm he'd shifted to had taken on large clients who opposed charter schools, so he had to get out of there. He found a position in a Bay Area research firm that had secured a small grant to do charter implementation work. Knowing the funding wouldn't last for long, they called it simply "the Charter School Project."

Not having a secure long-term revenue stream, he cobbled together various consulting contracts and produced tools that charter school founders would need. He did hands-on work with a handful of schools and wrote some policy papers, but "when I got tired of answering the same questions over and over and over again, I wrote a 'how-you-plan-to-start-a-charter-school' guide and 'how-do-you-put-a-budget-together-and-how-is-a-charter-school-funded' guide and 'how-do-you-incorporate-and-govern-a-charter-school' booklet." Early on, these were simply word-processing files, and eventually he slapped a cover on them and started selling copies.

When the grant for the Charter School Project dried up, he received an offer from Gary Hart, who had left his Senate seat to start a think tank within the state university. As Eric later recalled, the offer went something like this:

"We're still going crazy with phone calls on this charter stuff. We would like it if you would move to Sacramento. We'll give you free office, free phone, and we have a secretary and we only need about 20 percent of her and you can have the rest of her and we'll give you free space; the hook is we'll only buy 20 percent of your time, but we're not going to tell you what to do with it as long as you make the phone calls go away."

So he moved back to Sacramento.

Before long, in addition to helping charter founders in California, he started getting phone calls from people in other states. From 1993 through 1997, he spent half of his time working around the country. "My phone line was burning up," he recalled, "and I started flying to different parts of the country although it was really expensive for me to do that."

When I asked Eric why he would spend his own money to do that, he replied simply: "I just felt really strongly that based on my experience of going to college and getting my clock cleaned that this was a very important thing to do. It was just sort of—it was a cause. Still is."

By 2018, California had 1,323 charter schools in operation, serving 660,000 children.[119]

CHAPTER 6

"ALL CHOICE IS GOOD AND MORE CHOICE IS BETTER": TWO WARRIORS

Although some charter school supporters felt uneasy about vouchers, it was evident that the push for private school vouchers made the charter movement more palatable for cautious politicians. In state after state, charter laws passed because the idea of creating charter public schools was viewed as more appealing than spending public funds to send students to private schools. We saw this in New Jersey in 1995: when legislators introduced an omnibus bill that included both charters and vouchers, lobbyists from the teachers' union fought to have the voucher provision removed, and the charter law sailed through.[120]

In the early 1990s, two leading proponents of both charters and vouchers emerged as prominent voices in the charter school movement: Howard Fuller and Jeanne Allen.

In his 2014 memoir, *No Struggle, No Progress*, Howard Fuller explained how and why he became such a fierce warrior for school choice in every form.[121] Born in 1941 in Shreveport, Louisiana, and raised primarily by his mother and grandmother, he was painfully aware that he was growing up in the Jim Crow South. In fact, as a child, he was so afraid of the white police that whenever a police car rolled by, he would run and hide under the front porch. One time his grandmother saw him do this and called him out:

> "Don't you ever let me see you do this again," she demanded.

> I had done nothing wrong, and had no reason to run and hide from the police, she explained. I think the bigger lesson she taught me that day, though, was that I shouldn't fear anyone, especially people with power, and that has stuck with me throughout my life.[122]

That telling moment sheds light on both the societal challenges he would face and why he would stand up to confront them.

Howard's connection to Milwaukee began when he was five years old. His mother moved them north and found a job in a Kex towels factory. Although they were poor, the beneficence of an unknown philanthropist enabled him to attend a Catholic elementary school.[123] No doubt this opportunity planted a seed that grew into his perspective about the importance of offering educational choices to students who wouldn't otherwise have them.

He subsequently attended public high school, played sports, and graduated from Carroll College, where he was the only non-white student.

After several decades as a social justice activist, in 1984, he began working on his dissertation, titled "The Impact of the Milwaukee Public School System's Desegregation Plan on Black Students and the Black Community (1976-1982)." He later wrote,

> Ultimately, my research provided factual data for what I had long witnessed—that Black students and the Black community had borne the heaviest burden of the city's desegregation decisions with neighborhood school closings and busing plans that transported Black children far from their community schools.[124]

Deeply concerned about the quality of education available to children, particularly poor children in Milwaukee, he became an avid supporter of the city's publicly funded voucher program, which began in 1990. Around that same time, he first heard Ted Kolderie speaking about charters and got engaged right away. When I interviewed him decades later, he explained that he saw charters as another opportunity for parents to have choice.[125] He noted,

> I really was not approaching parent choice from an ideological perspective; it was more "I think people would be better off if they had more options." I always saw it as social justice issue as opposed to a "free market" issue. So when I heard about charters, it came to me that it would be a good addition to the "parent-choice basket," so to speak.[126]

While some voucher proponents thought competition from vouchers would pressure public schools to either improve or close as a result of losing their market share, Howard simply wanted parents and students to have more choices. That was why he ended up advocating for both charters and vouchers.

In 1991, as Howard became increasingly vocal about vouchers, a group of local ministers urged him to apply for the position of superintendent of Milwaukee Public Schools (MPS). He had completed his doctorate and had plenty of relevant work experience. At the time, he was the Director of Health and Human Services for the County, in charge of the hospital, the mental health complex, the Department of Social Services, and another small agency,[127] but he lacked the proper credentials to run a school system. The law actually had to be changed for him, and when it was, he became one of the first nontraditional superintendents in the country.

Although the MPS board voted him in unanimously in public, Howard discovered that the private vote had actually been split. He later recalled:

> Some of the board members were so angry that they had selected me as superintendent that they wouldn't even let me talk at the first meeting. It got so bad that I wrote an open

letter to the newspaper saying that I would quit. And that led to a three and a half hour meeting—let's-get-together-and-talk kind of thing—and we smoothed it out. So that was the politics: people were angry that I was a supporter of vouchers. The agreement that we came to was that I would not promote vouchers as the head of the school district, but they were also clear that I would not go out and oppose them.[128]

With that détente in place, Howard spent the next several years attempting to improve the school system. But he was frustrated by the lack of progress. "I made some efforts and took on a number of different battles, and I won most of the ones I took on, but it only moved the needle a little," he said. "It wasn't like it transformed the system and all the kids were really learning. That didn't happen."[129] The last straw—what ultimately propelled him to leave and pursue school choice advocacy full-time—was a failed building referendum. He recalled:

I had asked the taxpayers to pay additional taxes to build new buildings for the MPS, and that went down to defeat in part because the Mayor had said he was supportive and then in the middle of the campaign he changed his mind. He lied to me, basically. So I had to figure out, *What are you gonna do? You can't just sit here and mope.* At that time, Edison [Schools, a for-profit educational management company] wanted to come into Milwaukee and operate two elementary schools, and they had a great model. They were going to invest $1.2 million in each school, so I'm sitting there saying, *OK, so I couldn't get the money from the taxpayers, maybe I can bring private investment into the district?*

But that didn't work; the board wouldn't go for it. "The union and others immediately put a red stamp on my forehead called 'Privatization,'" he said. The union and others ran a board slate of four people against him and they won, and although he still had a 5-4 majority, he decided, *Hey, I'm not going to sit here and be brow-beaten.*[130]

In his resignation speech, he quoted William Daggett: "We must love our children's hopes, dreams, and prayers more than we love the institutional heritage of the school system."[131] He was done trying to work with what Ted Kolderie had referred to as "the exclusive franchise."[132]

He walked away from the district and launched the Institute for the Transformation of Learning at Marquette University to focus full-time on advocating for charters and vouchers. He criss-crossed the country and spoke passionately at hundreds of meetings, hearings, and conferences. Many state-based leaders viewed him as a key voice in conveying the need for school choice.

Decades later, while he was still at it, I asked Howard why he thought charters were not enough and why he kept pushing for vouchers, too. He responded:

> Number one, you still have to go to some entity to get the authority to create charter schools, so there's been those situations in some places where school boards have been the only entity that can authorize charters. The second thing to me is that you want to have as many different options as possible and you want some of them to put parents clearly in the driver's seat in terms of deciding on the allocation of the money. I still see vouchers in that sense as more powerful because it does totally empower parents. The other thing is, quite frankly, I think if there was no threat of vouchers and opportunity scholarships, there would be a lot more forces aligned against charters.[133]

> People come to charters for all different reasons: they hate vouchers; some people are free-market people; some of them hate free markets. It's such a wide variance of people who support charters, and there are also people in the charter school movement who don't view charters as part of the parent choice movement. They always want to distinguish themselves from "these voucher people." For me, it's about *all* of the options. It's about home-schooling and now virtual

schools; it's whatever it is that empowers people to be able to make different decisions about their children's education.[134]

In 1999, the Institute for the Transformation of Learning organized a meeting of 150 Black educators and parents, which led to the creation of the Black Alliance of Educational Options (BAEO) in December of that year. For Howard, this was a logical next step as he had long argued that educational choice reforms are essential for the African-American community to take advantage of the opportunities made possible by the civil rights movement. For years, in speech after speech across the country, he lamented, "We can sit down at the lunch counter, but our kids can't read the menu."[135] He exhorted audience members to not be satisfied, to keep pushing. Almost invariably, his speeches concluded with the words of Frederick Douglass: "If there is no struggle, there is no progress."[136]

Like Howard, Jeanne Allen believed in the power of school choice. Having grown up a first-generation American, she knew how important education was, and her parents had worked hard to choose a place where she and her siblings would get what they thought was a great one.[137]

She began as a congressional staffer on Capitol Hill in 1983.[138] Looking back, she recalled,

> I wanted to work on the Hill forever. That's where I thought I was going to make my mark. I thought I was going to be an attorney. Then I ended up feeling like, *Wow, these people aren't real people making decisions or, if they are, they're not listening to the right people locally.* I just had a sense that there's a lot of great things happening out in the world that Washington is clueless about.

In 1984,[139] when she was offered a spot at the US Department of Education, she jumped at it, thinking, *Okay, here's an opportunity to make a bigger difference.* After four years in the Office of Post Secondary working for an assistant secretary, she had learned how slow the federal government was to change—if at all.

In 1988, someone from the Heritage Foundation, a conservative think tank, called her. There was a position available.

At the time, Heritage was one of the few think tanks talking about school choice. Jeanne started going to meetings around the country and was surprised to discover that "there were a lot of considerably older people who had actually been hitting this issue for a long time." Though they were earnest in their views, she was stunned by their lack of political savvy: "I thought, *That's really weird.* I just found them very ineffective at making their case."

One day in 1991, she received a surprising phone call that made her realize she needed to change her life.

"This is Milton Friedman, do you know who I am?"[140]

A Nobel Prize-winning economist and a leading advocate for vouchers. Absolutely!

Jeanne had just published a piece in support of public school choice, and Dr. Friedman was calling to tell her how misguided she was. He wanted her to know that he'd found her latest piece very disturbing.

"My dear," he said, "charter schools are the palliative of reform. They're only a temporary solution. They'll deter us."

"Oh, no, no, you're actually wrong," she replied. "All choice is good and more choice is better."

"There's no research behind it, and you should not be talking about this. You're ill-informed."

"Respectfully," Jeanne replied, "I disagree that I'm ill-informed; I actually think I know a lot about it."

Decades later, having founded and run the Center for Education Reform, Jeanne recalled:

I got called into my boss's office, and he told me he just got off the phone with Milton Friedman and "he doesn't like how you just spoke to him." I said, "No, I actually was perfectly civil. I just don't agree." That's when I realized that there were actually a couple of different ideologies behind the idea of choice.

Some people preferred charter public schools, some private school vouchers. Others, like Jeanne, believed education opportunity was important in whatever way one could get it.

On a quest for thought partners, she met Ted Kolderie and Joe Nathan and began to learn about charter schools. She became very excited about the idea of expanding public school choice. These were early days. Although individuals around the country were collaborating informally,[141] there was no official national organization focused on charters or choice.

So Jeanne jumped in and started to take charge. Shortly after the release of Chubb and Moe's pro-voucher book, *Politics, Markets, and America's Schools*,[142] she used her platform at Heritage to organize a conference for voucher supporters and business people. That was where she met Jerry Hume, the CEO of Basic American Foods, who would become her founding chairman at the Center for Education Reform (She later introduced Hume to Ted Kolderie, and Hume invited him to speak to the California Business Roundtable[143]).

By 1992, she was beginning to feel very confined. She knew that ideas about charters and choice transcended the ideological divide, and she wanted to approach the issues from a more mainstream perspective. Also, she wanted to do more to support practice in the field.[144] She recalled:

Heritage was a federally-focused think tank that wanted papers done. I felt like I needed to be out talking to people and helping people get this done. There was no other group doing that. There was a legislative group. The think tanks that Heritage helped create were more conservative-leaning. Otherwise, there was the establishment. Very much the Democrats, except for Minnesota, were anti-school choice. That's the environment that I decided, you know what, this isn't really a partisan issue and it's not an ideological issue because the people I have met in Missouri and Chicago and Minnesota don't wake up in the morning thinking about whether they're conservative or liberal. They wake up thinking, *I want to do something.*

She lined up three donors and dove in. At first, the Center for Education Reform (CER) focused on figuring out what was going on in the field and finding ways to connect interested parties. As she described it, "All I did was call all the people that I'd been talking to all those years to find out what they were doing and then start talking to other people about it and showing up at meetings." Very quickly, CER became a dominant voice advocating for all forms of school choice. In the mid-1990s as Internet access became more widespread, CER's website became a vital repository for information about charters and choice, providing annual updates on charter school laws (with a tool for evaluating the "strength" of those laws), school data, and links to resources and research.

Like Ted Kolderie, Joe Nathan, Howard Fuller, and others, Jeanne traveled around the country (in her case, to more than 40 states over the years) to testify and meet with legislators to help them draft charter legislation.

One challenge for Jeanne and for the movement in general was the question of who, if anyone, would lead the charge. By default, because there were no other national organizations focused on charters or choice, she became a leading spokesperson. Journalists called her routinely to comment on education reform issues. Some charter proponents, however, thought she could not "represent" charter schools or their supporters for two reasons. First: not everyone agreed with her expansive views on school choice. Second: the charter school movement was a grassroots revolt against the status quo. Reformers didn't want to form bureaucracies or join any "official" national organization or association.

And yet, we did need to coordinate our efforts. How would we do it? (Chapter 13 tells that story.)

CHAPTER 7

THE PIONEER

After she'd been at the work for decades—supporting the creation of dozens of high-performing charter schools around the country—and even though she walked slowly, people still described Linda Brown as "a force of nature," "a dynamo," "a lovable mad genius," and "a little fireball who just by sheer force of will and sheer force of personality makes things happen." She herself would admit that she was "good at being bossy."[145]

Why did she get involved?

Like many others, Linda's story began with an itch to do something different. One day in 1993, she noticed an article in the *Boston Globe* about the pending charter legislation that used the phrase "independently-managed public school."[146] She'd been working at an independent school in Cambridge for many years, and it had become increasingly bureaucratic. This phrase made her think, *That means no school committee, no superintendent, no elected anyone. It means no hierarchy, no bureaucracy.*

She couldn't stop thinking about it.

The charm for Linda lay in the word *"public."* Like many drawn to the charter school movement, she was captivated by the idea of transforming and improving public education. She was very aware that for years, her private school had needed to subsidize low-income students who wanted to attend, and she felt as though the school was not doing enough for these children. The more integrated the school became, the more Linda realized a lot wasn't happening that should happen. She thought that maybe with this new *public* option, she could do more for the children who needed more help.

She started combing the newspaper more closely, and one day, she found a cryptic ad that said something about "director of an education center that would implement Mass GL number, number, number." She suspected it might pertain to charter schools.

She went for an interview at the Pioneer Institute, a conservative think tank, where she met Jim Peyser, the son of a five-term Congressman from New York, whose own charter story had begun as a result of his daily walk to work at an electronics company in Boston.[147]

Every morning, Peyser had walked past the large, dysfunctional Boston High School, and one day he decided to volunteer to do some tutoring there. Not long after that, his friend Charlie Baker, then co-director of the Pioneer Institute,[148] asked him to help another friend, Steven Wilson, who was writing a book about the Boston Public Schools and needed research support. As Peyser would later put it, "one thing led to another"[149] and he soon found himself launching the Charter School Resource Center under the umbrella of the Pioneer Institute.

When Linda Brown applied for the job, Peyser and his colleagues took note of her close-cropped salt-and-pepper hair and her progressive independent school background. They repeatedly asked her how she would feel working at a conservative think tank. It was fairly obvious they thought she was a hippie (She later reported: "And I was."), but she didn't care about the politics.

In her final interview, when Pete Peters, the Pioneer Institute's buttoned-up 80 year-old founder and chair,[150] asked Linda if her neighbors would be OK with her working at "a place like Pioneer," she looked him straight in the eye and said, "All I care about is the schools and the tremendous opportunity we have here to do something great for kids. As long as this movement is fed and watered and groomed, it doesn't matter to me who's behind it."[151]

The old man stood up and threw his arms around her.

Jim Peyser recalled, "Pete Peters absolutely fell in love with her. I'd never seen him hug anybody before! And that was it. The deal was done."[152]

In retrospect, this scene offered a human snapshot of the bi-partisan push for charter schools.

What truly sealed the deal for Linda was an experience she had after one week on the job.

She was sitting at her desk when suddenly Jim Peyser, carrying a yellow legal pad, walked in and sat down.

"What are you doing?" she said.

"We'll meet every week."

"Every week we're going to meet?"

She was perplexed. She had never met with anyone formally. She had been the associate head of school, and in the course of her career, the Head of the School had sent her exactly one letter, which stated: "We commend you for the placement of the dumpster. We realize now that we'd had it in exactly the wrong position." Recounting this story two decades later with wide-eyed amusement, Linda said, "I saved it because I couldn't figure it out: I didn't know if maybe it was code for something."

So when Peyser sat down that first time, she was terrified.

He went through everything she had done. Linda recalled: "He did what executive directors are supposed to do. He knew about what everybody was doing, and he was checking in, and finally I said to him, 'When's the other shoe going to drop?'"

Peyser replied, "What do you mean?"

"Well, all of what you're saying is very positive. When are you bringing in the negative?"

He said he was looking for where she might want his help.

She was stunned. She had never had this experience before with leadership. She realized that these new schools could be like this. People didn't have to have someone write to them once a year about a dumpster.

She was hooked.

Not long after Linda Brown and Jim Peyser started the Massachusetts Charter School Resource Center, they began to travel to other states to support the passage of charter laws. They also tried to figure out what to do to help launch charters in their own state.

Not many people were doing this work yet. The Massachusetts law gave them some time: charters would be submitted in 1994 with the caveat that they couldn't open until 1995. Linda went to Minnesota and met with Peggy Hunter, who was the resource provider there. Hunter worked very closely with Ember Reichgott Junge and Milo Cutter, who'd started City Academy, the first charter school in the country. Linda recalled, "Peggy worked to understand our law enough to teach us how to implement it."

In 1994, Linda attended a charter school conference in Minnesota, where she met roughly 100 people, including Ted Kolderie, Joe Nathan, and Eric Premack. She recalled: "We didn't even know how to describe what we did. We learned about each other; there was discussion. Nobody knew much."

Full of vigor, she returned to Massachusetts, where Jim Peyser urged her to write a how-to manual.

She had brought all of the handbooks and policy manuals from her independent school. Peyser found her a research assistant who could help with the financial section. After they finished that project, Linda made a point of telling everyone she talked to that the first thing they should do was write a handbook "because you learn so much." Hers became a model for charter support organizations across the country and was even published in German and Japanese. The Pioneer Institute distributed thousands of copies.

In addition to producing the handbook, Linda also spent considerable time on the phone. When she'd started the job, Peyser had handed her a stack of about 400-500 "While You Were Out" notes and told her, "All of these people need to be called." There was a huge demand for information from people in Massachusetts and also people from other states. Linda was happy to help. The way she saw it, if she helped people, then it meant she had more people to go to.

In 1994, Linda could not predict that over the next 20 years, she would become a prominent leader in the development of charter schools not only in Massachusetts but also nationally. Nor could she imagine that she would provide vital assistance to leaders of charter support organizations in other states, create a solid foundation of charters in and around Boston, and start a new nonprofit to help launch dozens and dozens of high-performing urban schools all across the country.

In 1994, her work was still just beginning.

CHAPTER 8

"WHO'S GOING TO HELP PEOPLE START THESE THINGS?"

My own story began, in a way, at 7:15 a.m. on Tuesday, May 21, 1996, when I pulled into a vast, mostly empty lot at Seton Hall University. The booth attendant had given me a special permit; this was as close as I could park to the building where New Jersey's first statewide charter school conference would be held, roughly 300 yards away. With a deep breath, I lifted my crutches from the passenger's side, opened the door, and swiveled so I could plant my right foot on the ground.

So much had happened in the past few months. In January, Governor Christine Todd Whitman had signed the charter school law. I'd been keeping an eye on how charters were spreading across the country, eager to see how our state would respond. I had already called a friend at the New Jersey Department of Education, where I'd spent several summers as an intern, to find out more. I was enrolled in a doctoral program at Rutgers and was thinking about starting a school. I was also trying to figure out what to do at the end of this school year. I was pretty sure I wouldn't stay at Southern Regional, the high school where I'd taught for six years.

One morning in April, a few weeks after I'd ripped my Achilles tendon while playing basketball, the superintendent saw me in the hallway and waved. I was in a wheelchair, attempting to propel myself to the library, so I had to stop in order to wave back. He came over and asked how I was feeling.

"I've been meaning to talk with you," he said. "Unfortunately it's not good news. We're going to have to cut the Humanities program next year."

I stared at him. He was a smart, good-hearted guy, and one of my favorite teachers when I was a student. In fact, his family was like family to me. His wife had led my Brownie troop, and more recently, I'd taught his son in Honors English. But now here he was, *in the hallway, almost casually,* telling me that the program I'd spent years developing with a history colleague was not going to be allowed to continue.

I felt like I'd been punched in the stomach. The Humanities program, a two-year interdisciplinary cycle we'd designed for so-called "average" students, had been one of the most meaningful things I'd done at this school. For several years, struggling students who'd hated their watered-down college prep classes had thrived in our project-based classes. And even though he was in the highest position of power in the district, he was telling me he was powerless. The school was too overcrowded. He couldn't give us classes of 25 because it would mean other teachers would have classes of 35. There was nothing he could do. He was sorry.

I need to get out of here, I thought. *I need to make a change.*

For weeks, that scene had replayed in my head.

Bracing myself against the car, I strapped on my backpack and began crutching toward the conference.

The energy at the sign-in table was palpable, buzzing like an electric force. Evidently everyone else had had the same idea: *Get there early.* Of course, many of us were used to it. On a normal day, I'd be checking attendance in homeroom by now.

As I waited in line for a nametag, I noticed a pale, lanky older gentleman—and was thrilled to discover that he was Ted Kolderie, the policy expert from Minnesota widely considered the "godfather" of the nascent charter movement. I wanted to talk with him, but I wasn't sure what to say. For a policy geek like me, this guy was a rock star. *Would it be too weird to tell him that I'd read his paper on chartering so many times that I could actually quote parts of it?* I could feel myself nodding in his direction as I recalled his explanations about why so many possible solutions were not really going to solve education's fundamental problems. School restructuring provided no incentives for systemic change.[153] *Yes, definitely a problem.* Strong leadership had transformed some schools, but public education could not be improved one school at a time.[154] *True, it would take forever.* "An organization with an exclusive franchise is under little pressure to change."[155] *I saw that firsthand in the hallway with my own superintendent.* Therefore states should "withdraw that exclusive franchise" and invite various public agencies to charter new schools. *I couldn't agree more. Sign me up!*

I tried not to stare, and vowed I would approach him later. Maybe then I'd think of something useful to say.

Every room was crowded. You could feel the excitement in the air. Billed as a gathering for anyone interested in starting a charter school in New Jersey, it was as though hundreds of inventors had shown up in one place, rubbing their hands together, nodding and scribbling notes in anticipation of what they might design. Everywhere you turned, there was someone who wanted to know what you did and what you were thinking of doing. The organizers had hoped for 200, 75 had registered, and 330 had shown up: an event planner's nightmare. But no one really cared if there were enough seats. They would stand. Something important was happening.

The session before lunch was as overcrowded as the others. I found a seat on the aisle and listened intently as Jim Peyser described how the Massachusetts Charter School Resource Center was working to help people who wanted to start charter schools: running workshops, identifying resources, developing a handbook, "doing whatever it takes to help launch these schools." Then two women from the New Jersey Department of Education spoke about the application process, which was still being developed. I kept listening for something I *didn't* hear, and a question rose in my mind.

"OK, now we're going to take some questions."

I stood up and gently braced myself against the chair in front of me. Someone pointed to me.

"Hi," I said. "I'm really interested in what the Charter School Resource Center is doing in Massachusetts. Who's going to help people start these things in New Jersey?"

Peyser turned deferentially to the women from the Department, and they looked at each other, raised their eyebrows, and shrugged.

"I guess that's a good question," Peyser joked.

I nodded and sat down. My heart was pounding.

At lunch, I found myself seated next to a genial-looking, white-haired lady who turned out to be Peggy Kerns, the House Minority Leader who'd co-sponsored Colorado's charter school legislation. We chatted as the keynote speaker, a handsome young man in a pinstripe suit, was introduced and then stepped up to the podium. According to his bio, Jon Schnur was the Special Assistant to the Deputy Secretary of Education, but he looked like he'd just graduated from college. In fact, the bio said he'd gone to Princeton. *What year?* I wondered.

"Already, we're seeing some amazing new schools opening up in Minnesota, where of course this all began," he said, "as well as in California, Colorado, and Massachusetts." New Jersey had become one of about 20 states to pass charter legislation, "and you have a law with great potential." He wanted us to know how much President Clinton supported charters: "He believes that charters offer tremendous professional opportunities to educators and could really transform public education." The goal was to create more schools that were public schools, high quality, and fair. The president and Congress also recognized that "you can't start something with nothing." Congress had allocated $6 million for charter school start-up funding in 1994, then $18 million in 1995, and now President Clinton was hoping to increase that amount even further.

I turned to Peggy and whispered, "This is a great speech, but he looks so young!"

She looked at me with a twinkle in her eyes. "I agree, but everyone looks young to me these days."

After Schnur finished speaking, I watched him wander to the back of the room. He sat on a bench against the back wall, sipping a glass of water.

Then Dennis Testa, the President of the New Jersey Education Association (NJEA), rose to the podium. "The NJEA believes charter schools are an *honorable* idea," he began.

I had taught *Julius Caesar* enough times to know where this speech was going. (He went on to say that although the union supported charters and hoped they'd bring new opportunities for teachers, we should remember that they were "an experiment" and the union would be "keeping an eye on them.")

I picked up my crutches, tugged at my backpack, and made my way over to Schnur. When I reached him, I leaned down and whispered, "Is it me, or does this speech remind you of Mark Antony's funeral oration?"

He chuckled.

I introduced myself and asked him when he'd graduated. He'd been two years behind me. He wasn't even 30 yet.

"Don't take this the wrong way," I said, "but *how did you get this job?*"

"I wanted to teach," he exclaimed. "I still want to teach!" He'd worked on the Clinton campaign and one thing had led to another. What he didn't tell me was why he had become obsessed with education in the first place. His mother had co-founded Milwaukee's first racially-integrated preschool, which he'd attended, and she also founded the first Children's Museum in Milwaukee (also one of the first in the country),[156] so, clearly he was brought up to value education. But as he would later describe it, "a key watershed moment" came in high school—specifically, at Shorewood Public High School just outside of Milwaukee. He was the sports editor of the school paper, and one day after he'd asked a freshman girl that he considered brilliant and insightful to submit an article, he was floored by how terrible her writing was. Even worse, some of his peers were laughing at what she had produced. This girl had gone to Milwaukee Public Schools through eighth grade and had never been taught how to write. He was stunned. *How could someone this insightful not learn how to write?* That incident set him on a mission. As a senior, he wrote a series of articles about the Milwaukee Public Schools, observing and documenting the so-called "reforms" that clearly were not generating adequate results. That early research became a lifelong quest to figure out what he could do to change the outcomes for students like the girl who couldn't channel her brilliance into a newspaper article.

As the years unfolded, Schnur became a key educational advisor to President Bill Clinton and Vice President Al Gore, and he went on to found New Leaders for New Schools. Then he advised a senator who later became President Barack Obama.

But for now, not yet 30, he was intent on expanding the charter school movement. And when I told him I was thinking of starting a resource center like the one in Massachusetts, his eyes lit up.

"We should talk more after this," he said. "I've got a bunch of people you could talk to. Let me give you a few names to start with."

Before I left the Seton Hall conference, I worked up the nerve to approach Ted Kolderie and tell him what I was considering.

His brows raised in interest. "Did you talk to Jon Schnur?" he said. "He can put you in touch with people who can help."

"Yes, he gave me some contacts and said we should talk more."

"Good. What about Peyser? Did you talk with Jim Peyser? He works with Linda Brown; they're doing some great things in Massachusetts. He's floating around here somewhere." He turned and scanned the crowd, then zeroed in on me again. "You should also talk to Jeremy—" he pointed to a young man with a thick beard, who was standing across the room, engrossed in conversation—"Jeremy Resnick. He's trying to put some things together even though Pennsylvania doesn't have a law just yet. He could tell you what he's working on." He pulled out a business card and handed it to me. "Keep me posted."

I made my way over to Jeremy, and when I asked him if he was any relation to Lauren and Dan Resnick, the famous professors, he ducked his head in embarrassment. "Yeah, they're my parents," he admitted.

"OK, I won't hold it against you," I joked, and we began to talk about the idea of a resource center. He told me he really wanted to start a school, but it seemed like people would need some infrastructure first, "and anyway, we don't even have a law yet." He grinned and crossed his fingers. "Soon, I hope."

Jeremy was in the process of launching "a little center" at Duquesne with the support of the deans of the Business School and the School of Education. Once Pennsylvania's law passed in 1997, he would leave the center to start a school, then later launch Propel Schools, a network of high-performing charters in and around Pittsburgh.[157] But for now, he was meeting with people from other states to find out what they were doing. "I talked to Linda Brown," he said excitedly. "She's really helpful. Did Ted tell you to talk to Linda? You should really talk to her."

I nodded. Jon Schnur had also mentioned Linda. Soon, I would understand why.

But before I could call Linda or anyone else, I needed to do some more local research.

Two weeks later, I went to a charter schools conference hosted by the New Jersey School Development Council, where the audience was a mixture of district superintendents curious about this new law and potential charter school founders hungry for any scrap of information they could get their hands on. I took a dozen pages of notes. Senator Jack Ewing, the feisty veteran legislator who'd co-sponsored the bill, led off with "the how and why" of the law. Though he didn't say it directly, he implied that it wouldn't be the worst thing in the world to subvert the teachers' union in order to provide better opportunities for kids who are stuck in failing schools. He lamented that charter founders would face some tough challenges because they would not receive any money for facilities. *How are they going to solve* that *problem?* I wondered.

After several other speakers discussed the particulars of the law and its possible implications, I had my first exposure to Gloria Bonilla-Santiago, an energetic, politically connected professor at Rutgers-Camden bent on starting a charter school in Camden. She said she had already raised $1.6 million. "And we will definitely need more," she said.

"It's like that Steve Martin joke," I whispered to the woman sitting next to me. "'Wanna know how to make a million dollars and not pay taxes? First, get a million dollars....'" *Wow*, I thought, *this can't be the only way to launch a school. These people are going to need a ton of help.*

Then Kevin Andrews, the Headmaster of Neighborhood House Charter School in Dorchester, Massachusetts, stood up and offered a different perspective. I quickly realized that charter school founders from other states could teach us a lot. Andrews had assembled a board of trustees who could provide pro-bono support, and the Pioneer Institute's Charter School Resource Center had helped him and his co-founders navigate the start-up process. "No doubt it was difficult," he said, "but it wasn't impossible, and"—he grinned and nodded in Gloria's direction—"it doesn't necessarily take a million dollars." He described some key features of his school—teachers on a 12-month contract, an Individual Learning Plan for every student, a Family Center to help the parents who in turn help the school—then he concluded: "Starting a charter school is running a business. While it's nice to have total *autonomy*, you also have to remember that you have total *accountability*." *How refreshing,* I thought. *It would be so nice to have both.*

After lunch, many school leaders hustled out. With my head spinning and my heel throbbing, I sat down at a table and tried to figure out what to do next.

That was when I first met Norman Atkins. He told me he was working with a small group to start a middle school in Newark. They were thinking of calling it North Star Academy. Though neither of us knew it at the time, this school, along with Norman's subsequent work, would have a dramatic impact on the field and on my own career.[158]

Later I learned more of Norman's story. He was a journalist who wrote about education, poverty, politics, culture, and social issues for *The New York Times Magazine*, *The New Yorker*, *Rolling Stone*, and *The Wall Street Journal*. He also had nonprofit experience. In 1989, his college housemate, David Saltzman, invited him to co-lead the Robin Hood Foundation, which had been founded by hedge fund manager Paul Tudor Jones, in New York City.[159]

As co-Executive Director, Norman tried to figure out where the foundation could have the most impact. He went around the city and visited every single soup kitchen, every homeless shelter, and countless programs for people with AIDS. Providing necessities to help people survive was valuable, of course. But he also became convinced that education was the only possible "up" escalator for low-income children.[160]

Many grant applicants were focused on youth development: running after-school programs, teen pregnancy programs, gang prevention programs. But at their very best, he thought, these programs were simply trying to mop up for all of the failure that was happening in schools during the day. It was ineffective and inefficient.

By contrast, when he visited low-tuition private schools—schools in Harlem, Bedford-Stuyvestant, and Brownsville—he felt that they had assembled complete packages. He would return to the office and tell his colleagues that he had found places that truly cared, that built living communities that were going to help kids succeed and go on to college.

His colleagues thought he was crazy. Those schools were not scalable, they said. They were not serving the poorest of the poor. They were incredibly expensive and barely a blip on the radar. His colleagues urged him to figure out a way to support traditional public education in New York City.

Norman later recalled visiting hundreds of classrooms in large, traditional district public schools in the poorest corners in the city, where he found too many adults "at best, standing in front of students without any particular learning going on." Too many others felt chaotic, "absolute bedlam." He didn't understand how to channel the modest philanthropy through an amorphous bureaucracy into what felt like an educational "sinkhole."[161]

That changed, in part, when he met Geoffrey Canada.

Canada, who had grown up in the South Bronx in a poor, sometimes violent neighborhood,[162] had—after graduating from Bowdoin and earning a Master's degree from the Harvard Graduate School of Education—decided to focus his life's work on helping children who, like himself, grew up in poor, distressed neighborhoods.[163] He ran the Rheedlen Centers for Children and Families, a nonprofit youth program that was working inside of schools. Norman saw early on that Canada's team and organization were stitching together comprehensive services for children and families in Harlem. He learned from Canada and a few others about the power of organizational autonomy, community building, and the limits of what even the best service organizations could do in partnership with district public schools.[164]

Canada and his colleagues were taking a comprehensive approach to education and family support, not just slapping on band-aids. Canada eventually transformed his organization into the Harlem Children's Zone, which included a charter network, Promise Academy Charter Schools.[165] By 2007, the Harlem Children's Zone spanned 97 blocks in central Harlem. Over the years, Canada received hundreds of requests from mayors and other leaders across the country to speak about his work.[166]

In the mid-1990s, this work gave Norman some ideas about what it would take to innovate and create change.

He began to dream of starting a school. What would it take to create a world-class school for inner-city children?[167]

As luck would have it, Jamey Verrilli, a former community organizer and educator in Newark, New Jersey, harbored exactly the same dream.[168] For twelve years, he'd been a teacher and principal at Link Community School, a private middle school for low-income students, and from the minute the first charter school law emerged in Minnesota in 1991, he'd watched the idea sweep across the country. He believed Link should be a charter.[169] He saw no reason for it to be within the private sector. They were serving kids well. Everything they were doing, a public school could do.[170]

Verrilli held onto this idea and waited impatiently for five years. Finally, the day after Governor Christine Todd Whitman signed New Jersey's charter legislation in 1996, he began calling around in the community to find other people to work with. Someone referred him to "a guy named Norman Atkins." Coincidentally, the moment after he hung up the phone from that call, the phone rang again, and the voice on the other end said, "Hello, this is Norman Atkins."

It seemed like fate. They went out for coffee and talked for three hours.[171]

As Jamey Verrilli later recalled, the day after he and Norman Atkins met for coffee, they spent the next eighteen months "working every possible second" to create their school.[172]

Philanthropy helped: they secured a $50,000 planning grant from the WKBJ Foundation, run by Bob Howitt, a Wall Street guy who became North Star's founding board chair. Atkins enrolled in a Masters program at Teachers College, Columbia so he could work on the application and obtain a principal's certificate. Verrilli cut back to half-time at Link in order to help draft the charter and take courses to obtain a supervisor's certificate.[173] He saw their goal as "providing the type of quality education that inner-city children deserve and are frequently denied."[174] They wanted to design a school on the needs of the child rather than designing it on the needs of the administration, union, or board. For him, the metaphor was that they should "cut the coat to fit the kid." For a long time, urban schools had "cut *the kid* to fit the coat," and clearly that hadn't worked.[175]

After the charter was approved, they observed and carefully selected teachers who would constitute the founding team: they all had at least several years' experience and were excited about working with Newark children. After a team-building retreat in the Pine Barrens, where they built a raft together and managed to get it across a body of water, they visited more schools, looking for best practices, including Dave Levin's KIPP school in the South Bronx.[176]

One of the most powerful pieces of advice they received, Verrilli would later recall, was from Brother Brian Carty at De La Salle Academy, an independent school serving economically disadvantaged 6th- through 8th-graders in New York City,[177] who told them, "You have to define what you are about, what you are, and also define what you are not. If you do not define yourself clearly and really stick to it consistently in every aspect of the school, you risk being defined by forces in society."[178]

From the very beginning, they focused on building an intentional culture. Norman Atkins recalled:

> One of the issues we were most engaged by as a group was not "What do you teach the kids?" but "How do you build community? How do you build positive culture? What is 'community'? What would be the kinds of rituals that would

be meaningful for the kids? What would be the ceremonies? What would be the values that we should impart?"[179]

They searched far and wide for answers. How could they build what Atkins liked to think of as "the music of the culture of the school" so that students would recognize very early that they were part of something special?[180] One morning while visiting Urban Day Academy, a voucher school in a poor section of Milwaukee, Atkins saw students playing drums to call their peers into the community circle and decided that North Star's day should begin like that. At Link, Verrilli had developed a call-and-response chant that captured the spirit of what they were attempting to accomplish. Over the years, thousands of visitors to North Star would see students performing it with pride:

Who are you?

A star! I shine brightly for others!

Why are you here?

To get an education!

Why else?

To be the great person I am meant to be!

And what will you have to do?

Work! Hard! Work, work, work hard! Work! Hard! Work, work, work hard!

What else will you have to do?

Take care of each other!

And what will you need?

Self-discipline!

Why?

To be the master of my own destiny!

What else will you need?

Respect for me, my peers, my teachers, and all people.

Where are you headed?

To college!

And will you succeed?

Yes!

And when you succeed, what will you do?

Give back to others!

At ease. What are we?

A community![181]

Sitting at the conference with Norman, I didn't know what was to come. But I sensed that whatever Norman wanted to accomplish, he would. It was obvious that he was insanely smart and determined to make a difference.

That night after the conference, I went home and sent Scott McVay a fax laying out my thoughts on why New Jersey needed a resource center, where it might be located, and what it would do. Scott had been a mentor since my first year of teaching, and at this point I wasn't asking for funding; I just really wanted to know what he thought of the idea. I also included some "added bonuses," which, in retrospect, revealed the potential I saw in the charter school idea: "Operating such a center would enable me to reach out to all sorts of innovative people, including Dodge Teaching alumni, Principals' Center members, and Teach For America folks. Conversations about starting innovative schools are bound to draw innovative people in, to expand networks that are begging to be expanded, to provide a springboard for who-knows-what projects, and to create unstoppable dialogues that will lead to educational reform on many levels. In short, this center could find ways to bring all sorts of intriguing people together to promote educational reform." As I pressed "start" on my fax machine, I thought, *Maybe charters will finally shake things up. And maybe I can be part of this.*

The next day, the phone rang. It was Scott. "Why don't you come to lunch on Tuesday?" he said. "We'd love to talk with you about this resource center idea, and we were thinking about hosting a charter school conference in September. Maybe you could help with that."

One immediate result of my lunch with Scott McVay and his colleagues at the Dodge Foundation was that I decided to take a leave without pay from my teaching job. I appeared to be the most likely candidate to run Dodge's September charter school conference. Possibly because no one else had requested the assignment.

That night, I went home and wrote to Scott: "This stuff is too exciting for me not to jump in, in spite of the risks (esp. that of having to find increasingly diverse recipes for peanut butter and bread), but it's like Tommy Lasorda said: 'You can make things happen, you can watch things happen, or you can say, *What happened?*'"

At this point, I had been teaching for seven years. Leaving my job without another one lined up was a bit crazy, but I'd already had the experience of taking time off for graduate school (twice, in fact) and had landed on my feet before. I was excited—a little scared, too, but mostly excited—at the prospect of becoming involved in something that might have an impact on public education more broadly.

Fortunately, I soon found help. In fact, a few hours after I sent that note to Scott McVay, Jon Schnur called to see how I was doing with the resource center idea.

Jon said that although he couldn't offer financial support for a center, he would do anything else that he could to help. "Maybe if you run that conference in September, we could help pay expenses for some speakers; I can't promise, but I'll look into that," he said. "And also there's a conference coming up in late July that we're trying to pull together in Minneapolis: I'm going to see if there's a way we can get you there."

He encouraged me to "keep calling folks and learn as much as you can."

In the weeks that followed, consumed with the idea of launching a resource center, I focused on three key questions: *Where would it be located? Who would fund it? How would it operate?* Along with reaching out to potential supporters in New Jersey, I contacted the handful of people in the country who had already started charter support organizations.

One was Linda Brown. Though she knew nothing about me except that Jon Schnur had referred me, she spent an hour explaining how to run a resource center. She gave me a lengthy to-do list and rattled off budget items ranging from the price of a newsletter mailing to the costs of different-sized conferences. She predicted that schools would require extra support around special education and governance issues. "You need to run roundtables, bring in experts, and bring people together from different schools so they can also learn from one another," she told me. "And don't forget to have food! Food is very important!" She also stressed the importance of bringing resources to the schools and connecting them with potential funders. Her most recent effort to "get people out of the box" involved putting 22 school directors on a bus so that they could spend two days visiting Sy Fliegel's small schools in Harlem.

"They have to see what's possible," she explained.

That was an important idea. Soon I would see why.

CHAPTER 9

"WE HAD NOTHING TO LOSE"

On a hot July afternoon two months after the Seton Hall conference [in 1996], I found myself checking into a Minneapolis hotel to attend what was billed as the first National Charter Conference, although arguably it might have been the second or third.[182] A portion of the federal charter school funding was allocated to support technical assistance providers, and Jon Schnur's office had helped with the arrangements. I was grateful to have my travel expenses covered because my only income for the summer was a stipend to plan and run the September conference for the Dodge Foundation. As I handed over a credit card for incidentals, I noticed a Mutt-and-Jeff couple standing near me at the front desk: a short woman with spiky salt-and-pepper-hair and a tall, dark-haired young man. The woman, of course, was Linda Brown.

Her towering companion was Scott Hamilton. After graduating from the University of Pennsylvania with a degree in Ancient Greek, Scott had worked at the US Department of Education as a policy analyst, then spent several years at the Edison Project, one of the first for-profit organizations that tried to run public schools.[183] Now, at the age of 28, he was in charge of the Charter School Initiative for the Massachusetts Department of Education. In other words, while Linda helped people to start and run the schools, Scott and his colleagues (including Ed Kirby, who would later play a leading role at the Walton Family Foundation[184]) were the authorizers who decided which applications were approved, which schools could stay open, and which would be closed.

In 1999, Scott became a key player in the national rollout of the KIPP Schools model.[185]

But on this sweaty summer afternoon in 1996, he'd come to Minnesota to share what he'd learned so far about how to hold charter schools accountable. He had quickly become a national expert on the subject. In fact, his three essential questions for assessing a charter school's viability would guide authorizers across the country for decades: *1) Is the academic program a success? 2) Is the school a viable going concern? 3) Is the school faithful to its charter?*[186] In 2014, Greg Richmond, the president of NACSA (National Association of Charter School Authorizers), looked back on Scott's work and remarked:

> Scott's three questions were influential because they indicated that it was possible for an authorizer to establish a set of clear, concise expectations. Notice that it was the authorizer who determined the questions. This was a shift in thinking for many in the charter community who thought that each school was supposed to decide how it would be held accountable.[187]

Ten minutes after we checked in, Linda knocked on my door and handed me a thick stack of papers, including a detailed organizational budget and dozens of agendas and flyers from various meetings and conferences she had hosted. "This is so you'll have something to start with," she said.

It was a promising beginning. That night, about 50 people from roughly a dozen states gathered for dinner, and it felt like my first time at an overnight camp: everything was so new, and I had questions for everyone. I introduced myself to as many people as I could, asked as many questions as they would let me, and stuffed my pockets with their business cards. I had no cards to offer. My bio in the conference packet said simply: "I have been a public high school English and Humanities teacher. I am taking this year off in an attempt to start a resource center for charter schools in New Jersey."

One thing the bio didn't mention was that, like many others who became involved in charter schools, I had an entrepreneurial streak. A few years earlier, after earning a Master's degree at the Harvard Graduate School of Education, I had returned home to teach and, with the assistance of my erstwhile boyfriend, opened a used bookstore on the side. Used Book Heaven ran smoothly for several years before I sold it. So I knew a few things about starting a new business and was not afraid to take risks. But I didn't know much about starting a nonprofit, fundraising, or designing an organization that could help people start charter schools. Mainly what I brought to the table was enthusiasm and an almost-desperate desire to learn as much as I could as quickly as possible. Oh and one more thing: as a result of my internship work at the New Jersey Department of Education, I still had useful contacts there. I figured that when I didn't know the answers to questions (which would likely be often), at least I would know some other people to call.

As the conference invitation had noted, we were meeting for several purposes: 1) to identify critical issues facing charter schools, 2) to share what had been learned so far about addressing these issues, and 3) to discuss possible steps that might be taken in these areas to help existing and new charter schools. Even for such a small event, it was remarkably informative. In two days, I took 21 pages of notes (which I saved for posterity, not knowing that more than a dozen years later, "posterity" would be this book) about start-up challenges, facilities challenges, governance challenges—well, pretty much everything was a challenge since it was all so new.

What struck me most at this point was how few of us were doing this work. We would definitely have to rely on one another to share what we learned. And in the months and years that followed, that was exactly what happened.

The next morning when the program officially began, I sat down next to Eric Premack, who nodded at me over the large cup of coffee that he was nursing. He'd offered to speak at the Dodge conference in September, as had Sue Bragato, who ran CANEC (California Network of Educational Charters), one of the first official support organizations for charter operators.[188] Sue had collaborated with Don Shalvey and others to design the San Carlos Charter Learning Center, the first charter granted in California, and she was eager to share what she'd learned with folks in other states. CANEC's charter school conference would become a model for the National Conference and other state conferences. Over the years, Sue would work with legislators and charter supporters to develop laws and charter support organizations in New York, Massachusetts, Colorado, Alaska, Texas, North Carolina, and Georgia, to name just a few.[189] I was grateful to have Sue and Eric lined up, but I knew I would need more presenters—both immediately and long-term—because people in my state needed to learn from others with more experience.

Then a short, slim Asian woman stepped up to the mic. Every social movement requires its rock stars—charismatic leaders whose stories inspire the audience and highlight important messages. One reason that charter schools have not been a passing fad is because of their dramatic, well-publicized success stories. If you were thinking about starting a charter school in the early to mid 1990s, you heard something about Yvonne Chan and the Vaughn Next Century Learning Center. Or you saw Yvonne in person. Over the years, in addition to receiving widespread media coverage, Yvonne traveled to 37 states to offer testimony and support.[190]

At the conference, from the moment Yvonne started to speak—with her vigorous, loosely constructed English (she speaks English, Spanish, French, and Chinese—both Mandarin and Cantonese[191]) and a tendency to chop at the air with her hands—it was obvious that she was a fighter. Given what she'd accomplished, she was a natural role model for those who were fighting to open schools. But it was more than that: she was fighting for her kids and their parents—the poor, mostly Hispanic residents of Pacoima, one of the poorest districts in Los Angeles[192]—to have a chance at the American Dream.

That was probably because of where she came from.

When Yvonne was 12, she and her mother fled communist China with the help of Christian missionaries. She ended up in a private school in Hong Kong. At the age of 17, she borrowed $100 from a classmate, bought a basketful of inexpensive Chinese herbs, and boarded a ship alone for the United States. In San Francisco, she sold the herbs for $300 and took a Greyhound bus to Fresno, where nuns from her former school had contacts. There she attended community college, lived with a family, and went to work illegally, washing dishes and packaging fruit.[193] Eventually she earned multiple degrees and became a teacher, then an assistant principal, then a principal.

In 1992, at the age of 47, she was assigned to be the principal of Vaughn Elementary, one of the lowest-of-the-low-performing schools in the LA Unified School District. The district had made repeated attempts to improve the school, but nothing had worked.

Twenty years later, when I visited her campus and asked her to tell me the story, she began by pointing to the low concrete walls they'd had to erect in front of the school because of the frequent drive-by shootings.

At the start, things were awful. In fact, the situation was very similar to what Sy Fliegel and his colleagues had faced in East Harlem. Recalling her earliest impressions, Yvonne said:

> We had nothing to lose! The school is so bad! Twenty-six teacher grievances, teachers received death threats, the principal received death threats. Kids are not learning. We're in the worst Title One listed as the worst school. Burned-down buildings, gangs, drugs, kids get killed right in front of the school. Monolingual teachers against bilingual teachers, black against brown. Desegregation bussing out 260 kids, just to get four white kids in. I mean, how can you do worse?[194]

Clearly, the school had hit bottom.

She found the situation astonishing: "I came to this country poor, little English, immigrant, no family, and made it. And how the heck that I am the principal of this school? A public school with these taxpayer resources could not make it with these kids?" Though she had confidence in her abilities, initially she was dubious about the prospects for rapid change: "I have confidence that I can turn risks into opportunities. But I don't have the confidence that after 40 years of failure at this school and the district's repeated tries that I can do miracles in one year, you know?" She wouldn't be able to make dramatic changes, she said, "unless I got the tools." Being an experienced principal, she knew that she needed more autonomy and tools to turn the school around.

Then the charter school law passed, and she had her tools.

To be clear, she had already tried to work *within* the system. In 1992, Vaughn was a school-based management school. They had tried to use the existing rules and regulations to improve their bilingual program. But they hit a roadblock. And right around this time, they heard about the charter school law. Yvonne noted: "Actually, some of my more young and militant non-credentialed teachers on emergency credentials brought it to my attention, because they heard about it from the assemblyman's office." The teachers called the union leaders in to explain the charter school law to them.

What happened next changed everything.

The union leaders actually mocked them. She recalled, "The teachers' union looked straight in my teachers' face and said, 'Are you kidding? You guys can't even run a decent school, and you think you can be autonomous and take over and turn it around?' That really angered my teachers."

Ironically, this insult united the previously-divided staff. "My teachers just felt so belittled after that meeting," she said, "then they felt that they had to step out of the box and go for it all."

As soon as district leaders realized that her teachers were serious about converting to charter status, they tried to dissuade them by offering more flexibility: "But my teachers and the parents—especially the parents of students with disabilities whose kids were all bussed out—and my teachers getting belittled, and the all emergency militant community base, minority teachers, said, 'No deal.'"

The staff was inspired to pursue a charter, but they didn't know how they could do it financially when the district offered them only $2,300 per student. Considering that a pending voucher bill offered $2,600 per student and that most students at Vaughn qualified for Title One funding, bilingual funding, and desegregation funding, this figure was outrageous. So Yvonne decided to scrape together some School Improvement Grant money, and she and eleven teachers flew up to Sacramento for a meeting with Senator Gary Hart and his aide Sue Burr "to hear it from the horse's mouth." After lunch, when almost everyone else had left the meeting, Yvonne and her team stayed because their flight back wasn't till 7:00pm. Then the "nay-saying lawyers" took over. Yvonne and her teachers felt battered by all of the "no can dos," but they didn't give up. Flying back, they put their heads together and decided that they could not go home and tell the other 36 teachers that it was a wasted trip. "So what we did is, instead of regurgitating what we heard, we overlaid that with educators' passion and dream list," she said. "We overlaid that with our sense of what the American Dream is. Because, of the twelve, many of us are first-generation like myself."

Yvonne hoped they could find an existing charter application to use as a model, but the only one available was from a start-up charter in Minnesota which had 20 students; Vaughn would be a conversion charter with 1,000 students. "So we had to make it up!" she said.

They decided to ask the staff: "What would you like the school to be? What's your wish list?"

Telling me this story 20 years later, Yvonne shook her head and laughed heartily: "And my God, the wish list had Baby College University, a museum, even had a petting zoo! The first thing was 'Get off multi-track year-round, so we don't have to share rooms.' Teachers' staff development, universal pre-school, school-based health clinic.... That list: we have done everything, honestly, in 20 years. The only one that we have not done is petting zoo!"

The staff voted 68 percent in favor of applying for a charter, and over winter break, Yvonne invited them to her house to write the application. One teacher, the Chapter Chair, brought all 26 volumes of the California Ed Code, and they sat in front of Yvonne's fireplace, divided into teams, each team studying a different part. After three days of this, one of the teachers exclaimed, "Why are we doing this? What is this charter about?"

The Chapter Chair replied, "Freedom!"

"So why are we copying this Ed Code? Read the law! What does the law say?"

The law said that charters were exempted from the Educational Code. This "mega-waiver," as Eric Premack liked to call it, specifically stated: "A charter school shall comply with all of the provisions set forth in its charter petition, but is otherwise exempt from the laws governing school districts, except as specified in Section 47611."[195]

Yvonne recalled: "Everybody took the 26 volumes, and all of them wanted to burn the darned thing!"

In short order, they realized they could use their school-based management expansion proposal as a launching pad and focus on three primary goals: 1) to improve the quality of their bilingual education program, 2) to "bring home the kids with disabilities, so they don't have to ride the bus to somewhere else," and 3) to improve the quality of instruction overall.

From the beginning, Yvonne made shrewd, savvy use of the media to achieve her aims. When she and her team went to the central office to negotiate with the superintendent, she brought along a reporter from the *Daily News*. Though the reporter was not allowed in the room, the deputy superintendent took the phone off the hook and left it on speaker so that the reporter could hear everything. This setup enabled Yvonne to make the case for her children simultaneously to the Superintendent and to readers of the *Daily News*: "This is 100 percent minority, this is a poor neighborhood, and if these folks just try to take destiny into their hands and do more for public education, why won't you let them?"

They got the charter, but their battles were just beginning. Starting a charter school might be an appealing idea, but it comes with many challenges—for one, how to pay for the start-up costs. Before federal start-up funding became available in 1994, some charter founders were compelled to take dramatic steps to launch their visions. In July of 1993, not long after Vaughn Next Century Learning Center became the first independent urban conversion charter school in the country, Yvonne found herself without funds to pay the school's bills. As she explained in a case study:

> When no government funds flowed to us in July, when our year-round school began, I mortgaged my house. All staff agreed not to be paid until August. When local banks refused to set up accounts due to our lack of legal status, we had to manage with our small donation account until the IRS recognized our existence. When the labor unions demanded their monthly dues even when the employees received no paycheck, I took out personal savings to pay all dues.[196]

Another problem was that the USDA reclaimed all of its kitchen implements. Even though all of Vaughn's students qualified for free and reduced-price lunch, the district sent three trucks to come in and pick up the pots and pans.

Yvonne's response? "You don't think I won't call [U.S. Senators] Diane Feinstein and Barbara Boxer? You don't think I'm going to take a red-eye to go to Washington D.C. and duke it out? I don't duke it out with LA Unified; I'll take on USDA!" She testified and won back the USDA funding, and in the course of the proceedings discovered that schools with 95% or higher poverty rates did not have to waste time and money collecting meal tickets,[197] a fact that would help other charters become more efficient, too.

But the problem remained: *Who would feed her students?*

On the plane ride home, she noticed that her sandwich was wrapped in paper stamped with the word "Marriott," and suddenly she knew what to do. The next day, she contacted Marriott and arranged for them to handle her food services. Then she found out that the USDA reimbursement for food was three times what it actually cost: in other words, LA Unified had been spending triple the amount she needed to in order to feed her students. Why? "To screen the applications, to print the tickets, to bag the tickets, to staple the tickets: all a big waste of time." Because, as she had found out, they didn't need the tickets.

Vaughn gained more national attention when Yvonne tried to buy computers for the school. Diane Sawyer was planning to do a "Primetime Live" episode on district waste and mismanagement, and she wanted to know if Yvonne had a story to tell.

Of course she did.

Even before Vaughn had gone charter, the school had raised $26,000 to buy three computers for the library to do automated check-in and check-out. Yvonne completed a big stack of paperwork, and the rest, as they say, is history. She recalled,

> The paperwork went in there, got lost. Next one went through four departments: they did not know where. It took eight departments to go through one order. But meanwhile, don't forget, technology moves fast, right? The prices change, the serial numbers change, the components change. So after three years, my librarian gave birth to a set of twins—actually, one boy and a set of twins. And still no computer. The money's still sitting there encumbered. So that's my story, okay? So now, my new story is: being a charter school, 1-800-Apple. I can get it at half the price the next day!

Diane Sawyer was hooked, but she still wanted to nail the district on it, so the next day she went to Yvonne's office and they called the technology department. Diane got on the phone with the guy and asked for his location. Then she and her crew packed up three trucks and went and filmed him miraculously "finding" the order. The next day, Yvonne had her computers. Or as she put it, "Now, 'no can do'? Done!"

In the course of launching the charter, Yvonne uncovered additional problems with the district's finances. For example, when the first payroll roster arrived, she discovered that her school had been paying two principals' salaries as well as the salaries of teachers who worked at other schools. She cleaned all of that up and maintained a tight rein on the finances. She did not realize that some federal money and desegregation funds would drop later in the year, so when that funding arrived, it was a pleasant surprise. She grinned as she remembered it: "In February, after paying all the bills, I told Diane Sawyer, 'I have a $1.2 million surplus!' And that's her story: 'Now she has a $1.2 million surplus.' With that surplus, the teachers could have asked for a raise, right? They didn't. They said, 'Let's buy that crack house!'"

Turning the crack house across the street into a schoolhouse was the first step in rehabilitating the neighborhood. It also brought more positive newspaper coverage. Another breakthrough came, ironically, when the massive 1994 Northridge earthquake struck. Yvonne recalled: "All of these poor kids, a lot homeless with no place to take a shower, and all of the LA Unified schools closed. But not us. We opened right the next day because we care about the community." She was not afraid of being sued. As she put it:

So what, let the lawyers sue or protect them! We open. And sure enough, [Governor] Pete Wilson came in and gave us those portables. They came. And showers, the Conservation Corps—I mean, we got all the food trucks, all loaded, and it hit the news that a charter school, using its tools, was able to open while the rest of the district cannot.

By the time I visited Yvonne in 2013, the school was a $97 million enterprise spanning a four-block radius. As we toured the campus, she pointed to an empty lot strewn with garbage:

This is what it all looked like before. We are buying these up.
A public school would never do that. Basically, we are the

community now. The charter school is changing it. We used to have underground pushcarts, but now they have buildings and signs. So from underground to above-ground, and now they're paying taxes! So therefore charter school and community change is possible if you concentrate in one area and impact it like hell!

Reflecting on Yvonne's efforts and impact, Linda Brown remarked:

We talk about changing economic situations by changing the education base. You go there, and you see it. You see people who have jobs who never worked in a year, five years; they work for her; they all know who she is. They've started dry cleaners, they have laundromats; everything around her schools is clean. She's taken a barrio and changed it into mixed housing.

Over the years, the media attention Yvonne attracted had multiple benefits: spreading the mission, instilling pride in the parents (that they live in a place that reporters would want to cover for positive reasons), and inspiring school leaders across the country to see what was possible.

CHAPTER 10

FROM SMALL SCHOOLS TO CHARTER SCHOOLS IN CHICAGO

For reformers to make change, they must have some vision of what they hope to accomplish. They need to be leaders or hear from leaders, and they need to imagine—or better yet, see—what is possible. To that end, it helps to have models.

In Chicago, before charters, there were small schools. And two brothers—one a notorious anarchist, the other a mainstream civic leader—led the development of the small schools movement in that city. In the early 1990s, while Howard Fuller was attempting to improve the Milwaukee Public Schools, Bill Ayers (yes, that Bill Ayers, the Weather Underground anti-war protester) was an education professor at the University of Illinois at Chicago, and his youngest brother, John, was Executive Director of Leadership for Quality Education (LQE).[198] They knew about Sy Fliegel's small-schools revolution going on in East Harlem, as Bill's three sons had attended Deborah Meier's Central Park East when he was a Ph.D. candidate at Columbia. They reached out to Tony Alvarado and Sy Fliegel and would regularly take Bill's graduate students and other interested Chicago educators to visit schools run by Meier and others.[199]

By 1995 when Mayor Richard Daley took over the schools, the Ayers brothers had helped to launch roughly 15 small schools (district-based, designed to be tightly knit), and when they proposed the idea of running a Request for Proposals (RFP) to expand Chicago's small-schools initiative, the mayor enthusiastically supported them.

"We had a betting pool going on how many teacher groups would respond to our system-wide RFP to provide money and support to start small schools," John Ayers recalled seventeen years later.[200] "I had the highest guess: I guessed 37 groups would respond; 82 groups responded. What we realized when that number came in was that there was huge pent-up demand in the teacher corps to do things differently and to let teachers lead." By the time the Illinois charter school law passed in 1996, 80 small schools were up and running, and as he put it, John was known around town as "The Small Schools Dude."

Although he would eventually become known for his support of charters, John was initially dubious about them. His Leftist older brother opposed the idea. The night that the charter law passed, John ran into Chicago Public Schools CEO Paul Vallas at an event. Vallas had been a backer of the small schools initiative, but tonight he had a new idea.

"John, did you hear they passed a charter law today out of committee? I want you to run it!"

John said he knew nothing about charters and added, "I hear it's a terrible law. I want nothing to do with it."

Vallas shrugged: "Who cares what's in the law?! We're going to do it anyway, and you're the man because you did such a great job on the small schools!"[201]

Telling this story decades later, John reflected: "Vallas is a smart and effective politician, and he sought a degree of control over the charter movement in Chicago." Although Vallas had not been personally involved in the charter legislation (which passed as a compromise to vouchers), he enthusiastically embraced the idea, viewing charters as a way to multiply choices to parents and students around the city.[202] One advantage Vallas had was that the district's enrollment was expanding—in fact, it swelled by 30,000 students during his tenure from 1995-2001.[203] Unlike in some cities where migration to charters would shrink the districts' enrollment and corresponding access to resources,[204] he had a growing budget and could support charters without adversely affecting existing district schools. "We had enough resources to not only open charter schools but also provide charter schools with the facilities they needed," he noted. "We provided them with schools. They didn't have to go in and fend for themselves."[205]

Philanthropists also stepped in to support the initiative. The day after his exchange with Vallas, John Ayers received a call from a program officer at the Joyce Foundation who wanted to give his organization (LQE) $50,000 to support charter schools. John recalled:

> I was stunned by this unsolicited offer of funds. At the time I was also interviewing a lawyer who'd just done an internship at Sidley and Austin (a big, prominent law firm), and she had a Stanford Law degree and she wanted to come work with me because she'd heard I was doing good stuff. I told her about this crazy thing where Vallas had said I should work on the charters, which I hated, and then somebody without asking dropped $50,000 on me and said I was the only hope for a good charter implementation and that he thought I should start a Resource Center, something that would teach people what charters were because nobody understood them, and this young lawyer said, "I'll work on that." That was Margaret Lin.

In retrospect, the phrase "I'll work on that" was an understatement. Margaret Lin would work on charter schools for decades, and her efforts to raise the quality of schools, beginning in Chicago, would eventually have national impact.

Margaret had known since high school that she wanted to do something to improve schools. She grew up in Mattoon, a small town in Illinois, a rural, blue-collar and farming community 180 miles south of Chicago:

> I knew that my public school education was very mediocre. I knew that even as I was getting it. We went through all the things like budget cuts where everything academic was cut. The only thing that was sacrosanct was sports, football in

particular. I remember being 15 and actually thinking seriously about getting my own apartment in the next town, which was a college town and had better schools.[206]

She also read the *Chicago Tribune's* coverage of the state of Chicago's public schools and was aware that even though things were bad, they could have been a lot worse: "I would read about horrible, dysfunctional, dangerous inner-city schools in Chicago and I felt awful for those kids. I always knew at least my school was functional and safe. I just knew we needed to do better for all kids."

While considering the job at LQE, Margaret read Illinois's new charter law. She had never heard of charter schools before, but as she read the law, she said,

I saw that you could drive a truck through it. It could either help create new opportunities in Chicago for the kids who needed them most – or it could be used to exacerbate *inequality* of opportunity. I could stand on the sidelines and watch things happen (and perhaps watch the law be hijacked), or I could get involved in shaping how this worked in Chicago.[207]

Once John Ayers read the law himself, his initial skepticism evaporated:

I saw that this was a powerful way to engage educators and the community in creating great schools because it gave everybody the power that they weren't given under the small schools, and that was the power over the purse, over the budget, and over governance, and so you weren't stuck working within a screwed-up bureaucracy. And I learned also that they'd worked with Paul Hill [founder of the Center on Reinventing Public Education] and Ted Kolderie on the general outline for the law, so my initial skepticism was wrong: there was actually some good stuff in there.

Right around the time that Margaret Lin arrived on the scene, another man who would have a tremendous influence on her career, Greg

Richmond, was trying to find a way to take over the charter schools division for the Chicago Public Schools (CPS).[208] As a policy analyst on Paul Vallas's Governmental Relations staff, he had helped to shepherd the charter legislation. It was very unusual for a school district to lobby in support of charters. Greg became more involved in the implementation of the law because Vallas had given the CPS charter school assignment to a woman who knew nothing about charters, and she'd brought Greg in to explain them. He joined her working group and became increasingly involved in helping to oversee charters. He was captivated by the potential of charters; he particularly loved the idea that schools could be held accountable for their performance.

John Ayers met with the CPS group every other week so that they could coordinate efforts to support charters, and John and Greg became fast friends. Authorizers and support organizations typically keep one another at arm's length, but that didn't happen in this case. As John described it, "Greg and I worked an amazing inside-outside deal because we were both on the same page 90 percent of the time. So it wasn't me fighting the authorizer. We each knew what the other could do in each of our spheres of influence. We simply coordinated efforts and that made some real good schools happen."

One of the first things they needed to do in the summer of 1996 was create an application for prospective charter school starters, and John offered that LQE could write it since he already had a model. His associate director Robin Steans and attorney Jeanne Nowaczewski had written the RFP for the small-schools initiative, and Robin used that as the basis for the charter school application.[209] Robin later led Advance Illinois, a nonprofit focused on promoting "a public education system in Illinois that prepares all students to be ready for work, college, and democratic citizenship."[210] Jeanne later ran the Illinois State Charter School Commission.[211]

In October 1996, when the charter application process was still being designed, Vallas fired the entire division (for reasons unrelated to charter schools), and as Greg recalled, "It meant that I was the only person who knew what was going on in the charter school thing that hadn't been fired.

So Vallas said to me, 'Figure out what that was and keep doing it, and once you get that application stuff done, we'll give it to somebody else.'"

But Greg didn't want to give it to someone else. He explained:

In the fall of 1996—until then, I had just been this nice government relations guy—I had to pick up this application process and prepare to receive applications and evaluate them and make recommendations to the School Board. I found myself working with people—educators—who had ideas for schools, and it was more interesting than working with legislators. I didn't want to hand it off, and I also knew that Vallas had figured out who he wanted to hand it off to, which was a division in CPS that was generally responsible for running the whole district, kind of the nuts-and-bolts division, and I thought, *Well, that didn't make any sense, to turn this charter idea over to people who were just fixated on running things the traditional way. So that would be bad for charter schools and I'm enjoying doing this,* so I just wouldn't let go.

In the first round, there were 64 applicants. These applicants didn't emerge by accident. LQE hired a professional PR/media firm, Katz Communications, which publicized the opportunity to educators and community organizations throughout the city. Billed as a CPS initiative (LQE was behind the scenes), at the time it was unprecedented to publicize a charter RFP.[212]

Then, even though it was unorthodox for a resource center to collaborate with the authorizer to evaluate applications, Margaret Lin found herself working side by side with Greg Richmond during the review process, partly because he didn't have any staff.[213]

Margaret Lin recalled:

We worked at breakneck speed because CPS was then under the mayor-appointed School Reform Board of Trustees, which chose to embrace charters as an opportunity (unlike any other district in the country) and wanted some charter schools to open in fall 1997 as a quick win. In addition to recognizing the urgent need for improvement in CPS, they were business-people who wanted to get things done fast. That's why we issued the RFP in summer 1996, held applicant information fairs in August and October 1996, and applications were due in December and approved (or not) on December 23![214]

The Illinois law at that time permitted only 45 charters—15 in Chicago, 15 in the suburban "collar counties," and 15 for the rest of the state[215]—so they needed to be very picky. Many of the applicants were progressive leaders of existing small schools who were seeking more autonomy.[216] Greg assembled teams of volunteer reviewers—including CPS central-office staff, successful CPS principals, and external leaders in school reform—and while most reviewers (who also interviewed applicants) were assigned 4-5 proposals to review, he and Margaret each read proposals and interviewed half of the applicants to help obtain a consistent and comparative view.[217] Looking back, you could argue that the National Association of Charter School Authorizers was born then. But we'll come back to that story. Greg and Margaret quickly learned a lot about how to evaluate the quality of charter school applications, and ten were approved.

Of course, that was just the beginning. Once approved, what would it take for these schools to succeed? John Ayers was just finishing an M.B.A. (at Northwestern's Kellogg School of Management), and as he saw it,

> The biggest problem was that visionaries and people who can write great charters and great proposals—we learned very quickly that many of them could not lead an organization day-to-day to those visions. And very quickly, we began to push for things like, "Well, here's your visionary over here, but where's your business manager? Who runs the budgets?"

He noted that several charters "crashed and burned very quickly, and I felt like that was the surest way of shutting down this idea altogether; I was scared to death of that."[218] Fearing that a lack of managerial skills would undermine the movement, he worked steadily to help strengthen charter school founding groups and boards by identifying potential funders (because start-up and capital funding were needed), providing board train-ing, and pressing charter founders to hire individuals who could handle the business aspects of running a school. He hired two Kellogg grad students, Matt Candler and Peter Harvey, as summer associates and then part-time consultants to support these efforts.[219] (Candler later played an instrumen-tal role in the KIPP national rollout, then in the growth of New York City's charters, then in New Orleans after Hurricane Katrina. We'll come back to his story.)

Greg Richmond knew that when the next legislative session began he would have to go down to Springfield and wouldn't be available to stay involved with charters, and if he weren't there, then this other "nuts-and-bolts" division would step in. So he and John Ayers collaborated (some might say "conspired") to maintain control of the work. John actually offered up an LQE consultant, Katie Kelly, to work on charters for free for the school district in spring of 1997. So when Greg was in Springfield, Katie worked out of Greg's office, figuring out what they needed to do to support the establishment of charter schools that had been approved but weren't going to open until the fall. Greg recalled:

> Every so often, the woman in this other division that was supposed to take this over would come up and ask me or ask Katie, What was she supposed to do? And we were like, "Don't worry, I've got it taken care of. No problem." For her, that was great: "This is a good day, all right: no work for me; I'm going back to my cubicle." She kept doing this every so often because she needed to be able to tell her superior that she was trying but that "Greg and Katie, they just won't let go."

At the end of 1997, after going through another full round of appli-cation reviews, Greg went in to Vallas and said, "I can't do both of these jobs anymore. I can't do them both well, so I need to do one or the other, and I'd rather do the charter schools."

Vallas agreed. Greg remained the Director of Charter Schools for CPS until 2001,[220] when Vallas left Chicago and his deputy, Arne Duncan, took over as CEO. Greg recalled:

Duncan decided to embrace the charter philosophy and make it a major strategy of the district and have a purposeful effort to start new schools—not only charters but also schools within the system as well that had more autonomy. So he came in and wanted to build upon the charter philosophy as a way we should approach any new schools that were starting, and he asked me to lead that effort.

By 2016, 16% of the city's schools were charters.[221] Greg Richmond and Margaret Lin went on to become national leaders in charter school authorizing. In 2009, Arne Duncan took the education reform lessons he learned in Chicago to Washington, DC when he became Secretary of Education under President Barack Obama. His passion for the charter school idea—for educational choice, for opportunities to innovate, and especially for autonomy in exchange for accountability—shaped the policies he advanced from that bully pulpit.

CHAPTER 11

HOW TO MAKE THE MOST OF A CRISIS: THE DC STORY

In 1995, there were no charter schools in Washington, DC. By the 2016-
17 school year, nearly half (46 percent) of DC's public school students
attended charter schools.[222]

How did that happen?

The story of how the District of Columbia ended up with charter
schools is important because DC is a major media market, so it drew more
national attention to the idea. And it is not a simple story: it's more like a
play with a large ensemble cast, full of competing interests and voices—
including, but not limited to, Congressmen and their staffers; DC City
Councilmen and their staffers; the Mayor; business leaders; parents; and
education reform activists. Fortunately, some of them saw opportunities in
the midst of turmoil. Without their efforts, the DC charter school chapter
could have been titled "Close, But No Cigar."

In the early-mid 1990s, many people in the city knew things had to
change, especially when it came to the public schools.

Kenneth Campbell, a US Reserve Army captain from Mississippi
who became the Director of the DC Committee on Public Education

(COPE), had already spent several years trying to lead a broad-based community effort to reform the DC Public Schools. As he described it,

> We had business leaders, clergy, community leaders: a little bit of everybody. All of the most important people in Washington were part of this effort, and we worked very closely with the superintendent and the elected board of education. It was one of those efforts where everybody comes together to try to make it work.[223]

But Campbell and his colleagues kept hitting roadblocks. Over time, he'd arrived at two realizations:

> The first one was that, despite having a lot of good people who wanted children to do well, we couldn't find a way to make things improve systemically. We kept moving superintendents from around the country in and out, and in DC, everybody would come in with great fanfare and great expectations and community expectations. It would always end in some kind of disaster.

> The second was the growing concerns that we started to hear from parents that no matter what we were doing, it just wasn't fast enough. We had just brought in a new superintendent at the time; DC Schools had gotten taken over by a Financial Control Board, and they hired retired Army 4-star General Julius Becton [in 1996[224]], who came in and said, "Failure is not an option; we've got to get this right," and shortly after that, getting his plan for improvement, a parent just came in and said, "Hey, this doesn't work for me. Everybody's all excited about some three-year plan or five-year plan. I have a seventh-grader. What is this plan gonna do for *my* child?" That was the first time that personally, I started to get it—the urgent need for parental choice. We have to do something for parents who are trapped; they literally cannot wait for a new plan to come to fruition. So while I understand people who want to continue to focus and work systemically, we have to

have a stake in getting kids in the best schools we can get them into as quickly as possible.

While Campbell and his colleagues were still attempting to effect change in the existing system from the outside, a political insider named Jim Ford was making preparations for more radical change. A self-described "short white guy who played pickup basketball on public courts and in an all-black softball league and believes public policy can best be influenced by going inside the belly of the beast," Ford was also well-known about town for his unorthodox relationship with his boss, and he had been hoping to bring charters to DC from the minute they were introduced in Minnesota in 1991.[225]

Ford admits that he is "a bit of a free spirit." He laughs when he says it. As the Staff Director for the City Council's Education and Libraries Committee from 1985 to 1996,[226] he worked for Hilda Mason, an African-American woman in her 70s (if not 80s), a member of the DC Statehood Party who was a veteran of the civil rights movement and also involved in anti-war and anti-nuclear movements.

"Our relationship was unique," Ford explained, "because she literally allowed me the right to introduce legislation [through her] that she didn't necessarily support. At times, during public hearings or debates on a bill, if we disagreed on something, she would occasionally hand me the mic and allow me to argue my position." He was known as a disrupter, and behind the scenes he had the blessing of two City Council chairs, John Wilson and David Clark, Hilda's longtime friends and fellow champions of the civil rights movement, who wanted him to help push public education reform. Wilson, on occasion, would track Ford down in the hallway, saying, "I haven't gotten any complaints about you for the last two days. Get to work!"[227]

Ford had a certain amount of power and a sense of humor—both of which were known—and he had a lot of community support. This became apparent at a public hearing at Hine Junior High School near the Eastern Market (before gentrification) where someone said that he didn't understand something because he "didn't live in the community":

The implication was that I lacked sensitivity because I was white and resided in Northwest DC. Fair enough. Then this guy that I had literally fought with, from the day I got in DC— we agreed on nothing—he shot out of his chair, and I am sitting there, thinking, *OK, I knew this day was going to come.* He stands up, and he says, "I have one thing to say, and that is that Jim Ford is not a racist! He is just an asshole!"

I, of course, responded by saying, "For once, we agree on something!"

The crowd burst into laughter and applause.

Hilda Mason was quite wealthy, and she gave money to many students so they could attend private schools or college. Ford recalled:

> Every year we had a routine influx of people coming in, asking her for gifts, for college and whatever, and also to get out of the DC school system. It got to the point where she said, "I can't afford this anymore," but people were desperate. All of us on the City Council staff used to talk about how there had to be some option here.

With that background, Ford watched with interest what was going on in Minnesota. He had met Eric Premack and Ted Kolderie because they moved in the same education policy circles, and when the charter law passed, he quickly contacted them for more information. He couldn't do anything dramatic yet, but he was getting ready. He assigned legal interns from the newly created DC School of Law to begin crafting a charter school bill for DC.[228]

For a while, their drafted bill went nowhere. Hilda refused to introduce it because she had been supported by the teachers' union. Ford noted: "She agreed with the concept of autonomy, but she also was old-school. She had been on the DC school board and she had been a teacher, so she came up through the ranks. To introduce a law like that would have been literally a slap in the face to many of her personal and professional friends."

Then a crisis caught her attention during a budget dispute between the School Board and City Council.

"Rather than make cuts in a bureaucracy that arguably was spending 25 cents out of every dollar on overhead," Ford recalled, "the Superintendent and School Board threatened to eliminate two strong adult education programs, possibly thinking the City Council would back off and restore the funds." One was the Carlos Rosario International Adult Education Center, located in Georgetown, which served an immigrant population. The school operated programs morning, afternoon, and evening, and served a community of 2,000 to 3,000 people, with a 5,000-person waiting list.[229]

The head of that school was Sonja Gutierrez, a well-known, revered leader in the local Latino community. She also happened to be one of Hilda's closest friends and allies.

Hilda approached Ford and said, "We have got to save the school. What do we do?"

He handed her the previously prepared charter school bill and told her that if the district shut down Rosario, it could be re-created as a charter school. He then alerted two Council members, Kathy Patterson and Bill Lightfoot, who had been working behind the scenes with him to write and introduce the bill that Hilda was ready to sign-on.[230]

Ford later remarked how grateful he was for Kathy and Bill's courage:

Neither of them had a personal need for better school choices or anything to gain from supporting the concept of charter schools—Kathy represented Ward 3, which had very strong public schools, and Bill was a fairly young African-American attorney who had made a lot of money in his law practice— the beauty of them signing on was that they really wanted to equalize the playing field throughout the city.

When Bill was attacked for his position, he basically said, "I am wealthy enough to put all my kids in private schools, and that is where they are going to stay because I would never, as a responsible parent, put my children in any DC public school. All I want to do is level the playing field and give parents who are not as affluent as I am the same choices."

What happened next was actually comical. Ford recalled:

Kathy, Bill, and Hilda scheduled a press conference to announce the bill—after it had already been filed, thank God—because in the 24 hours since the filing and the press conference, Hilda got bombarded with calls from many of her friends and constituents, including the head of the teachers' union, about what she was doing, so she proceeds to stand up in the press conference and say, "Once again, my staff deceived me!"

One of the reporters from *The Washington Post* said, "This seems to happen a lot, so why do you keep him on?"

To which Hilda replied: "He does great work, and I like him."

The City Council's Education and Libraries Committee debated the bill at length. Eleanor Holmes Norton, the District's representative on Capitol Hill who was very attached to the teachers' union, mounted as much opposition as possible. As Ford put it, "She literally engaged the entire educational bureaucracy." While the debate ensued, Kenneth Campbell worked his contacts at COPE to pull in support from the corporate sector.

A relatively strong bill passed through the Education Committee by a narrow margin, but efforts were made by dissenting Councilmembers to water it down significantly before it came up for a vote before the full City Council.[231] The local bill did not come up for a final vote—and approval—until after until Congress had acted.[232]

We now turn to the Newt Gingrich portion of this story. After the Republicans took control of the House in 1994 and Gingrich became the Speaker, he took several steps that expedited the creation of charter schools in DC. While he might be better known for his showdown with President Clinton that led to the government shutdown, Gingrich also proposed a four-pronged initiative for reforming DC, and improving education was one of those prongs.[233]

Not long after the 1994 election, a policy analyst named Ted Rebarber received a funny but important phone call.[234] When the phone rang, Rebarber wasn't quite sure who it was. The voice on the other end said, "Hi, I'm Steve Gunderson, can I talk to you?"

It didn't ring any bells.

"I'm sorry, who is this?" Rebarber asked.

"Steve Gunderson. I'm a member of Congress." (To be fair, Gunderson was a Wisconsin Representative known as "Mr. Dairy," Rebarber had never set foot in Wisconsin, and you don't expect members of Congress to call you directly.)

Rebarber's work up to that point had focused primarily on choice and accountability. As a research associate at Vanderbilt's Public Policy School working with Checker Finn (who later co-wrote the seminal text *Charter Schools in Action* with Bruno Manno and Gregg Vanourek[235]), he had organized a mini-conference in 1990 for the National Conference of State Legislatures (NCSL), where more than a dozen states had sent representatives to discuss educational policy ideas. There he met Ted Kolderie; in fact, some of those discussions convinced Ken Nelson, a Minnesota legislator, to support chartering, which ultimately enabled Minnesota to pass the nation's first charter law. From there, Rebarber had taken a position at the Federal Department of Education, working with Assistant Secretary Diane Ravitch on standards and testing in 1991, right after President George H. W. Bush and the governors came up with their National Education Goals.

Ravitch had urged Gunderson to call Rebarber.

Gunderson had won reelection as the Republicans took the majority, and he was hoping to make some dramatic changes to the Federal Department of Education (DOE). He told Rebarber that as the Agricultural Committee Chair, his vision was to unite the DOE with the Department of Labor (DOL), do workforce education, and improve coordination among related programs. In fact, he'd already drafted a bill to connect the DOE and the DOL and was hoping to move it forward.[236]

Intrigued, Rebarber agreed to take the post as Gunderson's legislative and communications director. Although probably neither of them realized it at the time, they were both perfectly positioned to help advance DC charter legislation—Rebarber because of his educational policy background, Gunderson because of his appreciation for the importance of community involvement, as well as a few other reasons. For one, he'd announced before the election that he would not run again. Although some constituents worried that he would be a lame duck, he felt free to pursue issues he cared about. As he saw it, "Knowledge is power in the halls of Congress, and if you have the ability and the time to become an expert on any area of policy, you will have influence."[237] Also, because he was close to Gingrich, who was counting on him to lead other moderate Republicans along with his pressing agenda, he felt like he could make a difference.

As a result, very quickly Gunderson and Rebarber both got pulled by the Gingrich tide, as it were, into the "improving DC education" pool. Gingrich created task forces as a way to go around or supplement the committee structure, which enabled him to recruit people he thought could solve an issue. In this case, as Gunderson later pointed out, Gingrich was actually *not* trying to work around Bill Goodling, who was then Chair of the House Education Committee. Goodling and Gunderson were allies, and Goodling was supportive of Gingrich's ideas. "But he had a thousand other things to do as chair of the committee," Gunderson explained. "He didn't have the time to dig deeply into DC schools, so that's why Newt wanted somebody like me to do that."[238]

Gingrich created a "DC Education Task Force" and held a televised press conference to announce that Gunderson would lead it. Overnight, Rebarber's job description changed, but he was really excited about that because it meant he would be involved in something real—as he put it, "more than moving deck chairs and rearranging boxes on the federal bureaucracy."[239]

Gunderson's office began receiving calls from all over DC. A day or two after Rebarber produced a policy memo for him to consider, Kenneth Campbell showed up and said, "Here's our plan." COPE's plan called for completely restructuring public education with charter schools. At the same time, Speaker Gingrich weighed in with his own preferences. As Rebarber recalled, "He thought vouchers were the way to go. He said, 'None of this is going to help unless we have vouchers. It's fine to do other stuff, but here's the piece I care about: make sure you get vouchers in there.'"[240]

Gunderson focused heavily on community outreach and held dozens of meetings to try to get his arms around what needed to happen. Years later, he told me that although he'd spent "hours and hours" in conversations with the superintendent and school board members, the meeting he remembered best was this one:

> I'm sitting in my office in the Rayburn Office Building late one night; Congress is in session. It's around midnight. The janitor comes in. He said, "Mr. Gunderson, can I have a word with you?"
>
> I said, "Sure."
>
> He said, "I just want to thank you for all that you are doing to help my kids get a better education." Honestly, I've never forgotten that.[241]

As he considered various proposals from the task force, Gunderson sought input from others. He met on many occasions with Albert Shanker, then the head of the American Federation of Teachers (AFT), and Ted Rebarber recalled one of those encounters vividly:

> Al Shanker came in, and Gunderson was thinking, "Is this [idea of charter schools] too radical? How hard should we push on these? Shouldn't we just be helping them buy computers or something? I don't know—but a more traditional kind of support for schools?" He was really trying to wrestle with that. So he said, "Al, what do you think we ought to do?

People have proposed that we have a limited number of charter schools, or something like that."

Shanker said, "Congressman, every school ought to be a charter school." Gunderson was really floored by that, that the head of the AFT would say something like that. Shanker said, "Well, of course. Teachers should be able to create schools, or educators, and they should be held accountable. I know this is my union, and people in my union that aren't excited with this, but this is my position, and it's for the kids."

So, after that, Steve decided, "If Al Shanker can say this, then we can be really bold."[242]

The rest of the story about how DC got its charter law probably deserves its own book. While Rebarber and others worked on the House version of the bill, staffer Richard Wenning worked just as diligently on the Senate side. Wenning, a detailee from the General Accounting Office (GAO), had led the first national study of charter schools in 1995, requested by Senators Durenberger, Kennedy, and Specter.[243] Senator Arlen Specter, who was interested in the private management of public schools, had brought Wenning in to shepherd his amendments.[244] Wenning was captivated by the idea of holding schools accountable for performance; years later, he would lead the development of the Colorado Growth Model, a game-changing tool for school performance evaluation[245] (discussed in Part III). As things proceeded, he found himself working with Senator Jim Jeffords on the DC Appropriations Subcommittee of the Senate Appropriations Committee. Among other contributions, he inserted language enabling residential charters, which ultimately facilitated the creation of the SEED School, one of the first residential charter schools in the country.[246] And later, once the law finally passed, he took on the primary responsibility for implementing it as the Senior Policy Advisor to the CEO of the DC Public Schools, including coordinating the launch of the DC Public Charter School Board.[247]

External agents also played essential roles in shaping and passing the legislation. Jim Ford and Kenneth Campbell provided vital input. Marc

Dean Millot, a policy analyst then at the RAND Corporation, also advised on the bill.[248] Jeanne Allen at the Center for Education Reform brought in Lisa Graham Keegan, the Superintendent of Public Instruction in Arizona, to talk about her state's legislation, which featured an independent chartering authorizer separate from the district; and as a result, the DC law also included an independent Public Charter School Board,[249] a decision that would have important consequences later.

The bill did not pass quickly. In fact, it almost didn't pass at all. Gingrich's insistence on a voucher provision became a sticking point. Also, the bill was attached to the DC Appropriations bill, meaning it could not pass unless DC received its funding, so when the federal government shut down, the charter bill languished not far from the piles of trash steadily accumulating on the district's sidewalks.

Even after all of that work, as attention became focused on reopening the government, it looked like the charter bill was not going to be included. Ted Rebarber recalled:

> Finally, there was an omnibus deal with Clinton on the whole government bill, and at that point, the question was whether any piece of this bill was going to get stuck in at all, because Gingrich had said, "You've got to have something on school choice." At that point, it was clear that was never going to happen, because that had lost in the filibuster in the Senate. So, I talked to Gunderson and he said, "I don't think anything's going to happen, because Gingrich said it's got to be vouchers."

I said, "Let me talk to the Speaker's office, and if we can persuade them to get something in, can we get the charter schools?"

He said, "OK, if you can persuade the Speaker's office, I'm OK with it."

We talked to them, and we said, "OK, no money, because the Speaker said, 'I don't want to pour more money into a failed system,' and all that. So, no money," but they never really understood the charter piece, so I tried to explain to them, "You can do this without new money. This is all about money that is redirected based on where the kids go. Let's just get this in with no new money, but at least let's do this."[250]

The aide said he would check.

At the eleventh hour, as the negotiations were nearly finalized to reopen the federal government, Representative Eleanor Holmes Norton realized that the charter bill was in there, and she was not happy. Rebarber recalled:

> She was running around saying, "You can't pass this, there's no deal on the whole reopening bill," but at that point she couldn't get any Democratic support, because everyone was focused on the vouchers [which were not included] and this was going to reopen the government. She didn't really want to keep the government shut, she wanted to change the charter law. She couldn't get any support, and at that point, the deal had been struck with Clinton to reopen the government, this is on page thousand-something of a 2000-page bill, and it just sailed through.[251]

In 1997, the leaders of COPE decided to create a new, free-standing organization: the DC Public Charter School Resource Center, initially led by Kenneth Campbell. When Campbell left DC to work with charters in Boston, Shirley Monastra, COPE Deputy Director, became Executive Director of the organization.[252]

By 2018-19, 123 of DC's public schools were charter schools.[253]

The Carlos Rosario International Public Charter School was one of them.[254]

CHAPTER 12

A POT OF MEATBALLS AMONG FRIENDS

While John Ayers and his colleagues in Chicago were busy assembling their piece of the charter school puzzle and Kenneth Campbell began putting together the D.C. Public Charter School Resource Center, I was still trying to figure out how to launch the New Jersey Charter School Resource Center.

I had three things going for me: determination, luck, and networking. After the 1995-96 school year ended, my only income was a modest stipend to plan the September conference. Having such a limited cash flow tends to focus the mind. I was willing to work around the clock to make the Resource Center happen. But of course I couldn't do it alone.

That's where luck and networking came in. When I'd first considered leaving my teaching job, I'd called David Mallery, an educational consultant who was a dear friend and mentor who liked to say that life was too short "so we should always order two desserts." A mutual friend once described David as being "determined to inspire every teacher within the sound of his voice," and he definitely had that impact on me. I'd met him at a Dodge Fellows Retreat a few months into my rookie year. He could see that I was barely treading water, and with great compassion, he helped me to reflect on what had brought me into the pool—my admiration for some amazing teachers I'd been lucky to have and my determination to do something meaningful with the excellent education I'd received—and then he kept encouraging me, through countless letters and phone calls (for decades, in fact), to "keep at it."

In April when I called him, David offered two pieces of advice: "First, make a list of everything you want in your next job. Dream big. Don't leave anything off, or else you won't get it. Second, take seven minutes—and no more than seven minutes!—and make a list of everyone who knows you and loves you, and send them that list, and ask if they have any ideas for you or know anyone who could help you get a job with the things on that list." One person I sent the list to was Alan Rosenthal, a family friend who happened to be on the board of the Schumann Fund for New Jersey. He told me I should talk to a guy named Tom O'Neill, who ran a nonprofit called the Partnership for New Jersey.

Tom turned out to be exactly the right person to talk to. His organization, formed right around the time that *A Nation at Risk* was released, brought together the leading CEOs in New Jersey to address key challenges in the state. From its inception, the Partnership had focused on trying to find ways to bring business resources and experiences to bear on school improvement and improving educational outcomes. One of Tom's first steps was to arrange for a group of CEOs to meet with Ernest Boyer (the President of the Carnegie Foundation for the Advancement of Teaching), who, as Tom later recounted, "essentially gave them a pep talk about how important it was, what they were going to be doing."[255] In the ensuing decade, the Partnership tried various approaches, with varying degrees of success and impact. First they developed a curriculum of training courses on a whole range of management topics that were offered by Partnership members to school leaders. Then in the city of Paterson, they launched several "I Have a Dream" initiatives (based on Eugene Lang's program, which began in East Harlem in 1981, when he told the sixth-graders at whose graduation he was speaking that if they graduated from high school, he would pay for their college tuition),[256] but owing to the high mobility of students, the success rate fell short of their aspirations, and they began to look for another approach.

They brought in the ubiquitous Sy Fliegel to explain what he was doing at the Manhattan Institute's Center for Educational Innovation (CEI), and when I met Tom, he was working on a proposal for an initiative that would emulate CEI, deploying "Senior Fellows"—experienced, well-known school officials whose record of school improvement was clear—to work with struggling schools in urban districts. Fliegel's success in District 4 was again having positive ripple effects.

The arrival of New Jersey's charter legislation added a new dimension to the work the Partnership was contemplating. "The idea of charter schools brought to light the free market approach to not only providing a school in and of itself that would have more energy and creativity than a typical public institution, but would serve as a competitive benchmark against which to evaluate the public institutions," Tom said. "It was 'The Bible According to the Harvard Business School.' The CEOs went for it in a big way."

He invited me to help expand his proposal, and a month after the September conference (which 220 people attended), we met with foundation program officers from Dodge, Schumann, and the Fund for New Jersey to discuss prospective board members for a new nonprofit called the "New Jersey Institute for School Innovation," which would function as the umbrella over the also newly-created "New Jersey Charter School Resource Center."

My days and nights quickly became a rushed blur of Parkway and Turnpike tolls, driving from one end of the state to the other, trying to help planning groups marshal resources and information as they prepared applications. The learning curve was steep because—let's face it—I had never started a school myself, so I was learning right alongside these people. Week after week, I spoke at dozens of community meetings, partly to get the word out and partly to beat back the myths and misunderstandings that bubbled up relentlessly: "Charter schools are private schools, right?" *Wrong; they are independently governed but publicly funded; in other words, they don't answer to the local district school board; they have their own board.* "Charter school students don't have to take the *state tests, right?" Wrong; charters are held accountable for performance, including student performance on state assessments, and—unlike failing district schools, which are rarely closed no matter how poorly they perform—charters can actually be closed if they fail to meet the terms of their charter.* "Charter schools can cherry-pick the students they want, right?" *Nope, if they have more applicants than slots available, they have to have a random lottery. It says so right in the law.*

It turns out there was one "good" thing about ripping my Achilles tendon: because it had prevented me from driving to grad school for six weeks, I was forced to sit through my Ed Law course a second time. Understanding education law—particularly the charter law and regulations—was crucial to my job. As Eric Premack had predicted in our first phone call, I also needed to become an expert in the arcane minutiae of school funding. "How much funding will we get, and when?" was a common query. "How are we supposed to pay for our building with no facilities funding?" was another. Even though some federal start-up funding was available at this point, it wouldn't kick in until a charter was approved. So how were founders supposed to get this thing off the ground? Writing the application took time and money: nothing was easy or free.

Eager to learn as much as I could about how to help applicants and new operators, I reached out to colleagues in other states. Collaboration across state lines was vital to our success. It wasn't like you could go to the library and check out a book about how to help people start charter schools. The Internet in 1996 was still in its infancy (Google.com wasn't even registered as a domain name until 1997[257]), so although some Web resources were available (mostly listservs), they were quite sparse. And schools of education were not exactly banging down doors to develop courses about charter schools. In the early days, Katherine Merseth at Harvard, who helped to plan the Dodge-sponsored conference in September, and Pearl Kane at Teachers College, who conducted a study of New Jersey's charter schools in the first year,[258] were among the few who appeared willing to devote attention to this budding movement. What held them back? My sense was that they didn't want to offend the mainstream educators who buttered their bread. Looking back, Tom O'Neill reflected,

> The higher education institutions that take an interest in K through 12 education are generally the ones that are married to the production of teachers who go into traditional public schools, and are generally run by people who come out of traditional public schools. Therefore, I think they have been less than helpful to the charter schools and the charter school movement than they otherwise would have been.

Partly because I needed their help and partly because I just wanted to hang out with my new friends, I invited about a dozen charter support leaders to my house. For a day-long retreat. With a pot of meatballs.

That was how I found myself standing in my kitchen, sautéeing garlic on a late June morning on Long Beach Island in 1997, when I heard slamming car doors, then voices.

"We're here!" someone called. Peering out the window, I saw Linda Brown tugging overnight bags out of the car with several other women.

"It smells like an Italian restaurant in here!" Linda exclaimed as I greeted the other guests: Patsy O'Neill, who ran the Texas Charter School Resource Center; Thelma Glynn, who ran a private school and a resource center in North Carolina; and Susan Hollins, who worked independently and was trying to help start charters in New Hampshire. A few minutes later, another car pulled up: Jeanne Allen, from the Center for Education Reform. Then another: Shirley Monastra, who'd taken over the DC Charter School Resource Center while Kenneth Campbell was away serving his military obligation.

"Funny how the women all arrived first," I remarked. We chuckled.

Not long after that, Jeremy Resnick showed up with his colleague Chenzie Grignano, who would run the Charter Schools Project when Jeremy left to start his first school.

Jeremy announced that he had "good news and bad news." Which did we want first?

We asked for the good news.

"Pennsylvania just passed a charter law!"

And the bad news?

"The law requires local board approval until 1999."[259]

We shook our heads in commiseration. Requiring local board approval was like asking Burger King to approve the opening of a McDonald's across the street. It meant that few schools, if any, would open.

We were still digesting this news when Eric Premack walked in. He looked skinnier than usual. I told him I was going to fatten him up with some meatballs.

"Well, you could try," he replied with a grin.

We migrated from the cramped kitchen and sat in a horseshoe in my equally modest living room. A few settled on chairs, a couple on the couch, a few sprawled on the rug—and then we began introducing ourselves. Some of us had talked on the phone but not met in person before.

Then there was a knock and the front screen door banged shut, and John Ayers walked in and waved to the group. "Sorry I'm late," he said. "I just drove down from New York, and the traffic was brutal. Now I understand why they call it 'The Parkway.'"

I set up an easel and we took turns sharing our most pressing questions. We made Ayers the poster scribe because he had the neatest handwriting or possibly because he arrived last. I also took notes on my laptop. Even the most mundane topics were up for discussion. When someone asked, "How do you communicate with all of the school founders, to keep them informed on a regular basis?" we were excited by Patsy's idea of the "Friday Fax." (This was before high-speed Internet and email.) No detail was too small. When Thelma explained the logistics of running job fairs and vendor fairs, she even told us how much she had charged per table this year ($75) and how much she planned to charge next year ($125).[260]

We learned that while there was clearly overlap in what we did—we all ran informational workshops, for example—we also approached the work from different angles. Jeanne said her office spent "65 percent" of the time on charters (the rest on other forms of choice) and described how she was trying to put together a media kit, keeping track of legislation across the country (and "what you need to do to get legislation passed"), and "trying to get the attention of non-charter people to inform them about charters." Shirley said she was planning to run workshops every other Saturday morning for planners, while Linda noted that her own focus had shifted from "Facilities and Funding, Buildings and Bucks" to "Leadership and Governance/ Management"—in other words, from launching to maintenance. She shared some charter school profiles she'd written to get the word out about effective schools, and urged us all to develop them in our state: "They're easy to produce," she said. "People need to see what's going on in order to understand it."

Eric agreed and chimed in, "You need a lot of horsepower around a coffee table for two years to get something really good off the ground. Everyone needs to understand that this is hard work." He said he was preparing briefing papers on special education and fiscal planning, and he wanted to align specific training with these papers. He was already running what he called "boot camps" for planners and operators; he wanted to do more.

We took a lunch break and walked to the beach even though Linda protested that we would lose momentum. She needn't have worried: we were still talking about what we were doing. The next day I would host my second major conference, and most of these folks would share what they knew with 150 people in New Jersey. Then they would go home and hit the ground running in their own states.

It became obvious that we needed to meet again. In the months that followed, a slightly different group, which included Margaret Lin and

Kenneth Campbell, met for two more retreats, both at Fort A.P. Hill, a site that Campbell secured through his military connections. Along with problem solving, we spent time cooking together and taking nature walks. Even in that relaxed setting, most of our conversations revolved around how to help charter school applicants and operators more effectively. It was pretty much all we thought about, around the clock.

Over the years, our interaction was very informal; no one ever directed us to talk or meet. We relied on one another simply because we had problems that were important to solve and we realized that we could solve them if we talked through them and worked together. We also recognized that everyone had a little something different to bring to the table. And there was no one else to ask for help. Building these relationships enabled us to call one another at any time, to share ideas and resources and to benefit from the lessons learned in other states.

Looking back, Linda Brown reflected:

We were in a naïve industry. I guess that's what you say about start-up. We were in an industry that didn't exist; we were causing the existence of it by what we wrote, by who we talked to…. We got to know each other. We were our own band of brothers. And those were some of the best relationships…. This group was ageless because we had common cause. That was the first time I really realized what could happen when you collaborate. You could smell the ideas; you could smell the burning brains.[261]

Kenneth Campbell added:

You had all these places that would literally come together to help us figure out how to do this work better and stronger. None of us had to do it, but in my view, there was a little bit of magic in that. I don't know that I've ever been involved with anything that had that same pioneering spirit of "If we work together, we'll figure out how to get this done."[262]

The sense of urgency at these gatherings was electric. We knew the stakes were high. We knew the work was important, and we all wanted to do our best.

Seventeen years later, when I bumped into Jeanne Allen at the National Charter Schools Conference, she told me: "I was just talking about that meeting we had in your living room! I was meeting with some educators in Kenya who wanted to know how the charter school movement had spread in our country. And I told them it was about bringing people together to share ideas, like that time that group of us met at your house. It was all about building a network."[263]

Who knew a pot of meatballs could have so much impact?

CHAPTER 13

HERDING CATS, PART I

The earliest plan to hatch a national organization for charter schools was launched, oddly enough, in the Mall of America. On September 12, 1996, a relatively mild fall day in Minneapolis, Ted Kolderie and Jon Schroeder met for lunch with two representatives from the Challenge Foundation,[264] William "BJ" Steinbrook, Jr., the executive director,[265] and John Bryan, who'd donated $30 million to the foundation.[266] Challenge was one of the earliest philanthropies to offer start-up funding to charter schools, and program officer Cathy Nehf[267] had encouraged her bosses to meet with Ted and Jon to hear what Ted, ever the Big Picture guy, was thinking now.

As the waitress set their drinks down, Ted began to make his case. More than two dozen states had passed charter laws, and the people who ran state associations and resource centers—he liked to call them "charter friends"—had lots of common concerns. He'd been providing informal support for a number of years now, but these folks—these "friends"— needed more help to coordinate their efforts. Jon Schnur was doing what he could from his post in the Department of Education to support the implementation of the policy, but it was clear that the federal government was not sufficiently nimble to respond to emergent needs and requests, nor could it properly address thorny issues related to different states' laws.

For a while now, Ted had been bouncing this idea around with his friend Jon Schroeder (who'd been working with a large nonprofit in Minnesota since leaving DC)[268] to develop a "Charter Friends National Network" (CFNN). He'd known Schroeder for more than 20 years; in fact, Schroeder's first paying job out of college was at the Citizens League with Ted. As noted in Chapter 4, Schroeder had spent ten years as a senior adviser to U.S. Senator David Durenberger,[269] and largely as a result of their efforts, Congress had approved the first round of federal start-up funding for charter schools.[270]

Ted believed Schroeder would be the perfect point person for several reasons: 1) because of his connections in Minnesota, he already knew many key players around the country; 2) he had useful contacts in DC; and 3) his humble demeanor would make it clear that he didn't want to boss people around, he simply wanted to be of use. Decades later, Schroeder recalled that he was very aware that people in the field "didn't really want anyone to be claiming to be the national spokesperson for the charter movement, either as an individual or as an organization." And that was fine with him. He remarked: "That was pretty consistent with my style and modus operandi. I have a pretty small ego and was very happy to play [again] a supportive role."[271]

As they sat at lunch, the four men chewed on the idea. Schroeder recalled:

It was sort of this weird thing: there were these four men sitting in this restaurant at the Mall of America and nobody was really taking responsibility for this decision. It was kind of like, *Well, we have Ted who is behind this and thinks that it's needed. It probably is, and it's probably a good idea. Even though we've been just supporting schools with start-up funding for charter schools, there's probably going to be a need for some charter funding for infrastructure.*

John Bryan finally spoke up and said, "Well, if BJ has confidence in Ted and Ted has confidence in Jon, you know, I suppose we can do this."

The Challenge Foundation committed $100,000 for the first year with the chance to renew several times, and the Charter Friends National Network (CFNN) was born. Several months later, the Walton Family Foundation joined Challenge as CFNN's second major funder.[272]

To keep its profile as low as possible, CFNN became a "project" of the Center for Policy Studies, a St. Paul nonprofit, which partnered with Hamline University to hire Schroeder. The Center contracted with Hamline for Schroeder's time, but CFNN had no members, board, or dues. Schroeder was simply CFNN"s "Project Director," reporting to a combination of the Center and Hamline. And all future personnel were engaged on a temporary contracted basis.

Almost immediately, Schroeder went on the road to start meeting and building relationships with state-based charter leaders. He began with a core group of resource center and state association leaders who would become mentors to emerging leaders in states passing and expanding their laws. From 1996-2004, his travels took him to 26 states, where he met with community and school leaders, spoke at state and national conferences, was interviewed by local and state media, and testified before state legislative committees.[273]

CFNN produced an array of papers on accountability, facilities financing, and special education to advance work in the field. One of the leading authors was a bright young man named Bryan Hassel, whose research and design of innovations would plant seeds for change in the roles of K-12 teachers in traditional public schools as well as charters. Hassel's story began in 1993, when he arrived at Harvard University to pursue a doctorate in public policy.[274] A Rhodes Scholar from North Carolina, he initially intended to study welfare reform, but his plans changed. He recalled:

> The welfare reform professors of Harvard went to work for [President Bill] Clinton in 1993, so there was no one there to work with. Also, when I got up there, I thought, *Welfare reform is kind of depressing*. So I needed to find something

else to do. There was some good stuff happening with job training, but it wasn't really life-changing, I didn't think.

I started thinking, *What's life-changing?* and that's what led me to education. I started casting about for topics and went to see Richard Elmore, a professor at the Ed School, and I said, "I'm interested in education reform, and I want to study something cutting-edge and interesting. Do you have any advice?"

And he pulls this memo out from this stack, and it's from Ted Kolderie, and he said, "This is what you ought to look at. This is really interesting. It's new. There's not a bunch of other scholars working on it. This is real. There's all this other stuff in education about site-based management and giving principals autonomy, and that's all a bunch of crap. It never really happens; it comes and goes; it's not real autonomy. This is real. You should look into this." So I did. Ted—indirectly, I guess—was the guy that got me involved because I read that memo and went from there.

One of Hassel's first steps was to go meet with Linda Brown, who explained what was going on in Massachusetts. He began working on his dissertation about early charter legislation, but he found "there was so little capacity in the field at that time that I started getting asked to do things—write things, help with meetings that were being organized.... There were really only eight people in the whole country that were thinking about charter schools. So it was very interesting to get involved, and it was exciting."

After completing his coursework, he moved back home to North Carolina, continued to work on his dissertation half-time, and started doing various projects, including writing CFNN-sponsored guidebooks for schools and state resource centers. In the course of studying and working with charter schools, he published dozens of articles, studies, policy manuals, and one of the earliest books on charter schools.[275]

Along the way, he became interested in trying to solve one of the biggest problems in the field: *How can we ensure that the most effective teachers are positioned to have the most impact?* He and his wife, Emily Ayscue, created a North Carolina-based nonprofit called Public Impact, and one of its primary initiatives was to create and study "Opportunity Culture" schools. Their vision for states, districts, and schools was two-fold: 1) to reach all students with excellent teaching, consistently, and 2) to reach all educators with outstanding career opportunities for on-the-job learning and paid career advancement, sustainably funded.[276]

While running CFNN, Jon Schroeder also tapped the expertise of Jim Griffin, the head of the Colorado League of Charter Schools. In addition to being instrumental to the growth of the charter sector in his home state, Griffin became a national expert on facilities financing and a key partner in the development of the Colorado Growth Model, a game-changing school performance evaluation tool (see Chapter 28).

The story of how Griffin became involved with chartering might be titled "The Accidental Volunteer." In 1994 (not long after Bryan Hassel arrived at Harvard), Griffin was simply looking for a topic for a law review article, and he thought he might have an idea.

A self-described "policy geek," he had followed K-12 reform avidly. He recalled, "I was always interested in a whole variety of policy areas. Through high school and college and beyond, I would read a couple newspapers a day; that was just part of it. And the idea of education reform always piqued my interest."[277]

He was in law school when Colorado passed its own charter school legislation on June 3, 1993.[278] Six months later, it dawned on him that he could write something for the law review about the implementation of Colorado's new charter law. While perusing the newspaper one morning in late January, he noticed an article about how the first round of charter school founders were struggling with the lack of understanding about how the law was supposed to work. *This is intriguing stuff,* he thought. The article mentioned that the Colorado League of Charter Schools was holding an informational session, and "Anyone interested in attending is welcome to join." He later recalled:

> I got up that next Saturday morning and went to this meeting, and at the end, I just stood up in the back and raised my hand and introduced myself and said, "Look, I'm a law student, and I'm looking to do a research paper or a research piece on the implementation of this charter school law," and I basically said, "I'd love to hang out with all of you folks and learn about your story, and if you'd let me, I'd love to interview a few of you and get the scoop, and maybe I can give some assistance to you in some way, shape, or form down the road."

> So the woman at the front of the room, who's moderating this whole thing, says, "Oh, boy, I think these people would probably be interested in talking to you. Maybe you want to give out your name and phone number and see where it goes."

> So I give out my name and phone number and all of a sudden I'm in the back of the room, and I'm watching all of these adults frantically scribbling my name and number down. And I'm like, *Oh, shit.* I'm 26 at the time, in law school; I don't think of myself as an adult; I'm living in what amounts to a young-adult fraternity house with a bunch of my high school goon friends, and here these adults are going to call my house on Monday morning, and one of my idiot roommates is going to pick up. Lord knows what sort of stupid thing they will say on the phone.

> Sure enough, Monday morning the phone started ringing. The next thing you know, one thing led to another and I was going to the meetings and I'm starting to go to other events for some of these new school groups that are inviting me to all the different things and the monthly get-togethers of the Colorado League of Charter Schools; I started going to every one, and after about two of them, it was clear that this group

was very hungry to have somebody take charge and lead and run this stuff.

At the time, the "League" was simply a group of people interested in charters. There was no entity; it wasn't incorporated; it was simply a name attached to a monthly meeting of interested parties.

So, as I'm finishing law school, they say, "Why don't you come work here? Why don't you launch this organization? We don't have any money to pay you, but we have some leads and a plan and energy and interest." At 26 and single, paying $250 a month for rent, I could afford to take a little shot at something different and interesting. So I did.

Beginning in the spring of 1994, he didn't get paid for four or five months. When visiting schools in outlying areas, he lacked money for hotels. On one particularly challenging November night, having maxed out his personal credit card, he slept alone in his Jeep at the base of a 9,000-foot mountain pass.[279] Eventually, he and Mary Ellen Sweeney (the woman who'd asked him to share his phone number) applied to the Gates Family Foundation and received a three-year, $100,000 grant in December 1994 to support the League's work.[280]

The audience's reaction from that very first meeting left a huge impact on Griffin:

They hear "law school" and they think I'm a lawyer. I didn't know anything about anything. It told me immediately two things: one is how powerful that idea about being a lawyer really is and how much stature you get even if you don't know a thing. It blew me away that reasonable adults would just hear that and think that I knew anything. And then secondly, in our specific field, how little anybody understood about any of this and that in spite of how little I knew, I still knew more than anyone else. And it didn't take very long before that was truly the case. Six months in, I realized how much I knew and how much I understood of it.

When I asked him how he figured out how to do his job, given that he'd had no prior experience in advocacy or legislative work, he replied:

> We just did it. We had to. It wasn't hard to figure out where the problems were and where the challenges were and what schools were struggling with. That was not difficult. On the legal and advocacy and the policy side, it wasn't hard to see where our problems were in terms of schools getting approved or in terms of facilities or in terms of legal problems and headaches and things our statute just got wrong. There's nothing like immersing yourself at any given time.

He worked with the 12 schools that opened that year[281] and was in daily meetings and conversations with the next set of applicants all across the state. He quickly grasped the problems with the statute, and he began devising a plan to address them.

Griffin and his colleagues developed a soup-to-nuts menu of services for charter school founders and operators. They helped groups prepare applications, provided legal advice, assisted in negotiations with districts, and designed model policies. On behalf of charters, they conducted statewide public relations and media work, advocated in the state legislature, and held meetings and conferences to train founders, boards, and operators.[282]

Nearly 20 years later, as he was inducted into the National Charter Schools Hall of Fame,[283] *Colorado charter schools were serving 10 percent of the state's children.*[284] His organization, the Colorado League of Charter Schools, had largely enabled that growth. His efforts, along with those of his colleagues and thousands of charter school founders and staff members, had led to the creation of nearly 200 charter schools serving almost 90,000 students.[285]

PART II

SCALING UP: QUANTITY VS. QUALITY

CHAPTER 14

EXPLAINING THIS NEW THING

Whenever something new appears in the world, people immediately begin to judge it. And the amount and quality of information they receive about the thing really matters. Charter schools are no different. One challenge for those of us trying to support the birth and growth of these nascent schools was that we needed to help other people see their potential even though not all of the schools were great—and some were in fact quite awful.

As soon as New Jersey's first thirteen charters opened in September of 1997,[286] my phone began to ring with invitations from business and educational leaders who wanted the Coordinator of the New Jersey Charter School Resource Center to meet with them. They had lots of questions.

It was difficult to show them what was going on because the technology at that time was so limited. You couldn't refer people to the Internet. At that point, it was not a reliable resource. Google didn't exist.[287] People had created some groups, listservs, electronic bulletin boards—pockets of information that were helpful if you knew where to look. But few schools had Websites. Everything was very hit or miss, and we couldn't even think about showing video: You Tube would not be invented for another 8 years.[288] The public relied on traditional media—TV, newspapers, and magazines—whose coverage of charters was limited.

Like most people back then, I didn't own a digital camera or a smartphone. Nor was it feasible to run a one-day field trip as Linda Brown had done in East Harlem because New Jersey charters were scattered too widely around the state. So I went out and visited every new school and met with every principal. I took notes and photographs, then had the film developed into slides and created an old-fashioned slide show, "A Tour of New Jersey's Charter Schools."

One morning in October, as I prepared to speak to the Middlesex County Superintendent's Roundtable (a group of about 40 superintendents), I was feeling a bit queasy. It was a potentially explosive situation. Two districts in the county had "denounced" the proposed Greater Brunswick Charter School and appealed its approval.[289] As I adjusted the focus on my slide projector, I scanned the room, looking for a friendly face. Several dozen sober-looking grey-haired men in dark suits stared back at me.

I turned off the machine and waited as the host called the room to order. He pointed out that though there was "a little bit of controversy" about charter schools (hahaha), he knew that everyone was eager to learn more about these new schools.

I nodded, took a breath, and dove in: "Thanks for inviting me. I want to begin by saying: I come in peace; I hope to leave in one piece." That drew a collective chuckle. Then I spoke about my background and my passion for public education (with evidence: my career). I talked about how the Charter School Resource Center played a tiny role under the umbrella of the New Jersey Institute for School Innovation and how my new boss, former State Commissioner of Education Mary Lee Fitzgerald, was planning to do many other things for public education, especially urban districts.

Then I showed my slides. The first three slides showed the view looking out from Camden's LEAP Academy Charter School: rundown buildings; an empty, overgrown lot; a large, ugly apartment building. The next three or four showed the amenities in the Sussex County Charter School for Technology, which utilized (and in fact was created to maximize) the facilities of the Sussex County Vo-Tech School: computers in almost every room, robotic equipment, an Olympic-size swimming pool.... The array continued: from bubbly-looking bulletin boards and forest-green plaid uniforms at the Robert Treat Academy (a K-8 started by well-known Newark political boss Steve Adubato, Sr.[290]), to casually-dressed students sitting on the floor, playing chess, at the Learning Community Charter School in Jersey City. I talked about how hard the teachers and school leaders were working to try to do something positive for these children, how thoughtful they were trying to be in forming new school cultures. I concluded with the story of the drum circle I had seen on the first day at North Star.

When I finished speaking, they actually clapped—not just politely, but with vigor. I was startled. I took questions, then it was time to break for lunch. Several superintendents pulled me aside to tell me that I had done a good job "especially with this crowd." Wow. That was a good feeling.

Of course, not every day in the charter world went as smoothly as that one.

In fact, about a year earlier, one of DC's first charter schools had blown up (figuratively) in a high-profile way. On December 20, 1996, the front page of *The Washington Post* carried the headline "D.C. Charter School Principal Indicted in Clash with Reporter."[291] Along with the principal, three staff members at the Marcus Garvey Public Charter School were indicted for assaulting a *Washington Times* reporter. The scandal bore racial overtones: the school had an Afro-centric curriculum, the principal and staff members were black, and the reporter was white.

In truth, the school was struggling and probably never should have opened. The DC law had created two charter school authorizers: an independent DC Public Charter School Board (which took some time to get off the ground, but then gained momentum and developed a strong portfolio of schools), and the existing elected DC Public Schools Board, which had been stripped of all authority except for its ability to authorize charter schools. Which they did. Badly.

This mess had fallen in Richard Wenning's lap. After shepherding the legislation as a Senate staffer, he had become the Senior Policy

Advisor to General Julius Becton, the CEO of the DC Public Schools. His new job was "to implement the charter legislation," which meant everything from negotiating with the DC government and Mayor Marion Barry about getting the DC Public Charter School Board operational, to ensuring that funds flowed to schools, to staffing the elected DC Public Schools Board.[292]

In Wenning's eyes, the elected board was "like a wounded animal."[293] The board members lacked the capacity to review, approve, and oversee charter schools, and they were not allowed to do anything else. Before he was hired, they'd chartered several schools. "They did a lousy job in approving the first set of schools with no real due diligence," he remarked. "And they continued to charter schools using a political process with sloppy authorization practices that no one liked."[294] One of his first acts in his new job was to shut down an approved school before it even opened. Then the Marcus Garvey situation erupted.

For months, this controversy boiled in the news and would not be stilled.

A few weeks after I showed my slides to the Middlesex County superintendents, *60 Minutes* announced that it was going to air an episode about the Marcus Garvey school. We all knew it would show charters in a negative light. Jeanne Allen, from her perch at the Center for Education Reform, urged charter supporters to Email *60 Minutes* and "express your dissatisfaction with the specific charter highlighted and represent the unified, nationwide coalition of activists who are actively promoting the charter concept."[295] It seemed like the story would never die.

Finally, in May of 1998, the *Post* reported that the DC School Board had revoked the Marcus Garvey Charter, citing "a pattern of fiscal mismanagement."[296] But the damage was done. Successful schools did not get as much press as failures. The people running good schools were too preoccupied to work on PR, and the media preferred to cover problems, anyway.

Many of us in the field felt like we were constantly under attack. Although the movement was growing rapidly, it remained very new and small. Not all charter schools are alike, so it does not make sense to judge them all based on the performance of one. But most people still didn't know what a "charter school" was, and half of the states didn't even have a law yet. Even charter school employees were often uncertain about the differences between a charter and a district school.

When failures like Marcus Garvey dominated the news, they jeopardized our efforts to build a solid foundation of strong schools. As much as we believed that failing schools should be closed, we wished even more fervently that they had never been allowed to open. Every struggling school called into question whether charters should exist at all. It was starting to feel like a death by a thousand cuts.

While much-publicized failures like the Marcus Garvey school enflamed the debate about the quality of charter schools, my colleagues across the country and I tried to remind people that a key premise behind charter schools is autonomy in exchange for accountability. Unlike failing district schools (which often receive additional funding), failing charter schools are *supposed* to be closed. We did not defend the Garvey school; we agreed that a dysfunctional school should be held accountable. And we didn't want the entire movement derailed by the failure of a few.

This chart from the *National Study of Charter Schools Second-Year Report* shows how small the movement was in the first few years:[297]

	Number of states with charter school laws	Number of charter schools operating
1992-3	1	2
1993-4	3	36
1994-5	6	101
1995-6	10	255
1996-7	17	433
As of Sept. 1997	24	693

In his State of the Union Address on February 4, 1997, when President Bill Clinton called for the creation of 3,000 charter schools by the next century,[298] we appreciated his support and optimism, but we knew that our existence was tenuous at best.

Also: that "next century" was only three years away.

CHAPTER 15

WHY AREN'T ALL CHARTER SCHOOLS GREAT?

For Linda Brown, John Ayers, Eric Premack, and the rest of us in the trenches running state-based charter support organizations, our work involved a lot more than trying to explain what charters were about. Day after day, we focused on how best to help charter school founders and operators succeed. Some schools became great, developing materials and practices that became strong roots taking hold in the field (described in Part III). But not all did.

Some people might ask—and in fact many critics have: *If chartering is such a great idea, why aren't all charter schools great?*

In the introduction to *Angels and Elbow Grease*, a charter school application handbook that I developed with support from Linda Brown and others, I noted: "Starting a charter school is not for the faint of heart. It is like starting a business—except that more people are watching and the consequences of failure could be much worse. It is a huge undertaking. Not everyone will appreciate your efforts."[299]

Charter school founders face an array of challenges:

1) Finding and financing the facility. Except in a few states, charters receive no facilities funding and must pay for renovations and facilities expenses.[300] It's hard to secure a bridge loan when your school isn't open yet and you have no collateral. Even if you happen to find a "free" building, as one charter school founder said, "Free isn't really free." You still have to pay for renovations and maintenance—even if the building comes with a janitor.

2) Start-up costs. In the beginning, it was difficult to start charters because so few people knew what they were. Potential vendors were suspicious of these unknown entities. Matt Candler, who helped charter operators in the early days in Chicago, recalled: "Back then you couldn't get someone to sell you textbooks because they were like, 'What's a charter school, and who are you, and why the hell should I take your money when you're not a district?'"[301]

Over the years, I met several founders who, like Yvonne Chan, had mortgaged their homes to cover start-up costs.[302] Before the federal government began offering start-up grants in 1994, the absence of start-up funding was not only challenging for founders individually; it also created some unanticipated problems for the movement as a whole.

3) Some bad apples. The state of Arizona, which suffered from a lack of philanthropy, was seen as fertile ground by for-profit EMOs (Educational Management Organizations). Unlike CMOs (Charter Management Organizations), which are non-profit and supported by philanthropists who want to replicate successful schools, EMOs tend by definition to be focused on the bottom line. "People thought EMOs had the magic sauce because they brought capital," explained Jim Ford, who consulted there in the late 1990s after working on the DC legislation. "So the Arizona State Charter School Board received a lot of political pressure to approve for-profit EMOs."[303] One consequence was that some people drew negative conclusions about the motivations of founders when they heard about the involvement of "for-profit" entities.

The perception that charter founders were "in it for the money" was exacerbated by the actions of some nonprofit community-based organizations and community development organizations, which treated charters as "cash cows" for their parent organizations: having students meant a guaranteed income stream. A Progressive Policy Institute study of Arizona's charter schools from 1994 to 2004 noted that there had been "serious problems at individual charter schools, ranging from egregious financial misconduct to illegal religious instruction to discrimination against children with disabilities."[304] The study also found that before the practice became prohibited, some districts "sold" charters to schools far outside their own boundaries, collecting fees but doing little to oversee the schools.[305]

Arizona saw rapid charter growth. By 2003, 495 schools—*nearly one out of four public schools in the state*—were charters.[306] Not surprisingly, there were questions about quality control. As of December 2003, only seven charters had been revoked; 36 had voluntarily surrendered their charter (or closed under threat of revocation), and three revocations were pending.[307]

As a result, Arizona became known as "The Wild West."[308] Some of the toxic seeds planted there grew into three sweeping lines of attack that critics have since used against charter schools *nationally*: 1) Charters were "private" or "just another attempt to privatize education and make a profit," 2) Charter founders "just wanted to start religious schools," and 3) "Many" charters were terrible. In the next chapter, we'll see how these problems led to a push for increased accountability.

4) Staff recruitment and retention. Finding talented educators is an ongoing challenge for the field, and as described in Part III, several key charter leaders began to address this problem by creating new organizations that target teacher training and leadership development—not just for charters but for district schools, as well.

Along with the routine difficulties of "getting the right people on the bus," as Jim Collins would say,[309] brand-new charters face an additional struggle: it's hard to recruit staff when your school doesn't exist yet. People want to know, *What am I signing up for?* Even once the school is open, you need people who are the right fit. Charters tend to be administratively lean, and many have longer school days and longer school years. Some educators thrive in start-up mode: they are willing to wear many different hats and devote long hours to the work. Others find the work unsustainable or "not what they expected," so they leave—sometimes abruptly. And in stark contrast to the business world, it's hard to find excellent replacements in the middle of the year: in teaching there is a distinct, limited hiring season.

5) Student recruitment. When you start a new school, you are asking parents to trust you to provide a great education for their children in a school that doesn't exist yet. Depending on what other choices are available to them, they might not want to take that risk. And if you fail to meet your student recruitment targets, you will be under-enrolled and therefore under-funded. In charter schools, the money follows the students. Fewer students means less money.

6) Governance. On the surface, it might seem as though charter school boards have advantages over district boards. One of the open secrets of traditional public schooling has been the inability of many elected board members to meet their responsibilities. Board corruption, nepotism, local feuds, and incompetence have plagued school systems for decades, often leading to high rates of superintendent turnover and causing instability in districts. Netflix founder and educational philanthropist Reed Hastings has argued that politically motivated board candidates who promise "change," then throw out the superintendent and churn through programs make long-term planning impossible.[310] At the 2015 California Charter Schools Association's annual conference, he proposed a solution to this traditional district problem: to create instead "a system of large nonprofits" running charter schools. In charters, appointed trustees have the potential, at least, to develop a stable governance structure.

Another promising aspect of charter boards is that they are legally accountable for school performance: if a charter school fails to meet the requirements of its contract, it can be put on probation or closed. Until recently, failing district schools could operate with impunity. But this distinction has begun to evaporate. In 2002, New York City Schools Chancellor Joel Klein tapped into the charter-based momentum for accountability and began closing schools.[311] Other district leaders—including Michelle Rhee[312] and Kaya Henderson in DC,[313] and Cami Anderson in Newark[314]—soon followed suit.

While this emphasis on accountability is important and might heighten charter board members' sense of urgency, it is not sufficient to ensure the effectiveness of charter boards. Although some charter boards have developed effective governance practices, *their collective capacity to govern remains mixed.*

Why? Because being appointed (as opposed to elected) is no guarantee of quality. And being "committed to the mission" is not enough, either. Board members must understand all aspects of their charter agreement, including, as governance expert Marci Cornell-Feist notes, "what the charter promises, the methods proposed to deliver the promises, and a clear sense of how these promises will be measured."[315]

Board members also need skills and training in order to conduct proper fiscal and academic oversight. Unfortunately, the training they receive is often inadequate or misdirected. In the mid-1990s when he was running the Central Michigan University Charter Schools Office, Jim Goenner brought in the District Association of School Boards to talk to his charter school boards, and he quickly realized that they did not know their audience. He recalled: "The whole conversation essentially centered around how do you do a bond issue, how do you calculate your millage tax." He told the presenters in frustration, "They can't even levy taxes. We told you that."[316] Charter trustees in New Jersey faced a similar experience: required by law to attend board training provided by the New Jersey School Boards Association,[317] for years, they received exactly the same training as district board members even though their schools could not float bonds or put budgets before voters. More targeted training would help set schools up for success.

7) Opponents. Although the idea of chartering has had bipartisan support among legislators, governors, Congressmen, and Presidents since its inception, it has also had staunch enemies. As Ted Kolderie observed, the idea "was just automatically, instinctively opposed by all of the associations representing the organized elements of K-12."[318] For years, charter schools have faced a continuous onslaught of legal and legislative challenges.

Opposition from teachers' unions (with a few exceptions[319]) has been unrelenting. In spite of Al Shanker's early advocacy, many state-level union leaders have worked aggressively to undermine charters, presumably because in most cases they are not required to be unionized (and therefore do not generate dues).

Even some activists who initially supported charters have developed concerns. Possibly the most famous flip-flopper is Diane Ravitch, a prolific writer on education reform issues who from 1991 to 1993 was Assistant Secretary of Education under President George H.W. Bush. Ravitch also served on the National Assessment Governing Board from 1997 to 2004 (appointed by Secretary Richard Riley in the Clinton administration).[320] Through the late 1990s, she avidly supported school choice and accountability. In a 1996 essay, for example, she and co-author Joseph Viteritti lauded charter schools as one of the "most notable initiatives" amidst a "burst of bold experimentation in the organization and governance of schools,"[321] and in 1997 they published an entire book, *New Schools for a New Century*, which elaborated on the promises of such reforms.[322] However, she changed her mind about things and in the early-mid 2000s began to express her opposition to ideas she had previously espoused.

Former New York City Schools Chancellor Joel Klein noted in his memoir:

> Ravitch played as big a part as anyone in calling America's school reform movement into existence by prominently articulating the core ideals—accountability, choice, and innovation—that animated it. But despite having been a strong supporter of [Mayor Michael] Bloomberg and the programs we were pushing, soon into my tenure she became the reform movement's and my fiercest critic.[323]

In March 2004, Ravitch and union president Randi Weingarten wrote an op-ed piece in *The New York Times* that called for rolling back the mayor's authority over the schools.[324] In 2010, Ravitch published *The Death and Life of the Great American School System: How Testing and*

Choice Are Undermining Education,[325] in which she recanted many of her earlier beliefs.[326]

Why was her reversal such a big deal? Ravitch had a large following,[327] and such a vocal opponent could influence the views of politicians, funders, and others whose work could either help or impede the efforts of charter school founders.

Diane Ravitch was not the only surprising opponent. In August 2016, the NAACP (National Association for the Advancement of Colored People) issued a call for a national moratorium on any new charter schools.[328] Howard Fuller (introduced in Chapter 6) quickly responded with a commentary in *Education Week*, noting that this call represented "a dramatic shift away from an approach that is working to advance the educational interests of people the NAACP has historically represented."[329] He argued that it would pit the NAACP against black families, many of whom are working-class and "in desperate need of the types of educational opportunities that are being provided by charter schools." He pointed out that the number of black families choosing to send their children to charters was actually growing. Black enrollment in charters was at 27 percent—almost double the 16 percent in traditional public schools. He added: "Many of the one million names on waiting lists to get into a charter school are black children."[330]

Fuller also shed light on a key reason why black parents were heading to charters in droves: because the schools were showing stronger results. Stanford University's CREDO 2015 Urban Charter Schools Report on students in 41 urban regions across the country found that low-income black students attending charter public schools gained 33 percent more learning in math and 24 percent more learning in reading each year as compared to their traditional public school peers.[331]

8) Ineffective authorizers. Ironically, one of the biggest impediments to charter school quality is the authorizers whose job it is to approve and monitor the performance of the schools. This is such a big problem that I am devoting the entire next chapter to it.

CHAPTER 16

"WEEDING IS HARD WORK"

It was a 25-mile taxi ride from Denver to the airport in 1999 that finally pushed Greg Richmond over the edge.

He'd known for a long time what the problem was.

"While public policy can make people do things, it cannot make people do those things well."[332] This insight from Frederick M. Hess, who has written extensively on educational policy,[333] applies to charter schools as much as any other policy. In state after state, laws enabled chartering but did not ensure that the idea would be implemented perfectly. And some laws, from the start, were poorly written.

As the lead authorizer of charter schools in Chicago, Richmond was acutely aware that charter authorizers—which, depending on the law, could be state boards of education, commissioners, universities, or districts[334]—lacked guidance on how to perform their jobs. Laws and regulations tended to address *what* authorizers were supposed to do (review applications, evaluate schools, and renew or close them) but not *how* they were supposed to accomplish those tasks. Also, because the laws were so new, there were very few experts on how to be a good authorizer. The hundreds of authorizers scattered around the country had no one to call.

Some didn't even *want* to be authorizers. Bureaucrats with zero interest in supervising new schools would say it was "not their thing."

Some only cared about getting "their cut," the percentage designated for services they were supposed to provide. And some were not effective at running their own district, so why would they be good at authorizing?

Indeed, the challenges that authorizers have faced are numerous. In a 2012 study, David Osborne enumerated nearly a dozen obstacles that *prevent* the closure of ineffective charter schools:

- Too few authorizers collect a robust body of evidence of charter school performance.
- Too many authorizers lack adequate staff and funding.
- Authorizers have incentives to keep schools open.
- Too many charters lack meaningful, measurable performance goals.
- Too many authorizers have no clear criteria for renewal and revocation.
- Sometimes, closing a charter school would send students to schools that are worse.
- In some states, appeals to the state board and/or courts reverse and inhibit authorizer decisions.
- Charter operators often make 11th hour turnaround attempts when threatened with closures.
- Sometimes a poorly thought-out charter law gets in the way of a closure.[335]

Quality control from the beginning was largely a function of authorizers' attitudes and capacity. While some states enacted charter laws with very tight caps, others were less restrictive. Allowing the creation of numerous schools became a problem in those states that took a laissez-faire approach to authorizing. In Arizona, one observer noted, "early on, the attitude was, *Let a thousand seeds blossom. Quantity will lead to quality. If we build it, they will come.* There was little in the statute about accountability; it was all about autonomy."[336] Between 1994 and 2002, the

Arizona State Board for Charter Schools (ASBCS) approved a whopping 76 percent of the applications it received.[337]

That approach enabled some ineffective schools to open—and because so many were approved, it was difficult to monitor them all. As Bob Bellafiore, the former head of the SUNY Charter School Institute (an authorizer in New York), put it, "You can let a thousand flowers bloom, but weeding is hard work."[338]

Twenty years after Arizona's first charter schools opened, Lisa Graham Keegan, the state's Superintendent of Public Instruction from 1995-2001,[339] acknowledged that autonomy had preceded accountability in her state. But she also felt some good things had emerged. "If I had a magic wand," she said, "and I could rewrite the way history progressed, I would have loved to have had accountability out in front of choice, but who knows? I think that Arizona 20 years hence is positioned to be one of the fastest-improving states in the country."[340]

From the beginning, Keegan strongly believed it was important to expand choice and involve community members in that process. The Arizona charter law for the first four years required that the state board have at least three members from low-income communities. In hindsight, she was aware of the trade-offs. "We had a much higher percentage of low-income kids in public charter schools at first," she recalled. "And, frankly, that's why we had so much failure: a lot of new schools were started by really well-intended community folks who had always worked in low-income communities, but they didn't know... how to run a school."[341]

When asked for her response to the critics who referred to Arizona as "The Wild West," Keegan replied:

> First of all, I believe in the power of great people bringing great things to the public and letting folks choose them. A lot of the education movement—even the reform side—believes in a central plan where "We're going to control all of this and we're going to make it happen the way we want it to happen. Our expertise is going to make everything safe for the world."

I don't believe that, and I think that is one of the key reasons that we had a lot of success in our public charter school sector.

We are one of the only states that spawned about a half-dozen really high- performing *suburban* charter school networks. Great Hearts, BASIS, the Sonoran Science Academies, EDUPRIZE.... They were able to do that because they had the liberty to move in those districts. A lot of folks constrained their public charter school movement to low-income areas. Surely that's the highest need, but you don't learn everything you need to know when you constrain them and there was no reason to. You could do all of it at once.

To a lot of people who were more comfortable with the incremental practice, that looked like "The Wild West." We did not have higher failure or closure rates than anybody else. We just had a lot more stories about what we were doing because there was so much of it.[342]

In truth, it is difficult to find the data to assess Keegan's assertion about the failure rate because so many of Arizona's charter schools were not included in the state's accountability system owing to their small size.[343] Some struggling schools might have been overlooked.

Arizona's problems were not solely a function of authorizer inclination or capacity. The law also contained a loophole that gave districts additional state funding simply for converting to charter status. "We had a major school district that literally sent a flyer out to all its parents saying, 'Nothing is going to change here, but we'll get $1,500 more per pupil,'" Lisa Graham Keegan recalled. "They just called their schools 'charter schools' and tried to draw down that additional assistance." The state eventually closed that loophole in 2014.[344]

Arizona was not the only state with high-profile problems.

After Texas passed its charter law in 1995, the State Board of Education established a lax application process, allowing many weak schools to open. In 1998, the Board—stunningly—approved all 109 of the 109 applicants.[345] Revisions to the law tightened up the application standards, but the damage was already done.

In 2005, when some charter school folks wanted to lower the standards so that weak schools could continue to operate, Patsy O'Neill, the Executive Director of the Texas Charter School Resource Center, stood before the Texas Education Agency and pleaded for better authorizing.[346]

"For the health of the whole charter movement," she said, "we must close charters that should not be open." She hoped that establishing higher standards would help clean up what she saw as charters' unfairly bad reputation. Of the 33 charters that had been revoked, returned, rescinded, or expired, 25 were from the round approved in 1998. By contrast, in 2004, only five of 55 charter applications were approved. She hoped that the new rules would strengthen the quality of the state's charters to the point that legislators would consider expanding the number of charters, which was then capped at 215.[347]

Meanwhile in Washington, DC, the Board of Education voted to give up its own authority after years of ineffective, politicized authorizing practices when its former Charter Schools Oversight Office administrator, Brenda L. Belton, came under federal investigation for possible misuse of funds.[348] (Belton was later convicted of stealing and illegally steering more than $800,000 in school system money and sentenced to 35 months in jail.[349]) The independent DC Public Charter Schools Board, which had maintained a more successful portfolio of schools, took the lead as the sole authorizer in the District. This was a step in the right direction.

During the late 1990s, Greg Richmond went to every major national meeting on charters looking for solutions to the problems that undermined charter school quality. He and his colleagues from Chicago, John Ayers and Margaret Lin, were struck by the fact that 99 percent of the people they met at these conferences were running charter schools.[350] "There was so much talk at those conferences about improving charter schools," Lin recalled, "and yet half of the equation was missing."[351]

Aside from Scott Hamilton, whose accountability work in Massachusetts drew national attention, the only other authorizer Richmond ever seemed to bump into regularly was Jim Goenner, an earnest, buttoned-down guy who led charter school authorizing out of Central Michigan University (CMU).

In 1995, Goenner—who was inducted into the National Charter School Hall of Fame in 2010 for his contributions to the movement[352]—was teaching at a local community college, coaching Little League, and pursuing an MBA when he received a call from Dr. Robert Mills, an old family friend, who wanted to know if he wanted to come to CMU and work in the Charter Schools Office.

Goenner's mother was a district schoolteacher, and his father, a university professor, had been a superintendent, so he told Mills he would have to think about it. "I asked around," he recalled. "Everybody said, 'Well, Jim, if you do that, you won't be able to work in public education again.' I thought, *Wow, that's a challenge. I'll take the job.*"[353]

He quickly fell in love with the work, and after a brief stint running the Michigan Association of Public School Academies (MAPSA),[354] he returned to CMU, and when he met Greg Richmond at a Charter Friends National Network meeting in Tampa in 1998, he confessed that one of his secret passions was to make authorizing a respected profession.[355] They agreed that traditionally respected professions like medicine and law have standards—so why shouldn't charter school authorizers, too?

Richmond went back to Chicago to confer with his friends, and they wrote a letter to Alex Medler, who ran the Charter School Grant Program at the U.S. Department of Education, suggesting that before the next national conference, the Department should sponsor a day for authorizers to improve their practice.[356]

Medler loved the idea. He'd been involved with charters since 1992, beginning as a researcher and policy analyst at the Education Commission of the States.[357] In 1995, he and Joe Nathan published one of the first research reports on charter schools (titled *Charter Schools: What are they up to? A 1995 Survey*),[358] and he spent a lot of time testifying at state houses about the idea of chartering. One thing that amused Medler on those trips was how the teachers' union leaders would invariably stand in front of legislators and proclaim, "Charter schools are evil," but then afterward, in the hall, they would tell him what they would do if they started their own charter.[359]

Medler was well aware of the challenges authorizers faced and agreed that they needed more support, so he set aside some funding and spoke to Jon Schroeder at the Charter Friends National Network about shepherding a pre-conference. Schroeder asked Lin to organize one, and as a result, the March 1999 National Charter Schools Conference in Denver began with a pre-conference for authorizers.[360]

More than 200 attended from all across the country, hungry for information.[361]

On his way back to the airport after the conference, Greg Richmond found himself in a cab with another authorizer. "She complained the entire way about 'these charter schools,'" he recalled, "and by the time I got on my plane, I thought, *What a shame; what a completely different attitude. Here I am thinking this is fantastic stuff.*"[362]

This was the last straw. *Something needs to be done*, he thought. *We need to know who each other are that are doing this work and find a way to be in touch and learn from each other.*[363]

Back in his office, he called Medler and asked for a list of everyone who'd attended the conference. He wanted to convene a meeting to see who was seriously interested in sharing ideas. Would the Department be willing to support such a meeting?

Yes, it would. Medler sent Richmond the contact list and found $20,000 in the US Department of Education budget for a meeting in Chicago, which was held in the fall of 1999. Roughly 30 people showed up—including Goenner; Ed Kirby, who had replaced Hamilton in

Massachusetts; Josephine Baker and Richard Wenning, from DC; and Bob Bellafiore, from New York.[364]

Richmond recalled: "We said, 'All right, we don't want to create an Association or anything like that because we've got enough work to do, but let's put some working groups together, get an Email listserv, etc.'" That was the approach for the 1999-2000 school year, but by the end of that term, it was clear that if they wanted to actually accomplish anything, they'd have to form an organization.[365]

First, they would need funding.

They faced an uphill battle. At the time, the dominant charter philosophy was that the best way forward was the "thousand flowers" approach—to open as many schools as possible as quickly as possible. There were two reasons for this. For one, people believed in the virtue of the model. For another, they were captivated by the ideas in the book *The Tipping Point: How Little Things Can Make a Big Difference*.[366] "There was a strong belief in this Tipping Point theory," Richmond recalled, "that competition will then cause the rest of the system to improve. Nobody knows what that Tipping Point is, but when a school district starts losing kids—15 percent, 20 percent, or certainly 25—they have to change in order to survive."[367]

Many believed that authorizers had little to do with the potential success of the movement. They thought the model was so good, you only needed somebody to stamp "approved" on the paper. Richmond recalled: "The notion that you would want to organize these people, who were mostly bureaucrats, and get them active and busier, was really questioned by folks in the advocacy community for charters, who thought that was actually a bad idea: 'You don't want to organize these people; they're bureaucrats. They're just going to threaten the model.'"[368]

Richmond and Jim Goenner set out to persuade the Walton Family Foundation to provide funding for an Association, and in July 2000, they met in Detroit to put together a founding board, wrote up some bylaws, and incorporated.

In November, they went to National Charter School Conference to introduce themselves to the rest of the charter school world with Richmond as the Founding Chairman.[369]

He recalled that the "roll-out" meeting was a little rocky:

There was a group of us, about seven people, essentially standing in front of a ballroom of other folks, saying, "You've never heard of us, but we are now the National Association of Charter School Authorizers, and you should follow us and recognize us as being the national association."

And it was like: "Who are you? Who gave you *this* authority?"

In order to be accepted, we had to not assert that we knew anything better than the other people we wanted to join this because if we'd asserted that we know what we're doing and you don't, there would've been no organization.[370]

Reformers who had left mainstream education to start fresh new schools were actively opposed to participating in anything that smelled like a moldy bureaucracy. The closest thing to a national organization, the Charter Friends National Network (CFNN), was not really even an organization.[371] We didn't have to pay dues.

So the emergence of a formal association was a bit startling, and the National Association of Charter School Authorizers (NACSA)—a non-profit focused on how to support authorizers, strengthen accountability, and improve the quality of charter schools—caused some folks to sniff with suspicion.

Margaret Lin became the Executive Director in March 2001.[372] For the first few years, Greg Richmond was very aware of the need not to be prescriptive. NACSA took what he described as "a librarian attitude" toward the work: "We just collect books and put 'em on the shelf; we don't tell you what books to read; you can come in and check them out if you want, but you don't have to. You can read 'em if you want, but you don't have to. We're just librarians."[373] The NACSA Website featured numerous documents from people in the field.

In September 2001, NACSA received a federal grant to promote quality authorizing activities, including producing a publication about what they were learning, which sparked a heated debate amongst its board members. Richmond recalled:

> "Would it assert that we know things, or not?" There were board members who were adamant that we should not be producing a publication that says, "These things are better than those things; these activities and these practices are better than those practices" because "that wasn't the charter way." Some of us who were around then joke about it to this day, that for the first couple of years of our existence, we couldn't even assert that we knew anything, and we put out a publication called "Critical Questions for Charter School Authorizers"—this is just the *questions*, not the answers.[374]

But as time went on and board members turned over, they learned more things, and in late 2004, they were finally able to publish NACSA's "Principles and Standards for Quality Charter School Authorizing."[375]

By 2005, Richmond had logged more than ten years at Chicago Public Schools (CPS), and although he and the other board members thought NACSA was doing well, they believed it could do a lot more. In March of that year, he left CPS to work full-time at NACSA as its President.

That August, when Hurricane Katrina and widespread flooding devastated New Orleans, Richmond's work took another turn (see Chapter 25).

In July 2012, still working to strengthen charter authorizing from coast to coast, Richmond wrote a letter to *The New York Times* that summed up NACSA's views about the importance of quality and the role of authorizers in ensuring it:

> Few can dispute that all parents should be able to enroll their children in a high-quality public school. Good charters provide that choice. But charter status doesn't automatically mean excellence; many are superb, some are not. The

authorizing bodies that approve and monitor charters have an essential role in seeing that they provide a quality education, treat all students fairly and spend tax dollars appropriately. With strong and smart oversight, charters are more likely to be excellent, and parents are more likely to be able to choose a school that's best for their children — a mission that all of us in public education can share.[376]

One telling indicator of how much things had changed: in the fall of 2013, Lisa Graham Keegan—the same person who had championed the "thousand flowers" approach years earlier—became the Board Chair of NACSA.[377]

Weeding had won the day.

CHAPTER 17

THE SUPERINTENDENT AND THE ENTREPRENEUR

The story of how Don Shalvey and Reed Hastings hatched a plan to lift the cap on charters in California is funny but also important. Their efforts ended up changing the charter school landscape across the country.

In 1992, while Eric Premack watched as business cards fluttered down in the California State Senate chamber,[378] Don Shalvey, the new superintendent in the San Carlos School District, was in the middle of a listening tour. The board had won him over with their very first interview question: "Our kids do pretty well here and the staff's pretty good, but neither the kids nor the staff are having any fun. What would you do to increase the amount of fun kids and staff could have in this system?"[379] Now he was trying to figure out how to answer that question.

Walking around, he heard complaints from the middle school teachers that they had "the worst possible life" of any teachers in the system.[380] They taught a longer day than the elementary, didn't have prep time like the secondary, and so on. And even though San Carlos was an affluent district in Silicon Valley, the budget was actually tight. State regulations restricted enrollment, which in turn pinched per-pupil funding.[381]

So as he faced these challenges of low morale, staff inequities, and declining enrollment, he looked far and wide for solutions. And when he laid eyes on the new charter law, he realized it could solve all three problems.

As quickly as he could, he assembled a team and developed a plan for a school that would be an R & D lab around technology and multi-age instruction. This "lab," the San Carlos Charter Learning Center, opened with 85 students in 1994.[382] As the first charter school in the state and because a district leader—*a district leader!*—had founded it, the school drew lots of media attention. As the years went by, it added grades and continued to thrive.

One morning in July 1997—a noticeably quiet morning as most of the staff was on vacation—Shalvey was sitting at his desk, calmly combing through some reports, when the phone rang.

His secretary told him: "It's the White House."

"Yeah, right," he said.[383]

But it was true: President Clinton was planning to sign a piece of legislation to create more incentives for charter schools across the country and wanted to do it at Shalvey's school.

On the day of the visit, Shalvey introduced the President, who—ever the consummate politician—began by complimenting him twice: praising first Shalvey's speech, then the depth of his commitment to the school ("If you look closely at his tie, you will see it is a pattern of golf balls and tees. And on this beautiful Saturday morning, he's here with us!"[384]). After a few more light remarks, he dove into the topic at hand: his longtime support for charter schools and his more recent efforts to help grow the movement with federal funding. There followed a roundtable discussion featuring business leaders and educators, then the first lady made some closing remarks, and the president offered additional remarks (beginning with, "First of all, let me say I agree with everything she said," which drew guffaws[385]).

Afterwards, as Shalvey stood smiling on the stage, watching the audience of 250 streaming out of the packed room, a dark-haired young man in his 30s with a goatee came up to him and said, "Hey, I've been following your career. Do you ever think that there'll be more than a hundred charters in California?"[386]

"I really don't think so," Shalvey replied. The state had been capped for a number of years.

The man with the goatee said, "Well, I'm not an educator—I'm an entrepreneur—but I've got a little bit of time on my hands. Would you mind—how would you think about going to lunch to talk about this?"

They shook hands. The entrepreneur said his name was Reed Hastings.

Two weeks later at lunch, Hastings explained that when Shalvey was starting his charter in 1992, he had been starting his first company, Pure Software. He'd started it for $400,000 and had recently sold it for $750 million. He couldn't work, he said, and since he had some time and really cared about education, he thought maybe they could work together to get the law changed.[387]

They formed a 501(c)(4), non-profit political organization, called Californians for Public School Excellence (CPSE).[388] Shalvey went to his board and took a 20 percent leave. Every Friday for several months, he and Hastings worked to prepare a proposition that would lift the cap. They hired firms to get all the signatures and qualify the proposition. Every Friday, they drove to Sacramento and tried figure out what to do. Having little political experience, they relied on a $9.00 paperback called *The Initiative Cookbook* that they'd heard some Green groups had used to pass earlier propositions.[389]

One Friday in March, in the midst of this work, when Shalvey got into the car, Hastings said, "I know what I'm going to do next."

"Well, last week you didn't know what you were going to do," Shalvey said. "What's the deal?"

Hastings had returned the movie *Apollo 13* to Blockbuster and they'd charged him a $40 late fee.[390] It was absurd. He thought he had a better idea.

That idea became a little company called Netflix.

Around this time, they were ready to run a proposition, and then the California Teachers Association came to them. As Shalvey later explained, "They said, 'We don't like what you're doing, but we don't hate it enough to want to spend our money to fight it. So, if you'd be willing to give us your million signatures, we'd give you our political clout and we'll work together to get your initiative and make it a bill. We'll see if we can get it passed.'"[391]

And in 1998, they did. Governor Pete Wilson signed the revised bill into law. Which is why, by 2018, there were 1,323 charters in California instead of only 100.[392]

At the same time, Shalvey and Hastings set the stage for an even more important innovation—in fact, a new phase of growth—in the charter school movement. The new law allowed one board of directors for *multiple* schools, which meant that people could create a new entity called a "Charter Management Organization" (CMO). Using $400,000 that was left over from the CPSE campaign fund, Shalvey and Hastings flipped the 501(c)(4) to a 501(c)(3) and created "Aspire Public Schools," the first CMO in the country.[393] They had learned from the first five years that they didn't want to create more school boards, but they did want to replicate good schools.

Aspire started a trickle which eventually—when combined with a major shift in how philanthropies allocated their dollars—became a torrent of CMOs: KIPP, Uncommon Schools, Achievement First, YES Prep, Strive Prep, Democracy Prep, Success Academy, MATCH Schools, and on and on.

It might be useful to consider why this shift mattered.

On the one hand, forming networks could help schools become more efficient. Before CMOs existed, most charters stood alone. It was harder for them to marshal and share resources, and school leaders had to become experts (as much as they could) in staff recruitment and all aspects of curriculum and instruction, not to mention reporting and operations. CMOs centralized some of these functions and enabled school leaders to focus more time on instruction.

On the other hand, the significant diversion of philanthropic support into CMOs meant there would be less support for so-called "Mom and Pop" charters, the stand-alone schools that had no desire to replicate. Some charter advocates worried that the emphasis on *replication* would mean less attention paid to *innovation*.

In the next few chapters, we'll look at how several influential CMOs were developed, and in Part III, we'll consider the impact they've had on the field more broadly.

CHAPTER 18

A COUPLE OF ROOKIES

While Norman Atkins and Jamey Verrilli were founding North Star Academy, two other educators—Mike Feinberg and Dave Levin—were laying the groundwork for KIPP (the Knowledge is Power Program), which became one of the largest and best-known charter management operations in the country.

But these two men did not originally plan to run even one charter school, much less 224 schools serving 96,000 students.[394] In fact, for a while, they were just a couple of rookies trying to survive. At several points, it was not even certain that they would stay in the field.

How did KIPP get off the ground?

In the summer of 1992, Mike Feinberg and Dave Levin joined Teach For America (TFA), a two-year commitment to teach in an urban or rural public school district. They had both felt drawn to teaching as a result of tutoring experiences—Feinberg with Ethiopian Jews in Israel,[395] Levin with inner-city children in New Haven public schools.[396] They'd also faced their own challenges growing up—Feinberg with stuttering,[397] Levin with decoding words[398]—and developed both grit and a sense of empathy for students who struggle.

After the TFA summer training institute, they drove from Los Angeles to Houston, where they'd been assigned, full of ideas and enthusiasm. As Jay Mathews notes in *Work Hard. Be Nice.* (his comprehensive narrative about how KIPP came to be), by the time they stopped on the Arizona border,

> they had completely dismembered and reassembled the public education system. They had figured out how to fix everything. They had detailed plans for better schools. They had ideas for financial incentives for students, families, and teachers so that more students could go to college. They even had a budget, about $150 billion, which they would take from the Defense Department, since it no longer had to spend all that money on the cold war.[399]

A few weeks later, when they began trying to teach, they realized how little they actually knew. Their classrooms were chaotic. Every day was a struggle.

Ironically, one solution—the power of home visits—came to Levin when he went to a student's home to apologize out of mortification for doing something that could have gotten him fired. The boy had been bullying others and completely ignoring Levin's remonstrations. One day when the boy refused to return to his seat, Levin—who was tall, strapping, and 22—abruptly picked him up, carried him back to his seat, and dropped him into it. When he explained to the boy's mother what had happened and apologized, her response surprised him.

"Do whatever you have to do," she said. "You're the first teacher that ever came to the house…. He doesn't listen to me. Do whatever you have to do."[400]

Levin of course did not take this an endorsement of corporal punishment, but as a signal that he should visit more homes. He began doing so routinely and found it had several benefits: it gave him more clues about what might motivate his students; it demonstrated that he truly cared about them; and it helped him build relationships with their parents, who would back him up when needed.[401] Feinberg, stationed at a different school, tried the same approach and found it equally beneficial.[402] When they later decided to launch their first KIPP class, home visits would become an essential tool for recruiting students and parents.

But home visits were not enough; after all, they did not strengthen teaching practices. Feinberg and Levin, like any other inexperienced teachers, needed effective mentoring and coaching, and they didn't have that—until one day when their luck changed.

Harriett Ball, a charismatic master teacher, happened to teach across the hall from Dave Levin. A few weeks into the school year, he worked up the nerve to ask her for help. She allowed him to sit in her room during his prep periods, and he took careful note of her mnemonic chants for math and grammar. He was in awe of the array of exercises she used to engage students in learning. He brought Feinberg in to watch, too, and they both peppered her with questions. Under Ball's tutelage, their teaching improved dramatically.[403]

Even so, in 1993, at the beginning of their second year, they felt increasingly disconsolate as they watched what happened to their former students when they entered middle school. Students returned to visit with dismaying stories about the low expectations they faced, and when Feinberg and Levin visited those schools to help prepare their students for 6th grade,[404] what they saw was often underwhelming and in one case, horrifying.

At one school, when an unfamiliar teacher asked Feinberg to stand in and cover his class briefly, he found students playing dice, chatting, and putting on makeup. One by one, he asked them if they had work to do; they all said no. The teacher was gone for fifteen minutes, and when he returned, he said, "Thanks. I needed to make a phone call."[405]

The system was clearly broken, and Feinberg and Levin did not see any way they could fix it. What was the point of raising students' hopes and expectations in 5th grade if they were going to be treated like this in 6th? How could they even hope to make a dent?

Again, luck intervened.

It is hard to imagine what Feinberg and Levin would have done after that school year if another TFA corps member, Joe Sawyer, had not convinced Feinberg to go hear Rafe Esquith, an elementary teacher from Los Angeles who had recently been named Disney Teacher of the Year and was speaking on that October evening at Lee High School. They were both somewhat in despair. Feinberg was considering law school, and Levin was talking about returning to New York at the end of this school year, when their two-year TFA commitment would be over.[406]

But they went. And in the space of 90 minutes, Esquith opened their eyes to a new option.

"There are no shortcuts," Esquith began. He didn't think he was better than anyone else; he just worked harder. His students attended school from seven to five o'clock for 50 weeks a year. He'd brought along two girls to demonstrate the kind of work his students did: they solved complicated mental math problems with ease and performed a skit from Shakespeare; they projected their voices with pride. Esquith said he was setting his students up for success in college. They came to him on Saturdays for SAT training. It wasn't magic. Just hard work.

As Esquith talked about what he did, Feinberg and Levin could barely contain themselves. This was exactly the message they needed to hear. They could do this. They wanted to do this.[407]

They went home. It was a school night. Their adrenalin was pumping. They cranked up U2's *Achtung Baby* on the stereo and wrote a plan for the program they wanted to run. By five o'clock in the morning, they had a draft.[408] They decided to call it KIPP—Knowledge Is Power Program—after Harriett Ball's chant, "Read, Baby, Read."[409] By December, they had reached out to Esquith to pick his brain further[410] and finalized a 27-page proposal to show Feinberg's principal, who would pass it up the chain for district approval.[411]

In early June of 1994, they began team-teaching KIPP summer school in the Houston Independent School District with 49 students in one room.[412] At this point, roughly a dozen states had charter legislation. Texas was not one of them. So chartering was not a possibility, at first.

That, along with many other things, would happen later.

CHAPTER 19

KIPP AND YES PREP

In 1995, near the end of their first year running KIPP as a program within a Houston public school, Mike Feinberg and Dave Levin started making plans to launch a second location.[413] Partly owing to the space limitations in the burgeoning Houston Independent School District and partly because Dave Levin wanted to move back to his hometown,[414] they began to explore the possibility of expanding to New York. Sy Fliegel, whose small schools work in Harlem had inspired the Minnesotans who pushed for the nation's first charter school law, again became instrumental. Dave Levin's mother happened to know one of Fliegel's board members at the Center for Educational Innovation,[415] so with that reference, Levin reached out to Fliegel to ask for help.[416] Fliegel met with Levin, found him impressive, and put him in touch with District 7 area superintendent Pedro Crespo, who agreed to give him two classrooms in a South Bronx school.[417]

Meanwhile, Feinberg continued to run KIPP classes in Houston for another year.

It soon became apparent that Feinberg and Levin hadn't been the only TFA '92 Corps members in Houston thinking about ways to shake up the system.

Chris Barbic, Feinberg's friend and occasional roommate, had also seen Rafe Esquith's presentation and left there with a new vision. He later recalled: "Seeing somebody that was actually doing this and saying, 'You can push beyond what you think is possible in the school or the classroom,' that was incredibly inspiring to me." As luck would have it, though, instead of going home and huddling around a computer with Levin and Feinberg that night, he went to visit his then-girlfriend (later wife).

Then he began to develop his own innovative program.

Barbic had gone to Vanderbilt and majored in English, but until his junior year, he was uncertain what to do with his life. *Maybe law school,* he'd thought. But he wasn't excited about it. One night while home on break, flipping around the channels, he came across a PBS special on Teach For America. This was the first year of TFA, which was placing recent college graduates into urban and rural school districts for two-year commitments, and the show followed around a few Corps members in New York and Los Angeles. He was immediately fascinated with the challenges he saw. *Man, that's exactly what I want to do.* He went back to school and in his senior year, while his friends were running around for job interviews, he submitted only one application, to TFA.[418]

Once he began teaching, he was even more hooked, and he knew almost immediately that he would stay beyond the two-year commitment. He landed a sixth-grade position at Rusk Elementary, on the east side of Houston in a predominantly Hispanic community, and he loved it. The only thing he didn't love was the stories his former students would tell when they came back from Jackson Middle School to visit. Much like Levin and Feinberg, he was frustrated with the system. He recalled:

> It was really disheartening because I'd teach kids in my class who, over the course of the year, had really made progress, and they were talking about college and what they wanted to do when they got older. They had dreams and were excited

about their futures…. And then they'd come back and they were shells of human beings and who they were.

After his second year, he began to wonder, *What can I actually do in one year? What's the best case of having kids for one year and having a great school year if there's no guarantee that once they leave my class-room there's anything else happening? It's just a little bit of a drop in the bucket. Some good memories and the kids will probably think fondly of their sixth-grade year. But beyond that, what impacts are we really mak-ing? What can we do? I can complain about it, but what can we actually* do *about it?*[419]

He started getting some parents together and showing them the data at the middle school. "This is where your kids are going to school when they leave here," he told them.

They began to meet regularly, and when they found out there was some extra space at Rusk, they thought: *What if we kept the kids here for seventh and eighth grade and they didn't go to Jackson?*

One day, a new regional superintendent, Hector Ibarra, visited Rusk while making his rounds to talk about change and innovation. Barbic approached him afterwards and said that he'd been meeting with a group of parents who were interested in keeping their students at Rusk for mid-dle school.

Ibarra nodded, "That's great."

Barbic added, "We are actually in fact having a meeting next week, and we would love for you to come."

Ibarra nodded again. "Great, I'll be there."

That gave Barbic another idea. Over the course of the week, he enlisted a handful of parents to do some organizing.

When Ibarra returned a week later, the cafeteria was packed with 200 parents. The look on his face revealed that he had been expecting a much smaller group.

Barbic ran up, grabbed his hand, and announced, "Everybody, this is the new regional superintendent, Hector Ibarra, and he's here to talk about how he could help us keep all of our kids here for seventh and eighth grade!" The crowd erupted into a cheer.

Barbic then launched into a discussion about what the parents wanted. Ibarra didn't commit to anything, but it was clear that they were a force to be reckoned with.

After that meeting, Barbic and a team of parents wrote a proposal to the district and arranged rides for 300 parents to attend the next school board meeting. As the board looked out at the jam-packed room, parents marched up to the mic and declared that they wanted their children to stay at Rusk through middle school, adding, "We are not leaving until you let us do this." A student also gave a passionate speech in support of the idea, and the crowd stood up to applaud her.

Barbic recalled:

The coolest thing about this whole story was that the year before I got there, the state had declared that Rusk was *the lowest-performing elementary school in the entire state of Texas.* In fact, they forced the district to basically remove all of the adults in the school. All of the teachers, the principal, everybody was gone, and this new principal had hired everybody else and was charged with turning the school around.

One of the board members said, "It's amazing to think that two years ago Rusk was considered the worst elementary school in the state and here we have three hundred parents that actually want to keep their kids at this school longer for middle school." So they approved it.

Thus began Project YES, which stood for "Youth Engaged in Service." First they added seventh grade, and the year after that, eighth. They tried to do service learning and project-based learning with fidelity, and their goal was to get students into magnet high schools.

Although a lot of YES students got into those high schools, there were two problems: 1) Not *all* of their students got in, and 2) Not all of the magnets were great. Barbic realized that they hadn't really fixed the problem; they had just punted it for a couple of years.[420]

In 1995, the charter school law passed in Texas.

Barbic approached Mike Feinberg because he knew Feinberg was struggling with facilities and the district kept kicking them into different buildings every year. Barbic said, "We could actually get out of the district; there is this thing called 'charters' now. What if we were a charter and we took KIPP and YES out of the district and started our own school?"

"What the heck's a charter?"[421] Feinberg replied.

Barbic went off to do some research.

In the meantime, Houston ISD Superintendent Rod Paige did something funny. He invited Feinberg and Barbic to speak to a gathering of the 200 Teachers of the Year and asked the two of them to discuss how they'd stalked him in order to get their programs going.

Then Paige turned to the audience and said, "See? These guys brought me their crazy idea and I helped them. I want you to bring me your crazy ideas, too. I want more charter schools like KIPP and YES."

Feinberg recalled, "When he literally said those words, 'I want more charter schools like KIPP and YES,' that's when we became a charter school."[422]

A year later, Paige encouraged Feinberg and Barbic to apply formally for state charters so that they could have more control over their own destiny. Feinberg was desperate for space. All of the district buildings were at 150 to 200 percent capacity, and the district was struggling to pass bonds.[423]

Barbic wanted to serve sixth through twelfth grade. He told parents that he would keep their children until graduation and he wanted to be held accountable. He believed if he had students for seven years, the goal should be college for every student. So he made college admission a graduation requirement.[424]

Because Barbic did not yet possess nonprofit status, he and Feinberg submitted one charter application for two campuses—a KIPP campus and a YES Prep campus—and once approved, applied for financing to lease-purchase modular classrooms. At the time, very few lenders were willing to take a chance on charter schools. The interest rate on their million-dollar loan was a staggering 12.5 percent. They had no other options. Barbic put up his Honda Civic as collateral.[425]

In 1998, Barbic opened the first YES Prep campus with 300 students in grades 6 through 10,[426] and Feinberg opened KIPP-Houston with 346 in grades 5-8.[427]

After Barbic secured a 501(c)3 in 2000, YES Prep spun off on its own, and for the next 11 years, he kept his head down and focused on establishing deep roots in Houston. He didn't think about expanding to other cities or states because as he saw it, the need in front of him was so great. The waiting list was huge, and he wanted to ensure that every school they opened was set up with quality. He wanted to have a tight network. He believed that as long as he could drive to a school within 30 minutes, he could maintain a sense of quality control. In 2012, it was evident that his approach had paid off: YES Prep won the first $250,000 Broad Prize for Public Charter Schools. YES was named "the public charter management organization that has demonstrated the most outstanding overall student performance and improvement," doing so "among the country's largest urban charter management organizations in recent years while reducing achievement gaps for poor and minority students."[428] In 2018, YES Prep was serving 13,300 students in 18 schools in Houston.[429]

In 1998, while Mike Feinberg stayed at KIPP-Houston, Dave Levin continued to work with his "KIPPsters" in a district school in the South Bronx. Chartering had not come to New York yet.

The governor of New York, Republican George Pataki, was trying to get charter legislation passed, but it was not happening. The

Democrat-controlled assembly, under pressure from the teachers' union, kept rebuffing his efforts. Pataki decided to play hardball, and threatened to veto their proposed pay raise. As Bob Bellafiore (then a key Pataki staffer) recalled,

> The law would never have been passed if the legislature didn't want its first pay raise in ten years. Which is how it eventually got passed in 1998, in fact on the last day of session in 1998… Governor Pataki, to his great credit, of all the things he could have asked for in exchange for something that the legislature would have sold its mother for, he said, "charter schools."[430]

Over the protestations of New York City Schools Chancellor Rudy Crew, who described the charter school plan as "fraught with peril," the bill passed.[431]

That is how, two years after charters emerged in Washington, DC, the chartering idea spread to yet another major media market. And with that, the question began to change from "What's a charter school?" to "Where are the charter schools?"

The biggest challenge for potential charter founders in New York City was that the law did not provide for either start-up or facilities funding, and it was difficult to afford a facility in the city without deep—really deep—pockets.[432] Rudy Crew could have offered to let new charters co-locate in district schools, but he chose not to. It would be *another four years* before New York City had a Schools Chancellor who supported charter schools and proactively offered to share district school space with charters (see Chapter 23).

In the meantime, the only real option was to *convert* a district school to charter status, which required keeping the school unionized. So that's what Dave Levin did.

KIPP Academy in the South Bronx would always be unionized unless 50 percent of the entire UFT teachers' union voted to overturn its status. So Levin hired teachers who had agreed to work longer school days and on Saturdays for an extra stipend. Looking back, he recalled, "It's hard to remember what it looked like back then, now. No one viewed it as like a movement. It was *one* school."[433] With the exception of school leaders such as Norman Atkins and Jamey Verrilli at North Star and Dacia Toll and Doug McCurry at Amistad Academy, who came to visit and learn from Levin, no one really knew what he was doing. In 1998, "KIPP" was not something the Average Joe had heard of. "Forget the Average Joe," Levin later joked. "My *mom* was like, 'What are you doing?'"[434]

Things changed dramatically on the night of September 19, 1999, when *60 Minutes* aired a segment about KIPP.[435] Almost immediately, mayors and governors began calling Mike Feinberg to ask if KIPP would consider expanding. Feinberg reached out to Stacey Boyd because he knew that she knew something about starting larger organizations. She had field-tested her Project Achieve software at KIPP and hired Feinberg's colleague (and future wife) Colleen Dippel.[436] Stacey immediately called her husband, Scott Hamilton, who had run the Massachusetts DOE Charter Schools Office and had just been hired to lead the Pisces Foundation[437] for Donald and Doris Fisher.[438]

Having recently retired from being CEO of The Gap, Donald Fisher wanted to use his wealth to improve K-12 public education. He'd told Hamilton that he wanted to support education projects that, like The Gap, had real potential for replication. "I want to do something that's scalable, where we can touch a lot of kids," Fisher said. "I don't want to support just one school; I want to support something that has a broad opportunity around the country. I don't care how long it takes you to find the right thing, but I want you to find it. When we find it, we'll know."[439]

Not long after Hamilton visited Feinberg and Levin and saw them teach, he became fairly certain that he had found it.

He showed Fisher the *60 Minutes* videotape, and although the clip brought tears to Fisher's eyes,[440] they were not sure what they could do.[441]

Hamilton had some ideas. He decided to bring Levin and Feinberg and a few others to Chicago for a daylong strategic planning session,[442] then took both Fishers to visit Levin's school in New York, then spent several weeks writing up the business plan. He estimated the start-up costs at $15 million. He was unsure whether the Fishers would go for it.[443]

They did.

In fact, Donald Fisher was quite eager to get started, and he soon brought Feinberg and Levin out to San Francisco to discuss the plans. When Fisher asked them, "So, you guys really think you can pull this off?" Levin famously responded, "Well, Mr. Fisher, I don't know, but we'd be more than happy to use your money to find out."[444]

In 2000, Feinberg became the CEO of the KIPP Foundation. He recalled: "Dave and I played one of our infamous basketball games to figure out who would move out to San Francisco. I lost, so I had to go."[445] He asked Lisa Daggs to be his chief of staff. A TFA '92 alumna with a Stanford MBA, Daggs knew a thing or two about replication. She was working with Kim Smith at New Schools Venture Fund, and they had focused much of their attention on helping Don Shalvey scale up Aspire Schools. The timing was perfect: she was ready to jump into the operational side of things.[446] She helped Feinberg build the staff. One of the first people they hired was Matt Candler, who'd cut his teeth consulting on charter school development in Chicago and was supporting charter start-ups in North Carolina. The charter world was still small: Candler's friend Bryan Hassel had referred him to Feinberg.[447]

For three years, Feinberg spent his days evangelizing for KIPP. He said, "I lived on planes. Literally. I would be in the office one day a week. Otherwise I would be taking either Sunday night or Monday night red-eyes to Chicago or St. Louis and then doing the walk of shame in that airport at five in the morning to hop on another flight and return Friday night in time to drop off the dry cleaning, wash the boxers, and do it all over again."[448]

As vice president of school development, Candler shared that lifestyle, walking through doors that Feinberg opened. He built a team called the "Trailblazers," people spread all around the country who did the prep work, writing charters and recruiting talent. He also had other teams focused on recruiting, finance, and facilities. The goal was to open as many schools as they possibly could. In the first year, they opened 10 schools in 7 states; in the second, 17 in 10 states (which Candler described as "just completely bananas"); and finally, a more measured pace of 10 in 4 states for year three.[449]

In total, from 2001-2004, they established 37 new KIPP schools across the country.[450]

In 2004, Feinberg returned to Houston, and Levin and Hamilton took over the CEO responsibilities for a few months until they were finally able to convince Richard Barth to take the job. Feinberg had felt too far removed from the students and schools and was grateful to be back closer to the action. He recalled: "We were just starting to think about what it looks like to not just put random dots all over the map but to make the dot bigger and have an impact on the public education system, and that very much intrigued me."[451] He launched KIPP's first primary school and first high school and began to put together what they called the "turbo-growth plan." (By 2017, KIPP schools in Houston served 14,406 students.[452])

In the summer of 2005, at first it seemed like things would go according to plan. They were in the middle of launching this new "turbo-growth" plan and had just begun to do a bit of turnaround work in New Orleans—phasing out a middle school there called Phillips and phasing in a brand-new KIPP school. They ran a KIPP summer school for the new 5th-graders for a month, then the students were gone, scheduled to come back in late August.

On August 29, 2005, Hurricane Katrina hit New Orleans. The levees failed, and the city was devastated. Feinberg began receiving calls from the school leader and teachers who were on summer break, scattered around the country. They wanted to know if someone could go check on their kids in the Houston Astrodome, where many displaced families were being sheltered. Feinberg assembled a team, recalling: "We found the KIPPsters; we found their brothers, their sisters, their cousins, and their neighbors, and I had a quick idea."[453]

It was the kind of idea that Jim Collins would call a "Big, Hairy, Audacious Goal."[454]

Feinberg called up Houston ISD Superintendent Abe Saavedra and said, "I know you've got this huge pickle of a problem on your hands: you've got about 10,000 kids that you have to start to serve next week. I imagine you need all of the help you can get. I can help a little bit. If there's a building that you're not using, let me try to bite off several hundred of those kids for you."

"I need all of the help I can get," Saavedra said.

Feinberg hung up and called his friend Wendy Kopp at Teach For America. "Wendy," he said, "we've got all these displaced kids in Houston that need to be taught; it occurs to me that there's a bunch of displaced TFA Corps members that would be natural teachers for them."

Kopp thought it was a crazy but interesting idea, so they promptly got the word out to the TFA Corps members around the country. Five days later, Feinberg and Kopp met with the New Orleans Corps members and told them, "You've got three options: you can go join the Louisiana Recovery Corps, and you're not going to be teaching, but probably be doing more, literally, digging the city out of this mess; there might openings in some other regions where we could quickly place you in; or if you're up for a real challenge, we're thinking about starting a school here in Houston in the next ten days for a bunch of the kids from the Astrodome."[455]

About 31 Corps members signed up for that crazy idea. Five KIPP teachers who had a month on the job were suddenly elevated to assistant principal, and the school leader of Phillips became the school leader for this new school, which was called KIPP New Orleans West (now College Prep). Feinberg and his colleagues ran around the Astrodome and signed up students and started the school in ten days.[456]

"It was the craziest and the coolest thing I think we've ever done," Feinberg reflected. "We had an amazing year with the kids. They grew a ton." At the end of the year, two-thirds of the students and parents moved back to New Orleans; and two-thirds of the teachers moved back to New Orleans. That new school became KIPP McDonogh 15, the first KIPP school in New Orleans. It became the highest-performing school in New Orleans, only to be eclipsed by KIPP Believe.[457]

Feinberg and Levin and their colleagues across the country kept at it. In 2014, KIPP was awarded the $250,000 Broad Prize for Public Charter Schools.[458] By 2018, KIPP was serving 96,000 students in 224 schools in 32 regions.[459]

CHAPTER 20

THE DISGRUNTLED GRADUATE STUDENT

Many people joined the charter school movement because of their dis-satisfaction with the status quo. Doug Lemov was one of these people.

In 1996, Doug was not yet famous. He had not yet appeared in a cover story in *The New York Times Magazine*.[460] He had not yet sold hundreds of thousands of copies of his first book, *Teach Like a Champion*.[461] He had not yet become, perhaps, the most recognizable name in the education reform movement, giving talks and trainings not just around the country but the globe. That was still fourteen years away.

Doug was simply a frustrated Ph.D. candidate who had come to the realization that he needed to do something different with his life.[462] As much as he loved English literature and liked the people in his program at Indiana University, he hated the idea of being a cog in the machine of academia. It bothered him that professors didn't get evaluated based on their teaching—their teaching didn't matter at all, in fact. And the labor market was so screwed up. You couldn't really choose where you went. You had very little power. There was an over-supply of candidates and very little transparency on the job market; people posted jobs, but they often already knew who they wanted to hire. It made no sense.

The one thing that felt right was tutoring. He ran a study table three nights a week where football players could come and do their homework.

He provided structure and support. He liked teaching and coaching—it was something he looked forward to; it made him feel useful.

One day, an administrator who oversaw academic support for the football team asked if he would help a particular student more intensively, three days a week.

"Sure," he replied, "I'd love to."

When Doug met the student, a red-shirted freshman from the Bronx, he liked him immediately. "He was such a nice kid and a gentleman, thoughtful in every way," Doug recalled,

"so I said, 'Write me a little something about yourself.'"

"He goes to a study carrel, pulls out a yellow piece of paper—I can still see that yellow piece of paper in my mind—and he came back five minutes later with a paragraph about himself without a capital letter in it, without a single correct complete sentence. I just remember looking at it and saying, 'Oh my God.' He wrote at the third-grade level, maybe."

Doug marched into the Athletic Academic Office and said, "I don't know what the solutions to this guy's problems are, but it sure as hell ain't me three afternoons a week for an hour and a half. And number two, how the hell did he get in here, anyway?"

The administrator said, "You know what? We're surprised, too. He's not even a sponsored student."[463]

"Sponsored" students, she explained to him, were athletes who were regarded as academically marginal. They were paired with a faculty member who agreed to vouch for them and take responsibility for them.

The administrator said that the young man had been admitted legitimately: he had good grades from his high school in the Bronx and great recommendations about his character, and he was an outstanding athlete, but, "he had bad SAT scores. But how many kids come out of inner-city schools with bad SAT scores? So we took him."

As Doug recounted this story years later, the outrage he felt on behalf of this young man was still apparent in his voice:

Because he was a good kid and he worked hard and he was an upstanding person and he had this dream of playing football, all of those years, no one wanted to ruin his dream by saying, "We have to fix the reading before we focus on the football."

So every year, they promoted him based on character, not on academic mastery.

In the end, the people who did that in order to support him in achieving his dream ended up destroying him. He failed out at the end of the first year.[464]

Doug decided that he wanted to help design educational entities to make them work better. He started calling people who might know what that could look like, and asked them what he could do.

One of those people was Stacey Boyd, a friend he'd known at Hamilton College. She had worked at Edison Schools and gone to Harvard Business School, and she told him about various think tanks and other opportunities. She also told him she was starting a charter school.

"What's a charter school?" he asked.

That's when his life began to change.

He told Stacey about the football player from the Bronx. He had very strong feelings about social promotion and the need for honesty with students. They didn't do this kid any favors when they didn't tell him what it took to be successful. He and Stacey bonded over that, and he moved to Boston to help her start the school.[465]

In 1997, Doug became an English and history teacher and the dean of students in charge of middle school discipline at the Academy of the Pacific Rim (APR). The school established high academic and behavioral expectations for students and quickly became known as a place where students studied Japanese and were sent home if they arrived out of uniform.

In 1999, Stacey—who had developed an information management system at Harvard Business School called Project Achieve—decided to market and build her software application for schools and districts.

At age 28, Doug became the principal.

He felt totally unqualified and, he later admitted, "scared to death." But the school was doing well, and Doug had the wisdom to recognize that he couldn't run it by himself. He relied heavily on his very capable colleagues. They all worked extremely long hours. He recalled:

I wanted to show that I was willing to work at least as hard as all of the other teachers in the building because that was all I had.[466] And they of course were doing the same thing. We were all staying late to show that we were the hardest-working person in the building. I remember one day sitting in my office thinking, *Why are they working so hard for my school?* And I realized, *Dummy: they're not working so hard for YOUR school; they're working so hard for THEIR OWN school....* They perceived themselves to have owned it and to have built it.[467]

Years later, he remarked:

Teachers need to have this equity stake in the organization, and I think that's one thing we've learned about successful schools. Successful schools break down the administrator-teacher barrier, the divide. Teachers have more autonomy to make decisions, and when there are problems, teachers help find solutions.... People need to have faith that when you sit down at the end of the day, when we'd have our staff meetings in that first year to figure out problems, there was no "them" that we could point to, as in, "They say that we have to..." In this school, the "they" was us. And that is a fundamentally transformative experience.[468]

Several of his colleagues went on to start their own outstanding schools. In 2003, Molly Wood launched KIPP Bayview Academy in San Francisco,[469] and in 2004, Scott McCue joined Linda Brown's Building Excellent Schools program and launched Boston Preparatory Charter Public School.[470]

After three years at APR, finding the work schedule unsustainable for his growing family, Doug applied to Harvard Business School. He was aware of the irony that going to Harvard would be easier than running a charter school. But before sending in his deposit, he took an abrupt, important detour.

He made a phone call to Bob Bellafiore.

Bellafiore had finished his work with Governor Pataki and become the head of the SUNY Charter Schools Institute (one of the three authorizers in New York), and he had hired Doug and other school leaders (including Norman Atkins) as consultants to help review charter applications. Doug had loved tearing apart the budget and the plans and exposing flawed thinking. It fit with his desire to create effective entities.

He wanted Bob's advice. Someday he hoped to work at an organization like SUNY-CSI, and he wondered if going to business school would make him eligible for that.

"I'm getting on a plane," Bob said. "Why don't we talk tomorrow?"

A short time later, Doug joined CSI.

Although Doug believed that Academy of the Pacific Rim was a good school, he also believed that up to that point in the charter movement, too much had been left to the discretion of the schools. Like Greg Richmond, he questioned whether charters were really following through on their promise to be more accountable and measure better. In Doug's view, "that was a plausible and hopeful exaggeration that we sold about *the people that we wanted to be* as opposed to *the people that we were.*"[471]

He and Bob set to work building an accountability system to address this problem. They did the best they could, but it was challenging without annual test data in every grade. This was in 2000-2001, when states tested students only in grades 4, 8, and 11. "The measurement infrastructure did not exist to able to be serious about what makes a school great," Doug said, "to be able to identify a great school, what makes a school great, what makes a teacher great, and how we can learn from effective institutions."[472]

In 2002, President George W. Bush signed the No Child Left Behind (NCLB) legislation, which required standardized testing annually in grades 3-8.[473] By mandating annual testing, NCLB dramatically changed the accountability landscape in K-12 education. Very quickly, it shined a bright light on academic achievement gaps and pointed out where students were being underserved.

Of course, not everyone in the charter school movement was as interested in how to measure school performance as Doug was. He recalled:

> There were so many charter schools that resented my feedback, that were angry and didn't want to hear that just caring about kids wasn't enough. You had to show they were learning, and that was hard. You couldn't just hug 'em to Harvard.
>
> And their accountability plan would say: "The kids will say that we love them more, and the teachers will say that kids think that we love them more."
>
> And I would say, "Great. Where are your objective assessments to prove that? Where are your objective measures? Who other than you is going to tell me that?"
>
> And they would get mad and say, "Standardized testing is a conspiracy!"
>
> And I would say, "That's great. You can add additional data as well, but conspiracy or not, it's the best tool we have to objectively show that every child has made progress."

After two years at SUNY, Doug went to business school, and when he finished that, his friend Norman Atkins had a plan for him.

CHAPTER 21

BUILDING THE UNCOMMON TEAM

Norman Atkins was never going to be satisfied with starting just one school. When he first met Jamey Verrilli, he recognized that Jamey was a strong, experienced instructional leader who possessed the spirit of a long-distance runner, and this gave him confidence that they could start a school together.[474] He knew that once they got started, Jamey would probably continue to lead North Star until someone dragged him out of there.[475] While Norman saw his initial job as helping to shape and build the school that Jamey imagined and wanted to lead, he had a sense that his own passion and talent was more in starting new things.

As a result of this thinking, while preparing the ground to grow North Star, they also planted seeds for the future. They needed a nonprofit to hold funds they would raise on behalf of North Star, and they called it "Uncommon Schools" instead of the "North Star Academy Foundation" because they thought the entity might end up supporting more than one school. The name was a play on Horace Mann's notion of the Common School,[476] which, Norman thought, "began with such promise and such public purpose in the town commons in Massachusetts and spread the idea of public education." He regretted that it "had devolved to 'common' in the worst sense, which is to say, plain, ordinary, nothing to write home about." He believed that schools should be *uncommon*: "They should be unusual, and they should be extraordinarily good and make a difference in the lives of their students."[477]

North Star jumped out to a strong start, gaining significant attention for its purposeful culture, rigorous instruction, and positive academic results.

After a few years, Norman began to think about activating Uncommon Schools as a broader network. North Star parents wanted to know what would happen to their children after 8th grade. They clamored for a high school. The school was originally planned to be a tiny middle school, serving 144 students in grades 5 through 8. But in 2000, Norman and Jamey opened a high school and began thinking about a second middle school that would feed into it.[478]

Around this same time, Paul Tudor Jones, the hedge-fund manager who had originally hired Norman to co-lead the Robin Hood Foundation,[479] asked him to start an all-boys charter school in Brooklyn that would begin with students in kindergarten, and he didn't want it to be a duplicate of North Star Academy. He wanted it to be a new kind of school for elementary-age boys, and it had to be in Bedford Stuyvestant.[480] So Norman began to think that this—Excellence Academy—would be another kind of Uncommon School.[481]

In 2001, several major funders and policymakers began to ask leaders of charter schools with outstanding results to think about replicating. And they had a very specific idea in mind based on the model of Aspire, the charter management organization that Don Shalvey had created after he helped to lift the cap in California.

Norman recalled:

The Walton Family Foundation, the New Schools Venture Fund, and others said to a dozen different operators like me, "We'll give you planning money if you build out a plan to convert your school into a charter school management organization." I didn't really know what that meant at the time. I had this impulse to grow North Star, but it didn't feel fully ripe to grow fast just in Newark at the time. I decided that I would rather partner with a bunch of other leaders from other schools in places like New York.[482]

Initially, Norman focused on starting Excellence Boys Charter School,[483] but he began to envision a way in which he could expand his work. He recalled: "I began thinking about this awkward phrase, 'a network of networks,' that I would bring together a dream team of accomplished school leaders and that together we would grow this organization."[484] In *Good to Great*, Jim Collins talks about "getting the right people on the bus"[485] as a way to build effective organizations. Norman realized that he had friends in other states who could help build this organization. And he would do everything he could to convince them.

One of the friends he invited onto the "Uncommon Schools bus" was Brett Peiser.

A native New Yorker raised in a family of educators, Brett had graduated from Brown University in 1990 knowing that he wanted to teach. He was aware that Teach For America (TFA) was launching, and he gave that option some thought, but he also knew he wanted to be in New York City and didn't want to leave his placement in anyone else's hands. So he did not apply to TFA. In the summer before he started teaching, he taught summer school at Phillips Andover. He figured that the best way to become a good teacher was to teach.[486]

That fall, he got a job through an assistant principal who knew there would be a potential opening. When, as expected, a teacher did not show up, the AP immediately declared an "emergency" and hired Brett on an "emergency cert" basis. Every year for four years, although he worked as a full-time history teacher, he was rehired as a "long-term sub." He later described the school as "a nice half-magnet, half-neighborhood school in Brooklyn," but the insanity of the workload was not lost on him: he had five classes, three different preps, 34 students in each class, only three minutes between classes. There was no place to work. It was tough, especially for an untrained rookie.[487]

One reason he became involved in charter schools was to change this. When he later started South Boston Harbor Academy Charter School, one of his key motivations was that it shouldn't look like this. Looking back, he remarked, "If we were to colonize another planet, this is not how we would build a school system."

In 1994, after teaching for four years in New York City, he went to the Harvard Kennedy School for a Master's degree focused on education policy. He found a part-time job working at the Pioneer Institute, where he did research and helped to write a book about inter-district choice in Massachusetts. Though only there once a week, he struck up a friendship with Linda Brown at the Charter School Resource Center. He recalled: "I worked nine to five, very precise hours; as a grad student I was paid hourly; and every day, Linda Brown, this small, loud woman, would yell out, 'Five o'clock: Brett's leaving!'"[488]

While Linda liked to tease him, she also appreciated how much Brett cared about education. In their conversations to and from the subway, she saw his potential. Not long after he graduated and had temporarily moved back to New York City to figure out his next steps, she placed a call that would alter the path of his life.

It started with a call that Linda herself had received, from State Senator Stephen Lynch. He'd heard that if he wanted to know anything about charter schools, she was the person to talk to. He asked her to come meet him at the state house. He needed her help.

He wanted to talk about the suicide epidemic. In the white, predominantly low-income community of South Boston, between December 30, 1996 and July 22, 1997, there were six deaths and 200 suicide attempts.[489] Senator Lynch wanted to do something. He told Linda, "That's my territory, it's where I grew up. I can't let this happen." He had heard about something called the Paraclete Center, which was having some success in supporting South Boston teenagers with after school programming. Maybe they could start a school that did similar things?[490]

Linda visited the Paraclete Center with Senator Lynch and answered his questions about how to go about starting a charter school. One thing was, they needed a coalition. And another, she told him, was that you needed a founder, "that one person who can take your dream and form it with you."

Senator Lynch said, "Let's do it! Do you want to work with me?"

Linda was completely smitten. She recalled, "I loved what he stood for, and loved that what he stood for was right."[491] She would do anything she could to help him. She said she thought she could bring together some people who might be able to take the lead on this.

She went back to her office and immediately called Brett Peiser. He was in New York, working for Kaplan.

Brett looked at his phone and saw it was Linda calling. *What could she want?* He was in the middle of work, but he knew he'd better take it.

"Hi, Linda," he said. "I hope everything's OK. I'm kind of in the middle of stuff. Can I call you later?"

"Absolutely not," she replied. "You have to talk now." She quickly explained what had happened and said, "I'm putting together a breakfast for tomorrow morning of the people who might be instrumental in making this work, and I think you'd be great running this school."

"I can't come tomorrow," Brett said. "Is there any time next week?"

"No," Linda said, "It's got to be tomorrow. I don't care how you get here. But you get on a plane, and then you get in a cab and you get here. I will see you tomorrow. Breakfast is at seven." She concluded: "Just do it." Then she hung up.[492]

It was hard to say no to Linda Brown.

The next morning, Brett flew up to Boston.

After that, things moved very quickly. Brett and a friend from the Kennedy School, Susan Fortin, worked with Senator Lynch and wrote the application. They applied in September of 1997, were approved in February, and South Boston Harbor Academy Charter School opened in September of 1998.[493]

Brett had several motivations for wanting to start a charter school. The suicide epidemic was of course the initial driver. But he also felt a strong desire to help students in urban areas and give families more options. He saw chartering as "the best and fastest way to build new schools." He also liked the idea of flexibility in exchange for accountability.[494]

He didn't necessarily believe that parents voting with their feet would automatically make district schools improve their offerings. But he saw charters as "one star in the constellation of larger ed reform" that would put pressure on the entire system to get better.[495]

And another thing: as a result of his experience teaching in New York, he wanted to professionalize the conditions for teachers. He believed if they could improve those conditions, good things could happen.[496]

In the course of running the school, it became apparent to Brett that there was no single panacea for the problems in education. He began to tell people, "We're never going to find the '100-percent solution.' Instead, we need to find a hundred little one-percent solutions."[497]

One day when Brett was speaking about standards and curriculum at a Teachers College Conference in New York City in 2000, Norman Atkins came up and introduced himself. He really liked what Brett had to say. They quickly realized that they were philosophically aligned around what schools should look like. In fact, their schools were very similar: North Star had started in 1997 with 72 students in grades 5 and 6; South Boston Harbor had started with 120 students in 1998 with grades 5 through 7.[498]

A few months later, Brett drove to Newark to visit North Star. Around 7:30 in the morning, he pulled into the cramped parking lot and walked into the back area where the turf field was, and suddenly he found himself surrounded by dozens of students who shook his hand and introduced themselves: "Hi, my name is Terrell; welcome to North Star! Hi, my name is Aliyah; welcome to North Star...." Almost two decades later, Brett remembered how their greetings gave him goosebumps, as did watching Jamey Verrilli leading a Morning Circle, "weaving his usual magic of telling a story from a long time ago and explaining how it related to the world today." In classrooms, he noticed that North Star's teachers used the same blackboard configurations as his teachers, but there were other little things, too: inspirational chants, students training their eyes on the speaker and using complete sentences, details that made a difference. He was tremendously moved and realized how much more he and his colleagues at South Boston Harbor Academy still needed to do. He went home with pages and pages of notes. For the next few years, his school continued to grow, and he kept adding to his list of one-percent solutions.[499]

While Brett toiled away at South Boston Harbor Academy (later renamed Boston Collegiate when it relocated to a different part of the city), two other energetic young men had begun to march along on a similar path.

Evan Rudall grew up middle-class on the South Side of Chicago and attended the University of Chicago Lab School through middle school. Although he did well academically, he began to act out in response to some family challenges. In 8th grade, he was expelled. He wound up at Kenwood Academy, a large public high school on the south side that served students who were 85-90 percent black and Latino and predominantly low-income.[500]

One day in his 10th grade law class, as he and his classmates filled in worksheets, he watched his teacher read the newspaper and then fall asleep. Several students walked out. Other students strolled in. Evan was overcome with the feeling that he and his classmates were not in a good place. He knew that a mile down the road, the Lab School was sending 100 percent of its students to the top colleges in the country, while fewer than half of his classmates would walk across the graduation stage with him. It didn't have to be that way. In that moment, at the age of 15, he decided that he wanted to do something to try to level the playing field in public education.[501]

After graduating from Wesleyan University, Evan landed a job teaching 7th grade social studies and at 23, he found himself running Summerbridge Louisville, a nonprofit where high school and college students taught middle school students. From day one, he was captivated. "I fell in love with teaching, I fell in love with education," he said, "and I had this feeling inside that it was possible to build an incredibly high-performing public school."[502] He wasn't sure how to channel that impulse until 1995, three years into the work, when he first heard about the charter movement. He'd gone to the University of Chicago for his first year of college, and coincidentally, one of his favorite professors there, Amy Kass, was the mother of Sarah Kass, a teacher who had co-founded City on a Hill Charter School in Boston.[503]

One of the first 14 charter schools in Massachusetts, City on a Hill (which opened in 1995 with 65 9th and 10th-graders) garnered significant media attention, and funders interested in urban education reform flocked to support it.[504] Before New Jersey had a charter law, the Geraldine R. Dodge Foundation provided funding to show the potential of the charter school idea.[505] Sarah and colleague Ann Connolly Tolkoff had tried to make things work in the Chelsea Public Schools, but frustration with the system had pushed them to create this new kind of school. Their students were now in smaller classes, expected to demonstrate specific competencies in order to earn their diplomas, and taught by teachers who would be held accountable for their performance.[506]

Evan Rudall decided he wanted to do something similar. In 1996, he went to the Harvard Graduate School of Education, determined to figure out how to start and run a charter school. He spent the entire year laser-focused on the charter movement, absorbing everything he possibly could, visiting charters around Boston, near Boston, and across the country whenever he had the chance. In a charter schools course led by professor Katherine Merseth, his classmates included Mike Goldstein, who later founded MATCH Charter School; Jay Altman, who launched First Line Charter Schools in New Orleans; and Emily Lawson, who founded DC Prep.[507]

Evan did his principal residency with Roger Harris, the head of Timilty Middle School, a Blue Ribbon school in Boston, and initially they planned to form a district-charter partnership. But shortly after Evan's charter, Roxbury Prep, was approved, Harris was appointed to run Boston

Renaissance Charter School, so a formal partnership never materialized. Harris supported Evan by joining the Roxbury Prep board instead.

The night before Evan submitted his charter application, he met another person who would become a vital partner in his work. John King, a history teacher at City on a Hill, had known Evan's wife in college, and he joined them that night for dinner. They talked for three hours. Listening to John's questions and insights about working with Roxbury students, Evan thought, *Wow, I'd really love to run a school with this guy.* He stayed up all night to rewrite parts of the application, and submitted it the next day. He began to speak with John on a regular basis, and after Roxbury Prep was approved, convinced him to help run the school.

John King—who would later become Commissioner of Education in New York and then U.S. Secretary of Education appointed by President Barack Obama[508]—understood on a deep, personal level the importance and power of great teachers. He had grown up in East Flatbush, Brooklyn, the son of two New York City public school educators. His father, born in 1908, grew up in Bedford Stuyvesant. In a career that spanned nearly 40 years, his father served as a teacher, a principal, and eventually deputy superintendent. In the early 1960s, he was the highest-ranking African-American educator in the country, and his sense of urgency for the work was palpable. Years later, while receiving the Robin Hood Foundation's Hero's Award for his own work, John related this story:

> My father loved basketball and one weekend, while play-ing, he broke his wrist. When he went to work on Monday, with his wrist in a cast, the principal stopped him and told my father—who never took a single sick day in his nearly 40 year career—that he could not teach with his cast. My father explained that he would be able to teach just fine. The prin-cipal explained that there was a regulation about not teaching with a cast and again told my father he couldn't teach. My father then walked over to the counter in the main office and slammed his cast down shattering it. He brushed the pieces

into a trash can, put his hand in his suit pocket, and went to teach his class.[509]

John's mother had come from Puerto Rico to New York as a child. She grew up in the Bronx, the daughter of a single mother who was a garment worker. Like his father, she saw education as a path to opportunity. She was the first in her family to graduate from college, and she became a New York City public school teacher.

When John was eight, his mother died of a heart attack. For the next four years, he lived alone with his father, who suffered from undiagnosed Alzheimer's disease. John recalled:

No one knew he was sick, and as a result, life with my father was unpredictable and often scary. I can recall one night he woke me up at 2 AM to go to school. I remember crying and clinging to the staircase banister as he pulled my arm and I begged him not to make me go. By 7th grade, I was doing the laundry, cooking meals, and signing checks in my father's name to pay overdue bills. As he got sicker, he didn't leave the house even to go to the store - so I was forced to sneak into his room to steal money so I could buy us food.[510]

Throughout that frightening period, school was his refuge, and several teachers took him under their wing.

When he was 12, his father passed away.

He first went to live with his half-brother, who was 24 years old, drove a sports car, and had a drinking problem. Although John loved him, he found himself very alone again—doing the cooking and cleaning, taking care of the bills, and fending for himself. He decided the best alternative was boarding school.

With strong recommendations from his teachers, he was accepted at Phillips Andover, and he loved the classes there, but he was miserable and overwhelmed and eventually got kicked out. He then went to live with his father's brother, a career Air Force officer who had been a Tuskegee Airman. Living with his aunt and uncle provided a sense of normalcy:

dinner every night at the same time, strict rules, and high expectations. He got back on track and was accepted to Harvard, where he volunteered in after-school and summer programs in a public housing development in Roxbury. That experience gave him the opportunity to do for other kids what his teachers had done for him—to provide them with a safe, structured, and caring learning environment.[511]

After graduation, he jumped at the chance to teach at City on a Hill, a new kind of school whose mission aligned with his values and beliefs. He'd expected that the students would need lots of help, but neither he nor the school leaders had anticipated the depths of those needs. Early on, Sarah Kass and Ann Connolly Tolkoff told Linda Brown that virtually all 65 of their 9th and 10th graders were reading at the 3rd-grade level. Linda asked if they'd all come from the same school, and the answer was no. *They'd come from 26 different schools.* The question Linda asked next would keep all of them awake at night.

How come all of them can't read?[512]

So it was no surprise that Evan's idea of starting with younger students appealed to John.

After Roxbury Prep's charter was approved in 1998, Evan had a little more than a year before the doors would open, and like any other founder, he worked feverishly to get things done.

Linda Brown's training sessions at the Resource Center were essential. "We wouldn't have done nearly as well without her," Evan noted. "She helped with all aspects of getting Roxbury Prep off the ground, from operational support to curriculum structure and support, to school culture support, to facility, to fundraising, to helping us create networks."[513] In those sessions, he sidled up next to Brett Peiser, who was in his first year of operating South Boston Harbor Academy, to pick his brain. He visited Brett's school several times and took copious notes.[514]

He also spent some time at Academy of the Pacific Rim with Doug Lemov.

In the fall of 1999, Roxbury Prep opened with 80 6th graders. That spring, Evan and John traveled to the National Charter Schools Conference, where Brett introduced them to Norman Atkins. In addition to his work at North Star, Norman served on the board of the WKBJ Foundation (founded by Bob Howitt), and he asked if they could come see Roxbury Prep; maybe WKBJ could offer a grant.

One morning a few weeks later, Norman, Brett, Bob Howitt, and another colleague signed in for visitors' passes. John happened to be out that day. Evan led them to a windowless conference room, then sat there for four hours of interrogation. "They grilled me on every aspect of the school," he recalled. "It was one of the most intense, rigorous conversations I've ever been a part of, and I loved it."[515] Evidently it went well: a grant followed shortly.

Pulled into Norman's orbit, Evan and John would be among the first people he called when he began to contemplate creating a network of schools.

So were Doug Lemov and Brett Peiser.

When Doug looked back on how he, Brett, Evan, John, and Norman shared ideas in the late 1990s, he described it as "an accidental group of like-minded people—a very, very small world of like-minded schools that thought similarly about academics and culture and had strong results.... We all very quickly ran into each other at the same conferences and holed up in the corner and would talk to each other about what we'd seen in each other's schools...."[516] When Doug went off to Harvard Business School in 2002, Norman made a point of keeping in touch.

Around 2004, the Walton Family Foundation offered $50K grants to individual schools that were interested in expanding. Brett Peiser (at the renamed Boston Collegiate), Norman Atkins, and Dacia Toll (at Amistad Academy in New Haven) all decided to apply. Brett recalled:

> This was a small thing that became important. These grants spurred on our thinking because everyone had been talking about doing this but everyone thought to themselves, *Boy,*

starting one school was hard enough; I can't imagine doing more. After receiving those grants to explore, Norman was particularly insistent that this was a great thing that we could do. He saw it in his head that this work would be done more effectively and powerfully if we did it together.[517]

At the time, there was not a clear model of how to proceed. Because Boston was about to reach its cap, they could not expand there. One part of Norman's vision was that Brett could bring the Collegiate model to New York City and build a "Collegiate Schools Network" in the city where he had grown up and taught. In addition to the prospect of returning to his hometown, Brett was excited about refocusing his energies on curriculum and instruction and professional development instead of what he'd been forced to spend the previous three years on: facilities financing.[518]

Meanwhile, under Evan and John's leadership, Roxbury Prep had consistently outperformed schools in the most affluent communities in Massachusetts. In 2002, when Evan's wife took a job as a professor in New York City, Evan had gone to work for Joel Klein at the New York City DOE and helped Norman and Brett write the charter application for Excellence Boys Charter School, then he'd enrolled at Columbia Law School.[519] In 2004, John had gone to Yale Law School because he wanted to figure out a way to do what they had accomplished at Roxbury Prep on a larger scale, but within a year, he'd come to the conclusion that the best way to contribute to changing the course of urban education was to work directly in schools. So he was thrilled when Norman asked him to manage the Excellence Boys Network.[520]

Along with the Collegiate and Excellence schools in New York City, Norman saw two additional avenues for the growth of what would become the Uncommon Schools charter management organization. He'd selected his successor at North Star, Paul Bambrick-Santoyo, and he could see Bambrick-Santoyo and Jamey Verrilli replicating North Star schools in Newark. He also foresaw a growing role for Julie Jackson. In 1997, shortly after they opened the school, Norman and Jamey had visited Jackson's middle school math classroom in Paterson, New Jersey, and were stunned by what they saw. "We almost couldn't believe how good she was," Jamey recalled. "The level of engagement and her students' pride in their work was amazing."[521] Jackson, a TFA alum in her fourth year of teaching, came to North Star the following year, and her modeling of high expectations and effective classroom systems translated into dramatic student achievement gains. "We had high expectations," Jamey said, "but we didn't truly realize what was possible until we saw Julie in action." Norman believed that great teaching was replicable, and he sent colleagues in to study her. They built systems around the way she ran her classes. "In the early years," he said, "a large part of my job was as a tour operator for the charter school sector, bringing thousands of visitors into Ms. Jackson's math class."[522] Jackson went on to become Dean, Founding Principal of the high school, Founding Principal of the first elementary school, and ultimately Chief Schools Officer for K-8 at Uncommon.

As he scoured the landscape for talent, Norman also wanted to find a way to work with Doug Lemov. He knew Doug "was brilliant, had high standards, was creative...."[523] In fact, Doug had written a business plan for something like a charter management organization as one of his business school projects.[524] But there was one sticking point: Doug wanted to work in upstate New York. He'd gone to college up there and was passionate about places like Utica, Troy, Rochester, and Syracuse.[525]

"Nobody in the world was interested in building a network in that particular place," Norman recalled, "so part of how I won Doug's heart was by embracing his vision for a network of schools in a part of the state—in a part of the country—where education reform had not been a real focal point."[526]

"Norman can convince you to jump over a fence even if you have no idea what's on the other side,"[527] Doug said. In short order, the two men were driving around upstate New York visiting different communities to decide where they would open the first school, which would be named True North Rochester Prep.[528]

Neither of them knew at the time that what Doug learned in his new job would change the way thousands and thousands of teachers did their work. (We'll come back to that story in Chapter 29.)

In 2005, Norman became the CEO of Uncommon Schools. He convinced Evan Rudall to become the COO.[529]

In planning how to structure their organization, Norman and his colleagues took some lessons from the KIPP rollout. Recognizing the challenges of being geographically scattered and wanting to maintain more centralized control, they decided to cluster their schools in a more limited way. They also went with a different balance of tight and loose management. "Even though we were going to let each of these schools and networks develop their own flavor and give managing directors a lot of authority and recognized that there were separate boards," Norman said, "we tried to centrally manage our organization, so we had an interesting mix of autonomy, free, founding schools, and networks with a central management contract."[530] The regional managing directors would act as superintendents and have programmatic and instructional autonomy to run the schools as they saw fit. In exchange, they would be held accountable for results and would have to buy into the home-office operations dealing with recruitment, technology, and fundraising.[531]

In 2013, Uncommon Schools was the second winner of the Broad Prize for Public Charter Schools. The Eli and Edythe Broad Foundation cited the following statistics as among the reasons why Uncommon was awarded this $250,000 prize:[532]

- In 2012, 100 percent of Uncommon's seniors took the SAT exam. These seniors achieved an average SAT score of 1570—20 points above the college-readiness benchmark of 1550 established by the College Board.

- In 2012... proficiency rates for Uncommon's low-income students ranked in the top 30 percent of their respective states when compared to low-income students in the rest of that state....

- In 2012... proficiency rates for Uncommon's African-American students ranked in the top 30 percent of their respective states when compared to African-American students in the rest of that state....

- In recent years, Uncommon closed 56 percent of achievement gaps between its low-income students and the state's non-low-income students across the available comparisons.... Uncommon also closed 56 percent of achievement gaps between its African-American students and the state's white students across the available comparisons....

By 2019, the organization was running 53 schools, serving 19,200 students in New Jersey (Newark and Camden), New York (New York City, Rochester, Troy), and Massachusetts (Boston).[533] The robust results continued: 98 percent of 2018 Uncommon high school graduates were accepted to a four-year college or university, and 78 percent of alumni had either graduated from or were attending a four-year college or university.[534] Uncommon's Class of 2018 had an average composite SAT score 100 points above the national college readiness bar. And in 2018, North Star Academy surpassed the New Jersey state average for economically *advantaged* students in both ELA (81% NSA vs. 69% NJ) and Math (70% NSA vs. 60% NJ).[535]

In Part III, we'll see how the work in these schools planted seeds that grew to influence the field more widely.

CHAPTER 22

"FROM MARGINS TO MAINSTREAM"

On July 17, 2003—twenty years after the release of *A Nation at Risk,* **six** years after Jamey Verrilli first hit the drum at North Star, and 18 months after No Child Left Behind was signed into law—roughly 100 leaders in the charter school movement gathered at the historic Boar's Head Inn in Charlottesville, Virginia to participate in a seminal conference that some would later describe as "game-changing." It was called "From Margins to Mainstream: Building a Stronger Charter School Movement."[536]

In 1999, I'd left the NJ Charter School Resource Center, done some consulting in Chicago, and returned home to launch the NJ Charter Public Schools Association. Norman Atkins (then co-leading North Star) had asked me to help found the Association because as New Jersey charters had attracted media attention, their opponents had become more aggressive. Charters faced increasingly distracting legal and legislative challenges. The teachers union had plenty of representation. Charters did not.

Although not wild about the prospect of advocacy work (I preferred teaching to testifying), I knew all of the charter school leaders and funders and could hit the ground running. I told Norman I would take the job under three conditions: it had to be part-time because I was trying to finish my dissertation; it had to be an interim position because I wanted to return to teaching; and there was one other condition which I don't remember. As I liked to joke later, none of those conditions was ever met. The Association work was all-consuming. And while I finished my dissertation[537] and began teaching English—also "part-time"—at North Star (where Norman and Jamey Verrilli had added a high school), it took nearly four years to find my replacement.

So I'd come to this meeting in Virginia to introduce my successor to other state support leaders.

From the minute we arrived, it felt like a high school reunion for policy wonks. Among the two dozen papers written for the conference were many familiar names: Ted Kolderie, Joe Nathan, Alex Medler, Jon Schroeder, Jim Peyser, Bryan Hassel, Margaret Lin, Rick Hess, Eva Moskowitz, and Wendy Kopp.

In the dark-paneled lobby, I bumped into Jon Schnur. It had been seven years since we'd first met. In the interim, in addition to advising Vice President Gore on education through his fateful presidential campaign, he'd co-founded New Leaders for New Schools, a nonprofit whose mission was "to ensure high academic achievement for all children, especially students in poverty and students of color by training transformational leaders and pushing for policies and practices to strengthen student achievement."[538] He would later advise President Barack Obama, but for now he was there to hear what people had to say.

We were both aware that the movement remained in a precarious position.

On the plus side, some effective schools had begun to replicate. Don Shalvey's Aspire, the first CMO, was several years along. Dave Levin and Mike Feinberg were a few years into the KIPP national rollout. Chris Barbic was opening his second YES Prep school and would open a third in 2004. In 2002, New York City Mayor Michael Bloomberg had secured control of the schools, and his Schools Chancellor, Joel Klein, was drafting a strategy to bring more high-performing charters to the city (see Chapter 23). Several major funders had approached school leaders such as Norman Atkins, Brett Peiser (at Boston Collegiate), and Dacia Toll (at Amistad Academy) to encourage them to widen their reach.

In Massachusetts, Linda Brown had also started something new. In 2001, after running her Resource Center for eight years, several factors had caused her to reconsider the nature of her work. The first was that instead of raising the $38,500 she needed that year for her budget, she'd raised $330,000.[539] Another was that she'd met Dr. Lorraine Monroe, the dynamic, rebellious New York City principal who'd founded the Frederick Douglass Academy, a public school in Harlem.[540] Dr. Monroe's students were performing off the charts, and Linda had taken a busload of charter school founders to visit her. Linda was struck by Dr. Monroe's attitude toward school leadership, which was essentially, "It's better to ask for forgiveness than permission." As Linda later recalled, one moment capsulized this mindset:

> We were sitting and talking to Dr. Monroe in her office and she answered the phone, and it was a family member, and I said, "Oh, was that the switchboard?"
>
> She said, "I'm not connected to the main switchboard."
>
> I said, "How can you not be connected to the main switchboard? You're a district school."
>
> She said, "They don't know what I've got down here. I just called the phone company and put in a phone."[541]

On the ride home, Linda reflected on how Dr. Monroe had taken advantage of an incompetent system to do good work. *Charter school founders needed to be bold like that.* When she got home, she began to think about how she could use the extra money she'd raised. One option was to start a lab school. Another was to become "a bank" supporting charter school facilities financing, which was much needed. The third option was to start a fellowship that would train participants to start and lead charter schools.

She and her colleagues conducted focus groups and collected data which confirmed that their resources could best be used pre-emptively: instead of trying to help existing charter schools, they could have more impact by incubating great schools. Linda liked the idea of paying people to pay attention to her advice. She concluded: "I chose the bossy [option] because what I've always been sure of is that I'm good at being bossy."[542]

In 2003, they launched Building Excellent Schools (BES), a non-profit that would recruit and train charter school founders for years to come.[543] By 2019, there would be more than 120 BES-founded charter schools in 29 cities across 19 states, serving more than 33,000 students.[544]

Perched on the cusp of these promising new initiatives, the future of the charter school movement nevertheless remained uncertain. Twelve years into the work, many people still had no idea what a charter school was. Critics raised concerns about the schools' quality and their impact on the field, and the research showed mixed results.

This was why Andy Rotherham, the Director of 21st Century Schools Project for the Progressive Policy Institute (PPI), had convened the "Margins to Mainstream" gathering.[545] He had followed charters since the first law passed, when he was employed first at PPI, then in the Clinton White House (from 1999-2000), then back at PPI again. He was excited about the energy of the movement. But it was clear that not all of the schools were good, and some states were doing a better job because of policies and decisions they were making. He and his colleagues had begun to wonder if they could do anything about the issue of quality.[546]

He talked to Bruno Manno, who was then at the Annie E. Casey Foundation, and they cooked up a plan. Manno was a natural thought partner. After holding several senior positions at the United States Department of Education[547] and a stint as Senior Fellow in the Education Policy Studies Program at the Hudson Institute, he'd co-authored (with Checker Finn and Gregg Vanourek) *Charter Schools in Action: Renewing Public Education*, one of the seminal texts about charter schools.[548] From his post at the Casey Foundation, he was trying to see how he could support the movement, and convening a hundred or so of the key leaders seemed like a great idea.

"From Margins to Mainstream" was designed as a "town-hall meeting" that focused on how to grow the charter school movement most effectively—not just in quantity but also in quality.

In one of the most prescient papers written for the conference, Ted Kolderie noted that "the purpose of chartering was not to produce a particular kind of school....[It] is an institutional innovation, a new way to create schools." The way he saw it, chartering needed to scale up in order to have an impact as powerful as the standards movement.[549] Indeed, the standards movement continued to gain momentum, and in 2010, the National Governors' Association and Council of Chief State School Officers would release the Common Core State Standards (CCSS).[550] By June 2014, 43 states,[551] the Department of Defense Education Activity, Washington D.C., Guam, the Northern Mariana Islands and the U.S. Virgin Islands had adopted these standards in ELA/literacy and math.[552]

Another paper that telegraphed the future was penned by Eva Moskowitz, the chair of the education committee on the New York City Council. She pointed out that we fight monopolies in the United States everywhere except in education. She also noted that charter schools offered the potential to help keep the middle class in the public school system, adding, "Look at the most broken public school systems in the country and you will find that the loss of middle class families led directly to the schools' decay. Keeping these families in the public school system means constantly and consistently pushing the schools to grow and adapt."[553] A few years later, she launched Success Academy, which became a network of high-performing charter schools that drew more middle-class parents to stay in New York City and shined a bright light on the failures of the city's district schools. Moskowitz became a lightning rod for critics and supporters of the movement, particularly in her high-profile battles with New York Mayor Bill de Blasio (see Chapter 26).

On the issue of how much impact charters could have, Jim Peyser observed that while not much district-charter collaboration was going on in 2003, two things would enable charters to scale up: 1) replication of successful schools, and 2) cultivation of successful school leaders.[554] His predictions proved true. Funders began to support the creation and expansion of more CMOs (charter management organizations) like Aspire and

KIPP, as well as leadership training programs such as New Leaders for New Schools and Building Excellent Schools.

Other authors recommended steps that could strengthen the movement—and in time, they would. Wendy Kopp and Abigail Smith of Teach For America (TFA) wrote about the need to build pipelines of great teachers, who could in turn become strong leaders. At that point, more than two dozen charter schools had been founded or were being led by TFA alumni.[555] Jon Schnur and his colleagues at New Leaders for New Schools stressed the importance of leadership and the need to be strategic about developing school leaders for high-need public schools.[556] While 85-90 percent of New Leaders-trained leaders went to district public schools, a crucial subset became leaders of charter schools.[557] Margaret Lin asserted that "the single most influential policy reform to enhance the quality of charter schools across the country would be to improve the execution of authorizing at the foundation of the charter school infrastructure."[558] For the next decade and beyond, she and Greg Richmond continued to push that idea forward through their work at the National Association of Charter School Authorizers.

While this conference crystallized challenges that charter advocates faced and gave them more ideas about how to move the ball forward, it also highlighted some major tensions in the movement.

When Andy Rotherham looked back on the meeting nine years later, he made three observations. The first was that the movement seemed to be splitting into three disparate camps:

> *The libertarian camp,* who said, "If parents are choosing it, that's good enough"; *the quality camp:* they were really serious about quality, and choice was a mechanism for that, so choice was not the key thing they were about; and then the sort of *"choiceniks,"* and they were different than the libertarians: this was more about a larger movement. The "choiceniks" were public school critics, and so forth—more private school choice people like Jeanne Allen; this was a place for them, there was a lot of action going on in the charter world,

and they were charter supporters, but their project was a larger, different project.[559]

He left there thinking, *These groups are going to start to operate more and more uneasily with one another.*[560] When your movement is smaller and everybody's against you, you stick together, but as a movement grows and becomes more mainstream, factions tend to form. As he saw it, that was starting to happen in 2003. In 2012, he remarked, "We see those disagreements; those things are still playing out today in the charter world."[561]

The second thing he noticed was the emergence of the CMO idea. "You could get a sense that these networks—something was going to happen; it wasn't clear what, but something was going to happen," he recalled.[562] And something did. Within the next few years—to some degree as a result of this gathering—several major funders shifted their priorities and threw their support behind the idea of replication, and CMOs became a more dominant presence in the movement. (This decision would have consequences for independent, stand-alone charters, sometimes referred to as "Mom and Pop" charters, as we shall see in Chapter 24.)

Rotherham's third key takeaway from the meeting was that "we really did have a quality problem. The more you talked to people, people got it, that it could be traced to policy. There were things that policy makers could do, but they weren't doing them."[563]

As a policy analyst, he found that enormously frustrating. When the first charter laws passed in the early 1990s and states in the mid-1990s repeated some of those mistakes (such as lax authorizing), that was somewhat understandable. But a decade later (in 2003), "when states are still basically passing laws and repeating these mistakes, it means we don't have a good policy feedback loop and bad things are happening. We actually learned a lot over the last decade, and no one's paying attention to it."[564]

By 2012, the problem had become even more intractable. "Now it's all politics," he said. "You've got all of these charter critics who don't want to sit down and have a conversation about what you can learn about how to make the policy better; they want to end this. Our education debate has become so vitriolic that in the second ten years, you've still got that problem but it's even harder and harder to have those conversations."[565]

As time wore on, the combination of rising factions within the charter movement and hostile external forces continued to challenge charter advocates who wanted policy changes.

CHAPTER 23

"HOW MANY SCHOOLS CAN YOU OPEN?"

When New York City Mayor Michael Bloomberg (then a Republican) gained control of the city's schools in 2002, he told his team that he wanted a new Chancellor who would be a fighter and do bold, controversial things.[566] His decision raised some eyebrows. The man he picked was not an educator. He was an energetic attorney who had won a Justice Department antitrust lawsuit against Microsoft.[567]

It turned out that Joel Klein's experience in fighting monopolies was actually perfect preparation for the job. His work over the course of eight years would reshape the city's high-profile educational landscape and shine a bright light on the notion of having a "system of schools" as opposed to a "school system."

Early on, Klein recognized that one problem was that New York City had very little data on how the schools were performing. This was the year President George W. Bush signed the "No Child Left Behind" legislation, which expanded K-12 accountability measures,[568] but those measures had not kicked in yet. Klein secured a $4 million grant from the Eli and Edythe Broad and Julian Robertson Foundations so that he could hire policy and finance experts along with consultants from McKinsey & Company to figure out what problems needed to be solved. He also launched a massive community outreach program to solicit input from parents and other interested residents on what they thought needed to be fixed in public schools. That outreach—to some 50,000 people—bought him a lot of goodwill and was a vital early step in preparing the community for the radical changes that lay ahead.[569]

He decided to call his agenda "Children First," with the vision of "not a great school system, but a system comprised of great schools."[570]

Recognizing the importance of strong school leadership, Klein gave principals more autonomy and support, and enabled them to hire their own assistant principals for the first time. He also anticipated that philanthropy would be needed, and asked Caroline Kennedy to head up the Office of Strategic Partnerships. One of her first steps was to secure $15 million from the Wallace-Reader's Digest Fund to launch a Leadership Academy that would select and train new leaders.[571] She continued to shepherd a dramatic influx of philanthropic support for the Children First initiatives. Klein would later acknowledge that he could not have accomplished as much as he did without this robust stream of private funding. Another factor in his success was the talent pipeline being pumped by nonprofits such as Teach For America, New Leaders for New Schools, and The New Teacher Project, which drew well-educated and highly-motivated teachers and principals into the city.[572]

Along with supporting school leaders, Klein wanted to close underperforming schools and replace them with new, smaller district schools. He figured that taking this approach first would be less controversial than pushing charter schools because the small district schools would be staffed by union teachers. For this project, he solicited funding from the Gates Foundation, which was a little awkward given his legal history with Bill Gates, the CEO of Microsoft. Ultimately Gates provided $51 million.[573] (A colleague later joked, "Imagine what Gates would have given you if you hadn't sued him!"[574])

After he launched this new fleet of small district schools, Klein turned to charter schools, which he saw as a key contributor to a system of great schools. The national charter movement was eleven years old, and in New York it was four. While the number of schools had grown across the country, few had opened in New York City because it was so difficult to find an affordable facility. He addressed this problem by offering charters space in the huge, empty superintendent offices that he had shut down and in district school buildings where classrooms were available. In *Lessons of Hope*, his memoir reflecting on his time as Chancellor, he explains why he made this decision:

> Teachers and administrators in those buildings might not want to lose the space or have their work compared with the efforts of a charter school in the same building, but we believed the space belonged to the kids, not the schools, and if the kids wanted to choose a charter school, they should command their share of the space as well.[575]

In addition to providing real estate, Klein signaled his support for charters by publicly declaring that he was determined to turn New York City into "the Silicon Valley for charter schools."[576] He turned to philanthropists again and raised more than $40 million from the Robin Hood Foundation, Julian Robertson, and Joe and Carol Reich to launch the New York City Center for Charter School Excellence, a nonprofit that would provide charter support and advocacy in the city.[577]

On October 30, 2003, Mayor Bloomberg unveiled plans for the center and asserted that they were committed to opening at least 50 new charter schools in the next five years.[578] Matt Candler, who had largely led KIPP's initial national rollout, was hired to staff this incubation center.

One of the first schools to open under this new initiative was Excellence Academy, which Norman Atkins founded with the philanthropic support of Paul Tudor Jones.[579]

Chancellor Klein began to avidly recruit high-performing charter operators such as KIPP, Achievement First, and Uncommon Schools to open new schools in the city. He believed that competition would motivate the traditional public schools, choice would benefit families, and "to the extent that the charter schools did well… they would put pressure on the public schools to stop making excuses about why they weren't successfully educating kids from poor communities."[580]

He also hoped that the CMO model could become "a template" for how to reorganize traditional public schools. As he saw it,

> Charters had much more operational freedom than traditional schools because they weren't smothered by the micromanaging rules and regulations of the bureaucracy and union contract. They were, instead, pretty much free to determine their own course so long as they got good results for their kids. In short, charter schools were built on a model of empowerment and accountability, which made great organizational sense.[581]

A dozen years later, Dave Levin, whose KIPP schools were able to multiply in the city as a result of Klein's support, looked back and remarked:

> It's hard to remember, but before then, the idea that someone would come to you and say, "Hey, we want you to grow what works. We want to help you, we want to hold you accountable" [felt strange]. Obviously, I've since gotten to know Joel well, but I didn't know Joel then. So, to get called in by the Chancellor and told that they actually wanted to work with you, that was a shocking experience. Joel's leadership in growing what works on behalf of kids in New York City is—it is hard to capture the significance of it and the change that it represented.[582]

Dacia Toll and Doug McCurry, co-founders of the Achievement First network, were similarly startled when they first met Klein. Dacia, a Rhodes Scholar, had enrolled in Yale Law School in 1996 with a plan to pursue civil rights law or economic development. But several factors had led her to become involved in charters. One was that after examining numerous job training programs, including Jimmy Carter's highly-regarded Atlanta Project, she felt that even the most highly-rated programs for people 18 to 35 years old "were really training people for jobs that we wouldn't want for our own kids and that didn't have a lot of promotional opportunities."

And when people had an inadequate education and inadequate skills, it was incredibly difficult to remediate that later on.[583] A *New York Times* piece on class in America, which showed that Americans actually had less social mobility than they did in the 1950s, further convinced her that many of the inequalities that she cared about "really traced back to unequal investments we were making in kids that were further exacerbating these differences."[584]

Around this same time, she read a study that said if you could close the test score gap, you could close the wage gap. She concluded that if you actually equipped people with education and skills, then they could access the American Dream, but "in the absence of that, it was all a myth."[585]

Some education reformers had begun to refer to the achievement gap as "the civil rights issue of our time,"[586] and Dacia agreed. She decided to focus on public education, and enrolled in Yale's Teacher Prep program while still in law school. A classmate who shared her concerns, Stefan Pryor, joined her. The son of two public school teachers,[587] he had won a seat on New Haven's Board of Aldermen as a senior at Yale.[588]

Dacia found teaching 7th and 8th grade social studies at Fair Haven Middle School very eye-opening. "Issues that had been about statistics and policy matters became very personal," she recalled. "They were very real kids that I was struggling to teach how to read so that they could access the social studies content. And I was doing it very inadequately."[589]

Looking for ideas about how to strengthen her teaching practice, she went to visit Dave Levin's KIPP School in the Bronx, and she was "totally blown away by KIPP and by Dave and by what was possible." She and Stefan and a few others at the law school approached Reginald Mayo, the superintendent, and offered to help. But he wasn't sure how to use them.[590]

Connecticut had passed a charter school law in 1996, and Dacia began to consider this option. She started going to New Haven Board of Education meetings to figure out how to make herself more useful, and at one of these meetings, during a discussion of the district's 1997 test results, it became clear what she needed to do.

Looking back fifteen years later, she said:

The district had gone up one point in this subject and two points in that subject and was maybe flat in another subject. At best incremental progress was being celebrated with the end results being something like two-thirds of the kids or more were not at grade level in every grade and subject. In the high school, it was even worse than that: it was something like teens performance.

The worst part was at the end. Well, there were two really bad parts. Then came an expert from Yale who unfortunately said, "One of the straightest lines you'll ever see is the relationship between socioeconomic status and student achievement." And [he said], "Basically, New Haven's a poor city and the kids are facing all of these other challenges, so these are the results you can expect; the district's doing quite well under the circumstances." It's really hard to imagine today, but this was *so* accepted in 1998. It was *so* accepted.

So that was disheartening, and then came the public comment portion. And the worst part about it is, there was NO public comment. So here the community received the devastating news that 70 percent of its kids were not at grade level in core subjects of reading, writing, and math, and there was NO community reaction. And worse, there was this validation that "we're doing as well as we could." That was just it. There I became convinced that having a school that served the same kids but showed what was really possible (fresh off the visit from KIPP-Bronx) could make a huge difference.[591]

She and Stefan Pryor and a few others decided to start a charter school. She was 25. Stefan was 26. Fully aware that they didn't know everything, they enlisted community support and looked for models to emulate. They visited schools that had a track record of taking students who were below grade level and bringing them up to grade level—schools such as KIPP in the South Bronx; North Star in Newark; an Accelerated

School in California; and Calgary Academy, a special education school in Canada.[592] Just as Norman Atkins and Jamey Verrilli had done, Dacia and Stefan collected best practices to incorporate into the design of their school.

As they prepared to launch Amistad Academy, they hired Doug McCurry as the lead teacher and soon thereafter promoted McCurry to run the school's academic program. Doug and Dacia had known each other in the Morehead Scholars program at the University of North Carolina, and while earning a Master's degree at Teachers College, he'd heard about what she was doing and reached out.[593] He'd done some consulting and taught at a private school in North Carolina, but he wanted to make a broader impact.

In 1999, Amistad Academy opened with 84 students (randomly selected from more than 550 applications) in fifth and sixth grades.[594] The original plan was simply "to start a great school in our community,"[595] and they did that: in 2001, *their 8th-graders, 87 percent of whom received free or reduced-price lunch, achieved at the same level as their suburban counterparts on the Connecticut Mastery Test*; they exceeded the state-wide average in writing and math, and were close to the state average in reading.[596]

After a few years of early success, they wanted to have more impact, but they weren't quite sure which path to take. "We always talked academic excellence and character-building," Doug McCurry said, "and we always talked about public school reform: it was always the third leg of the mission. We never really knew what that meant; we were like, *Look, we want to share, we want to be partners; we don't know how to expand the impact of this little school beyond one school*. It was unclear."[597] For a time, they were torn between the idea of starting more schools or starting a teacher-training center. Calgary Academy, which had functioned as a mentor school to them, had opted to stay as one school and had started a teacher-training center. Some Amistad board members liked the idea of opening a "center South." But Doug opposed that idea, he said,

> not because I don't believe in teacher training, but I was like, *Right now, lots of people are doing professional development;*

what there's a shortage of is high-performing schools. This was 2002, 2003, before there was a proliferation of high-performing charter schools, and there weren't any really that had done it at any scale. So I believed it was much more important for us and others to grow to scale, to scale excellence, but also to make it really clear that this could be done.

People [who supported the PD approach] were saying you could impact 2,000 teachers a year; if all of them reached 100 kids a year, that would be 200,000 kids a year you could reach. Never was that appealing to me because I was like, *Yeah, you could reach 200,000 kids, but I don't want to be measured by that number. Of those 200,000 kids, I'd want to know, What number of them are having a fundamentally life-changing experience?* I just didn't believe we could get that without controlling all of the variables, without running the schools. That's where we decided to start more schools.[598]

Along with Doug's argument, several key factors had influenced their decision. For one, they were receiving about eight applications for every seat. Dacia recalled: "One grandmother said to me, 'You mean, whether my grandson gets a great education depends on *luck*?'"[599] The unfortunate answer was *yes*. Dacia wanted to change that.

The second factor was that they had a teacher who, as Dacia put it, "was so obviously ready to be a great principal" that they felt confident he (Marc Michaelson[600]) could take the reins of a new school.[601]

Third, even though Amistad had achieved "suburban-Greenwich-level results," they kept hearing "Yes-buts": "*Yes, but* it's the particular school leader," "*Yes, but* it's the particular group of hand-picked teachers," "*Yes, but* they must cherry-pick the students...."[602]

They opened Elm City College Prep—which became a middle school and an elementary school—less than a mile away. The new school began to out-perform Amistad, which surprised Dacia. She had feared that any attempts at replication would be "more like a photocopy machine—where each copy was a slightly-faded-with-a-couple-of-splotches version of the one before." After the success of Elm City, she and her colleagues began to think, *Actually this could be more like software development and if we do this right, the second school will learn tremendously from the first and the third will learn tremendously from the second, and it's more like Version 1.0, Version 2.0, Version 3.0....*[603]

Then, somewhat out of the blue, Joel Klein invited them to come to New York City for a meeting.[604] He greeted them in the newly refurbished Tweed Courthouse, in a large room filled with tables. As they sat down at one of the tables, Klein said, "So I've done my research on Amistad." He pointed to an array of performance graphs that tracked the progress of their students from year to year.

He wasted no time. "I want you to go into some of the historically low-performing communities in New York and show what's really possible," he said. "What do you need?"

Dacia looked at him. Then she said, "Well, we need facilities, we need funding, we need political support."

"OK, I'll do all that. Done." He nodded. "How many schools can you open?"

They hadn't expected this.

Doug looked at Dacia, Dacia looked at Doug, and Dacia said, "Um, three?"

Klein said, "OK."

Dacia said, "Who do I follow up with to start the conversation?"

Klein grinned. "*Start* the conversation? We just *had* the conversation. I need you to open three schools."

Dacia and Doug left that meeting and went to work. They opened those three schools, then 20 more in New York. As of 2019, those 23 Achievement First schools continued to thrive—with students' overall proficiency double that of their host districts and exceeding state and city averages by more than 24 percentage points. In math, every Achievement

First school's eighth-grade class performed in the top 3 percent of all New York schools.[605]

Norman Atkins and Dave Levin also multiplied the Uncommon and KIPP schools in the city. As the years passed, these four leaders collaborated on other projects, including one that became the Relay Graduate School of Education. We'll return to that story in Part III.

In 2010, after eight years of pressing his agenda to develop "a system of great schools," Joel Klein resigned. One measure of his impact as Chancellor was that by the end of Mayor Bloomberg's tenure, the city had opened more than 150 new charter schools, and their waiting lists reached into the tens of thousands.[606]

CHAPTER 24

HERDING CATS, PART II, AND THE DOUBLE-EDGED SWORD OF PHILANTHROPY

By 2000-01, four years after Ted Kolderie and Jon Schroeder had launched Charter Friends National Network (CFNN), it had become apparent that there was a growing need to represent charter interests more robustly, particularly in Washington. There was also a willingness on the part of key state charter organization leaders to consider organizational arrangements that more closely mirrored CFNN's growing role as a leading voice for charters on key issues including accountability (e.g., "Goals 2000" and "No Child Left Behind") facilities financing, and the federal charter grant program. And a degree of trust had emerged within CFNN and among the growing number of state organization leaders who participated in its activities. (The number of state and local "Charter Friends" groups grew from a dozen or so in the mid 1990's to more than 80 a decade later.)[607]

Staffed by "project leader" Jon Schroeder and a couple dozen consultants who were contracted to work on specific projects, CFNN had accomplished a great deal in just a few years. It ran a small grant program funded by the Walton Family Foundation to help start and strengthen state charter support organizations. It also organized working groups on federal policy issues, financed research projects, published 20 resource guides, developed an extensive website, produced frequent updates on topics of interest to charter supporters, and convened networking meetings of state charter organization leaders. In 1999, CFNN convened a working group that recommended—and then organized—the nation's first "National Charter Schools Week" that was held in May of 2000. The kick-off event was held at the nation's first charter school—City Academy in St. Paul—where President Bill Clinton gave the keynote speech. Over time, CFNN also gained recognition as a principal voice for charter schools with national and state policy makers and media. It helped plan several U.S. Department of Education national conferences. Schroeder testified before a U.S. House Subcommittee on reauthorization of the federal charter school program. And CFNN engaged a DC-based contract lobbyist to help guide its work on federal legislation.[608]

Although many grassroots activists remained skeptical about the prospect of forming a national charter school organization that would speak for the movement, there was growing pressure on CFNN to expand its capacity to represent charter interests on federal policy matters and appropriations. About a dozen state organization leaders—including Eric Premack and Sue Bragato (CA), Jim Griffin (CO), John Ayers (IL), Bill Phillips (NY), Patsy O'Neill (TX), Howard Fuller and Senn Brown (WI), Dan Quisenberry (MI), Shirley Monastra (DC), and I (NJ)—felt strongly that we needed to kick things up a notch. We were so busy with state-level challenges that it was difficult to find time to address federal-level concerns.

To be clear, no one was unhappy with the work that CFNN had done. The decision to create a more formal entity was simply an acknowledgment that the charter movement had matured to a point where it needed national infrastructure with more capacity, formality, and legitimacy than a "project" run out of a small Minnesota-based nonprofit could provide.[609] While Jeanne Allen and her colleagues at the Center for Education Reform (CER) kept a nationwide inventory of charter schools and laws, CER's mission to support school choice more broadly (including vouchers, which some charter advocates opposed) meant it could not represent charters specifically.

As state-level leaders began to meet informally to discuss what to do, one obvious question was: *How will we fund this thing?* There was some talk of collecting dues and developing revenue-generating programs and services, but in the early stages, we would need to rely on philanthropy.

While some may believe that philanthropy is always unambiguously helpful, others—including some in the charter school movement—view it as more of a double-edged sword. The truth is that philanthropists have both supported the movement and sometimes reshaped its path in controversial ways.

To be clear, the charter school movement could not have begun or survived without the support of private funders. State-based supporters— particularly those of us who ran nonprofit resource centers—were almost completely dependent on foundations. While we could charge fees for events we organized, these efforts covered only a small portion of the bills.

The schools themselves typically receive only a percentage of the local per-pupil funding from the district, and in most states, they receive no facilities funding at all. In the first few years, before federal start-up funding became available in 1995, charter school founders had to rely on philanthropic generosity or—in the case of Arizona, where philanthropy was limited—the involvement of for-profit managers whose bottom line was the bottom line.[610] Charter applicants and operators often dug into their own pockets to pay for start-up costs, and some—like Yvonne Chan—even went so far as to mortgage their own homes.[611]

In the early years, local foundations led the way in promoting charters and the growth of the movement. Before New Jersey even had a charter law, Scott McVay and his colleagues at the New Jersey-based Geraldine R. Dodge Foundation supported the City on a Hill Charter School[612] in Boston.[613] As soon as New Jersey's legislation was signed, McVay and his colleagues began plotting ways to advance the movement in their home state—first by running a major conference, then by collaborating with other state-based funders to help launch the Charter School Resource Center.

On a national level, CFNN relied on an array of local and national foundations—such as Challenge, Kinship, St. Paul, Labrador, the Walton Family, and Annie E. Casey—and was also awarded several grants from the U.S. Department of Education to lead or partner with others on studies or projects on special education, facilities financing, authorizer practices, and grassroots input on the design of the USDOE national conference.[614]

In 2001, when talk of forming a new national organization became more serious, the Walton Family Foundation provided funding for strategic planning, engaging a search firm to hire a CEO, and transitioning to the new entity.[615] Jon Schroeder provided staff support for a steering committee of state organization leaders.[616]

Without getting too far into the weeds (full disclosure: I chaired the steering committee), this process took a while, for several reasons. As Jon Schroeder noted,

> The national organization steering committee held a number of meetings via conference call and in person—including meetings of sub-groups it created on membership, governance, functions, services, and finances. Its pace was slowed, however, by the multiple commitments of its members and the complexities of balancing the need for a national organization with what was felt to be the need to represent the state organizations and local schools.[617]

Another challenge was that the funders and those of us "on the ground" had different views about what the new organization should look like and how it should be governed. The tension became apparent not long after the *first* national organization emerged.

In March 2003, we rolled out the National Charter School Alliance, a membership organization with a blend of state association leaders and national advocates who would be elected to its governing board by the state-based membership.[618] Howard Fuller was the chair. Dean Millot (who had previously conducted research with RAND) became the executive director and began to set up a Washington-based office and staff.[619]

But a few months later, several foundations active in the financing of new schools (including some that had supported CFNN) expressed a desire for a "leadership organization" rather than a membership organization. This sentiment was pushed further along at a follow-up meeting in early August in Philadelphia. The sense was, as one consultant privately put it, that for chartering to realize its potential "the little people" needed to give way and be replaced by "the heavy hitters."[620] Translation: They were less interested in herding cats and more interested in telling the cats what to do.

The foundations decided not to fund the original design.[621] The organization was dissolved. The Walton Family Foundation asked Howard Fuller to chair a new group of board members to come up with a plan that would be acceptable to the funders.[622]

That took another year.

In October 2004, the Charter School Leadership Council appeared as the new Washington-based national leadership organization, with Nelson Smith at the helm. In August 2005, the organization was renamed the National Alliance for Public Charter Schools.[623]

Nelson had been involved in charters since mid-1996 when he succeeded Ted Rebarber as Representative Steve Gunderson's aide. During the last six months of Gunderson's term, he worked with Richard Wenning on amendments to the DC School Reform Act (the charter law, which passed in April 1996). Probably the amendment he was most proud of was extending the term of DC charters to 15 years, which, he said, "we did because there were reports that charters around the country were having difficulty getting facilities funding because bankers were scared of the five-year terms." The amendment included a high-stakes review every five years.[624]

In 1997, he worked for the emergency trustee board set up by the District's Congressionally imposed Control Board to oversee DC Public Schools. This job gave him "a bird's-eye view" of what was wrong with DC Public Schools. He recalled:

I used to get into the office early. The phone would ring and it would be a parent who had some kind of issue with the local school, and they would scream into the phone. After a while, it became apparent to me that they didn't really believe that anything was going to change, but they had to scream. They were so frustrated. The impression that it made on me, which I've carried for a long time now, was *they really do care.* There is this mythology about charter schools getting all of the concerned and diligent parents, and the school system getting all the layabouts: not so. The parents who used to read me the Riot Act every morning were desperately trying to do the right thing for their kids: they just didn't have any place to go with it. They knew damn well that the system wasn't going to respond, but they had to try and fight anyway.[625]

This impression stuck with Nelson as he moved forward in his career, increasing his empathy for parents whose children were stranded in failing schools. Recognizing how widespread the problems were, he became even more passionate about the need for schools to be held accountable for their performance.

After a year at the Emergency Control Board, he became Director of the Public Charter School Board, an independent body separate from the DC system, and he spent the next three years[626] as the second authorizer of charter schools in the District. Unlike the DC School Board, which consisted of politicians who did not necessarily have the capacity to review charter applications, the Public Charter School Board under Nelson's leadership became known for being more selective about the quality of the schools it approved.

Subsequently, he spent three years at New American Schools, working with Richard Wenning and others on policy issues, particularly on No Child Left Behind and its effect on the charter community. "When we talk about growth measures these days," he noted, "a lot of the really seminal thinking came out of New American Schools at that time between Rich Wenning and Harold Doran. That later morphed into a grant that we worked on at the Alliance, and then that became the foundation of the Colorado Growth Model."[627] The Growth Model would have widespread impact on how states measured school performance, not just for charters but all schools (See Chapter 28).

In light of Nelson's experience with helping charters create systems that would enable them to do high-level accountability, it was perhaps not surprising that he was selected to become President of the National Alliance. The funders—some of whom had previously advocated for a "thousand flowers to bloom"—had become increasingly focused on the idea of "high-quality" schools. The Alliance formed a task force of "distinguished charter leaders and policy thinkers to help fashion a forward-looking strategy to realize the full promise of chartering" and in January 2005 released a report, *Renewing the Compact*, which Nelson shared with funders at a retreat that August on Mackinac Island.[628] This report clearly signaled the direction that the Alliance would take, as five of the seven "principles of quality chartering" emphasized quality over quantity, academic achievement, and accountability (The remaining two stressed the need for talented personnel and equitable funding).[629]

After launching the Alliance, funders continued to shift their priorities, and their actions had far-reaching and lasting consequences for the movement. By taking a more corporate/bureaucratic approach, they also took some of the heart and grassroots energy out of the movement. They de-funded a number of state and local charter support organizations (notably in California and Washington, DC). "Strategic planning" grants became available to organizations willing to fall in with the new initiative. By March 2008 most of the early state-based members had either resigned or been removed from the Alliance board.[630] Since many of us were taken down by the funders' decisions, our role as relationship-builders and community-builders within our states was derailed. In some states, the infrastructure to help improve existing schools evaporated. In addition, the support for individuals who wanted to create new schools was diminished or removed.

The funders then turned their attention to charter management organizations (CMOs) and replication efforts. This shift was dramatic. In 2000, individual charter schools received 71.5 percent of all [philanthropic] charter school dollars, with CMOs receiving the remainder. In 2005, the inverse was true: CMOs received 73.8 percent of all charter school money. By 2010, CMOs received 81.1 percent.[631] I am not trying to suggest that increasing funding for CMOs was a bad thing. Many of them had (and continue to have) excellent track records. But it is important to note that this funding shift likely affected the opportunities for individual start-ups and may have limited some chances for innovation. When the funding of the movement shifted, to some degree, so did the movement itself.

All of that said, the positive, powerful effects of philanthropy on the charter school movement should not be overlooked. The movement would never have emerged from the starting blocks without philanthropic support.

How might that support affect the future?

One potential indicator came in January 2016, when Marc Sternberg, a former high school principal who directed education philanthropy for the Walton Family Foundation, announced that the foundation planned to spend $1 billion over the next five years to improve public education by backing new charter schools and helping programs already up and running. At that point, Walton had already spent more than $1 billion on K-12 education in the preceding 20 years, including $385 million to help start charter schools in poor communities. Sternberg said that the new money would be spent in places where the foundation already had ties — creating new schools and developing "pipelines of talent." He added, "People in poverty need high-performing schools. Our goal is that all families ... have better schools. To be the rising tide to lift all boats."[632]

In June 2016, Walton announced another initiative, tacking on an additional $250 million to help charter schools build and expand their facilities.[633]

We shall see.

CHAPTER 25

THE KATRINA EFFECT

At the July 2003 "Margins to the Mainstream" Conference, as partici-pants wrestled with how best to expand the movement, Mike Goldstein, founder of MATCH Charter School in Boston, suggested that instead of focusing on how to multiply the *number* of schools, we should focus on *market share* and "put our energy into tipping those cities where everybody is used to shopping for schools."[634] It sounded perfectly logical, but no one had deliberately done it yet.

Then came Hurricane Katrina.

Prior to August of 2005, most schools in New Orleans were low-performing. To be more precise, in 2004, Orleans Parish public schools ranked 67th out of 68 Louisiana districts in math and reading test scores.[635]

The storm and broken levees led to a dramatic transformation of the schools in New Orleans. But that isn't the whole story. While it is true that the disaster changed the landscape, things would not have improved if committed citizens had not stepped up. Their individual and collective actions made a difference.

One could argue that the first step of the change process happened in 1992, when Leslie Jacobs decided to run for the Orleans Parish School Board. A native of New Orleans who ran an insurance brokerage firm with her brother, Leslie chaired a group of business partners that supported the schools. Leslie became so frustrated by how bad schools were that she was willing to volunteer 30-40 hours a week to try to fix them.[636] After she was elected, she grew even more frustrated with the system, recalling, "All I succeeded in doing was stopping bad things from happening."[637] She added:

> As school board members, if we showed up, we spoke to each other well, and we didn't self-deal and were honest, we were considered good board members. The public really didn't want controversy. And the fact that we were warehousing children [not teaching them] would get rolled up into the report of district-wide data.[638]

She tried to convince each of her colleagues to take ownership for one failing school in their district and help redevelop it, but they refused. She later realized that had they agreed, reporters would have had a field day with their choices and the results. The way she saw it, board members were "rewarded for not taking risk in the face of massive failure."[639] As a business person, she believed this "off-kilter risk-reward ratio" was a problem that needed to be solved. No one was being held accountable.

When Governor Mike Foster (a Republican) appointed her to the Louisiana Board of Elementary and Secondary Education (BESE), Leslie decided to address this problem by developing an accountability system for the state's schools. In 1999 (several years before President George W. Bush signed "No Child Left Behind" legislation, which expanded K-12 accountability measures[640]), BESE began issuing "school performance scores," and New Orleans was flagged as having a huge percentage of failing schools. The accountability system included assistance for schools, but that support, sadly, had zero impact. Leslie recalled:

> We gave the district extra money, we helped them with school improvement plans, we gave them distinguished educators.... We had a ten million dollar federal grant for Orleans Parish School Board to turn around their middle schools, and the bottom line is they got worse. Nothing was improving. The

district had eight or nine superintendents in the decade prior to Katrina.... It was just a totally dysfunctional system.[641]

A particularly low moment came in 2003 when the valedictorian of Fortier High School could not walk across the stage and get her diploma because she couldn't pass a minimal skills exit exam.[642]

Leslie and the governor agreed that the state should not *take over* the district because in addition to fraud and corruption (the FBI had actually set up an office on the West Bank campus of the Orleans Parish School Board[643]), there was also systemic dysfunction, and as Leslie saw it, incompetence was much harder to fix than corruption. She proposed the idea of a "Recovery School District" (RSD), a government innovation modeled loosely on bankruptcy law. She explained: "When a business files for Chapter 11 re-org, the court has tremendous power. It has the power to sever contracts, it has the power to sell parts of the business, it has the power to waive the rights of some creditors so the business can exit bankruptcy court as an ongoing viable concern."[644] With the RSD, the State would declare a school academically bankrupt or failing, take it away from the local school board, and put it inside the RSD. Taking the school away would remove the governance structure and all contracts, including the collective bargaining agreement. What would remain was "the building, the students, the money, and a fresh start."[645]

Unlike the more commonly seen "district takeover" model where the state and/or mayor's office would take control of a district and bring in a "rock-star" superintendent, the RSD approach acknowledged that the state was not equipped to run schools. Instead, the state department of education began chartering schools. If a school had failed for three or more consecutive years, the state had the "right but not the obligation" to put that school into the RSD.

When the levees broke on August 29, 2005, five New Orleans schools were already in the RSD, all charters—that is, district schools that had been turned over to charter operators.[646]

At this point, largely under water and in crisis, the city was shuttered. Some 110 of 127 schoolhouses were unusable.[647] With no local revenue, the schools were closed and more than 7,000 employees, including teachers and support workers—many now homeless—were initially put on "disaster leave without pay" and later terminated.[648] Though some were rehired, many lost their jobs permanently. (Their legal appeals demanding back pay went through various courts for nine years. Ultimately the Louisiana Supreme Court dismissed the lawsuit, and on May 18, 2015, the U.S. Supreme Court refused to hear the case.[649])

Immediately after the storm, Democratic Governor Kathleen Blanco took several dramatic steps to reboot the schools. One was that she pushed for Act 35, which passed in a special session in November (2005). Act 35 amended the RSD law to effectively put all but a dozen Orleans public schools into the RSD. Act 35 required that if a district was in "academic crisis,"[650] BESE now had the "*obligation*, not the option," to put any school below the state average into the Recovery School District.[651]

At the time, New Orleans was the only district in Louisiana that met the criteria for being in academic crisis. More than 100 Orleans Parish schools were summarily put into the RSD.[652] Governor Blanco also signed an executive order suspending the laws that required a vote of the faculty, the parents, and the students to convert a school to a charter. This allowed the schools that stayed with OPSB to convert to charters in the fall and winter of 2005. Of the dozen schools that OPSB kept, only four initially opened as "direct-run" schools. The others reopened as charters.[653] Leslie Jacobs remarked, "Although her base (the Black Caucus and the teachers' union) was opposed to these steps, Kathleen Blanco thought it would be terrible to reopen the schools to the failure we had before. She showed incredible political courage."[654]

To address the local funding shortfall, Senator Mary Landrieu reached out to U.S. Secretary of Education Margaret Spellings to see if any unused federal charter school funds could be accessed.[655] Jeanne Allen at the Center for Education Reform was actively involved in recovery efforts and made a similar pitch.[656] Additionally, State Superintendent Cecil Picard sent Secretary Spellings a detailed request for funding and waivers.[657] On December 30, 2005, Spellings issued a policy letter that announced three new grant programs to assist school districts and schools in meeting the educational needs of students displaced by Hurricanes Katrina and Rita and in helping schools that were closed as a result of the hurricanes to reopen as quickly and effectively as possible.[658]

Still, the devastation was massive. Four out of every five houses were flooded, and the city's infrastructure—the water, sewer, electricity, and transportation—was destroyed.[659] For months, uncertainty percolated about when and how the city might be reopened and rebuilt.[660]

In the months following the storm, several dozen charter school activists from around the country traveled to New Orleans to help community leaders revive the educational system.

One early meeting was held at Samuel J. Green Charter School. There was still water in the boiler room when Tony Recasner, the school's founder, greeted the visitors.[661] His was one of the few schools open. He'd converted the failing Green Middle School into a college prep charter that had opened one week before Katrina.[662] In January 2006, he'd agreed to reopen the school and serve more students than originally planned even though he wasn't fully ready.[663]

Several dozen local community leaders and outside charter leaders went up to the third floor and sat hunched in student desks in a classroom, and Nelson Smith, then head of the National Alliance for Public Charter Schools, facilitated the discussion. Their focal question was "What needs to be done to make this thing work right?"

There seemed to be consensus that chartering was the way to go. But there needed to be a rethinking of the support structure for it.[664]

At the end of the meeting, Smith suggested that they would have to think about some sort of new entity, a new support organization. He said: "We need to do some planning around it. Who would like to take part in that?"[665]

The first person to raise a hand was a young woman named Sarah Usdin. She'd grown up in Louisville, Kentucky, joined Teach For America (TFA) in 1992, and taught in Baton Rouge for several years. Like Kaya

Henderson (who would later run the DC Public Schools), she'd gone on to work as a regional executive director for TFA. In 1997, Michelle Rhee hired Usdin and Henderson to take The New Teacher Project (TNTP) out from under the TFA umbrella and expand it into a national teacher recruitment pipeline.[666] When Usdin raised her hand, she had just taken the summer off from TNTP to spend time with her family and was trying to decide what to do next.

Now she knew. "New Schools for New Orleans" was born.

Usdin's days and nights in the chaotic world of post-Katrina New Orleans—where the traffic lights didn't work and grocery stores were only open for a few hours a day—became even more hectic: trying to raise funds, trying to figure out how to build up an infrastructure of support.

Jim Peyser, then at the New Schools Venture Fund, dove in to help. Usdin recalled, "He convened a multi-day meeting and brought in the 'Who's Who' in the charter sector to determine the most effective way to launch a new charter campaign." Among those present were Nelson Smith, Greg Richmond, Chris Nelson (from the Fisher Fund), Jim Shelton (then at the Gates Foundation), Kevin Hall (at the Charter School Growth Fund), Mike Feinberg, Norman Atkins, John King, and Dacia Toll.[667]

Peyser asked them to share what they had learned. *If they had to do it all over again from scratch, what would they have wanted? What would have helped them do their work? What would have made it easier to launch and run their schools?*[668]

Sarah Usdin recalled:

That was a pivotal moment for us: out of the tragedy, getting folks to be able to stop and think that way, for us to learn from their own experiences and not make the same mistakes ... because we were putting together something new and we were doing it very hurriedly but also had this great good will and guidance and mentorship and input of so many folks.[669]

Usdin had thought New Schools for New Orleans (NSNO) would support back office services—helping schools with supplies and food vendors, and so on—but it soon became apparent that after the hurricane, you didn't have a choice of a vendor: there was one or none. In a way, this was fortuitous because it enabled Usdin to focus on issues related to academic quality. She recalled:

> The national team who was advising and helping us was like, "Honestly, you figure all that stuff out. What's more critical is the recruiting of teachers, the training of teachers, the pushing of academics, of understanding how to get better interim assessments and the things that will make the academic difference in classes and classrooms." So that's what pushed us early into that direction, which was absolutely brilliant and how it should have been.[670]

As Usdin worked to build the organization, Nelson Smith at the Alliance lent some manpower and the Broad Foundation sent some Fellows. In fact, one Broad Fellow stayed in Usdin's guest room for months because there were no hotels open in the neighborhood.

Among the many educational leaders who came to town was Jon Schnur. After working for the Clinton Administration and advising presidential candidate Al Gore on educational policy, in 2000 he had co-founded New Leaders for New Schools,[671] a nonprofit to recruit and train principals. A week after the storm, his phone began ringing, and he flew down to help. Schnur was not some disinterested outsider: his wife had grown up in New Orleans and his in-laws still lived there. Not long after Katrina, he and his wife decided to move there, too. In addition to participating in meetings to help rebuild schools, he did whatever he could to "fill the gaps." He brought New Leaders for New Schools to the city and hired New Orleans native Tyra Newell to come back to lead a local New Leaders program recruiting and providing intensive training to develop principals and other school leaders in New Orleans.[672] While visiting neighborhood centers and churches where people were finding refuge, he was struck by how awful the conditions were and how little support there was. This led him to recommend and advise on the creation of a humanitarian recovery corps, a government-chartered agency and nonprofit.[673] He later recalled how moved he was by the determined spirit of the people of New Orleans:

> What was really inspiring is as devastating as it was, neighborhood by neighborhood, there were citizens in New Orleans who were so dedicated to rebuilding their city. They knew this was life or death for their city…. They were like, *We're going to do this; we're going to build this*…. There was this level of civic engagement and commitment and willingness to envision and build something new that was inspiring…. The stakes were very high for people in the community of New Orleans, and their leadership and commitment to rebuilding their city was indispensable.[674]

Another key player who relocated to New Orleans was Matt Candler. After shepherding KIPP's initial national rollout from 2001-2004, Candler had gone to work at the New York City Center for Charter School Excellence, to support school start-ups in a more manageable geographic situation. Reflecting on the work in New York City, he remarked:

> It was a lot like what I was doing at KIPP, but all I had to do was take cabs and subways as opposed to planes. And I got to see a lot of different types of schools. That was the other cool thing: I wasn't just building KIPPs; I was working with a lot more politicians and community activists who wanted to start schools, as well as helping KIPP and Amistad and Uncommon expand. I got to know the in-district politics, and it was fascinating to think about what the city needed….[675]

After participating in numerous strategic meetings to support the New Orleans schools re-boot, Candler moved his family down from New York City in October 2006 to join Sarah Usdin at NSNO. It turned out that determining the resources and conditions needed for reform to work in New York City was excellent preparation for launching a new fleet of schools in New Orleans. In fact, Candler came to see the role of NSNO as being a "harbormaster—as in, *This is where you come to plug into the New Orleans challenge*."[676]

One obvious challenge was the need for a talent pipeline. Many people had fled the city and not returned because their homes and businesses had been destroyed. After Katrina, New Orleans lost more than half of its population, dropping from 484,684 in April 2000 to an estimated 230,172 in July 2006.[677]

One day in the spring of 2006, as Sarah Usdin was leaving a meeting at a school, she bumped into a Yale law student who had come down after the storm to volunteer. His name was Neerav Kingsland. He told her he wanted to see what he could do to help the schools. They went out for coffee, and he explained why he was there.

As a Tulane undergrad, Kingsland had tutored at a New Orleans district school. "To this day it was probably one of the saddest, lowest-performing, just tragic schools that I've ever been to," he recalled. "Security guards everywhere. It was a middle school. You walk in the classrooms and teachers are reading the newspaper. Nobody's paying attention."[678] He worked with third- and fourth-graders who could not even recognize letters. He knew that they needed much more help than he could provide. Later that year, the tutoring program was abruptly canceled after an execution-style shooting at the school. It became very clear to him that the experiences some students had in public schools were radically different than others, and when he went to law school, he divided his time between international human rights and educational reform.[679]

Kingsland offered to help Usdin provide legal advice to charter leaders. Although he still had one semester of law school left, he really wanted to be down in New Orleans. He decided to move there during his last semester (from August 2006 to January 2007), and threw himself into an all-out push to recruit teachers and school leaders. He skipped all of his classes, then flew back and took his finals (somehow managing to graduate). As NSNO expanded its efforts, he directed the human capital work and became increasingly responsible for the growth strategy. In 2012, when Usdin left (before she ran for office and was elected to the Orleans Parish School Board[680]), he became NSNO's CEO.[681]

Human and fiscal resources came to New Orleans through various organizations and individuals. Veteran educators in the community stepped up, and NSNO reached out to Teach For America, which tripled in size after the storm, and The New Teacher Project, to build the talent pipeline.[682] In addition to Jim Peyser at the New Schools Venture Fund, a group of major philanthropists delivered support: the Eli and Edythe Broad Foundation, the Doris and Donald Fisher Fund, the Bill and Melinda Gates Foundation, the Walton Family Foundation, and the Robertson Foundation.[683]

NSNO's work became one of the key levers that transformed New Orleans from being a city in which only 5 percent of students attended charter schools in 2005[684] to a city in which, ten years later, 93 percent did.[685]

A related lever, as schools began to reopen, was the push for *better* schools. As Matt Candler liked to say, "Our job is not just to create schools that *suck less* than the previous schools."[686] He and other charter school leaders who provided their expertise shared Leslie Jacobs's belief that starting new schools offered an opportunity to create *high-quality* schools. In this regard, the National Association of Charter School Authorizers (NACSA) played a vital role.

Greg Richmond had just begun leading NACSA full-time when Katrina hit.[687] Nelson Smith reached out and invited him to some meetings. That fall, Greg flew to New Orleans repeatedly to offer support.

At an early meeting that Senator Mary Landrieu convened in Baton Rouge on the campus of Louisiana State University with about 50 people around the table, when Greg introduced himself, he drew an analogy between his experiences in Chicago and what had happened in Louisiana up until that point. He recalled:

> Louisiana up until this point had just a handful of charter schools and it was this small, mildly interesting education effort in the public education system. And it was somewhat

similar to my experience in Chicago: for a number of years, charter schools were just this small, somewhat interesting thing on the margins, but when Arne Duncan came in [in 2001[688]], we made them a major strategy of the system. And now what Louisiana was doing was also shifting gears from a small, interesting thing to making it a major strategy.[689]

That fall, Greg met with State Superintendent Cecil Picard, a traditional educator who had been a teacher, wrestling coach, and principal at his high school in rural Louisiana. Picard was in his late sixties and had been diagnosed with ALS the summer before the hurricane hit. He continued to work although he knew he had probably fewer than 18 months left to live. "That was part of the human drama of this," Greg recalled. "He knew this was the last thing he was ever going to do, was to try to save New Orleans public education."[690]

Picard was initially skeptical about charters. But he'd heard that Paul Vallas had done some good things in Chicago, so as they sat in his office one day, he asked, "What happened in Chicago with charter schools? What was the deal?"

Greg replied, "Well, number one, we turned down about 80 percent of the proposals that were submitted to us because we had very high standards."

Picard uncrossed his arms and leaned forward. "That's what I want you to do here," he said.[691]

Picard asked Greg and NACSA to help design and lead the authorizing process in Louisiana. Not long after that, the state hired NACSA to evaluate all charter school applications.[692] In the first round, in spite of the pressure to open schools for returning families, NACSA recommended only six of 44 applications.[693]

The original plan was for NACSA to run the application process a few times and then turn it over to the state, but NACSA was asked to manage *twelve* post-Katrina charter application cycles. Between 2006 and 2012, Greg and his colleagues led a team of skilled national and local experts in the review of more than 250 charter school applications.[694] In 2012, Greg wrote a letter to BESE and the department stating that NACSA was stepping down from its role, noting that the department had demonstrated that it was now "fully capable of managing the application evaluation process on its own."[695]

Cecil Picard passed away on February 15, 2007, but his work carried on.

experts in the review of more than 250 charter school applications.[694] In

Paul Pastorek, Picard's successor, needed someone to lead the RSD, which had gone from a handful of schools to more than 100 overnight.[696] Robin Jarvis had been assigned the role of overseeing a "few" schools on top of her job as Deputy Superintendent for Accountability, but it was not humanly feasible for her to keep doing that. "She worked harder than anyone I've ever seen in my life (in terms of hours)," Greg Richmond recalled, "but it was just too much. The RSD was like a nameplate up till that point, but it didn't really exist, it was just a unit within the State Ed Department."[697] Now it needed its own unit with its own leader.

In March 2007, Senator Mary Landrieu called Paul Vallas, who was then running the Philadelphia Public Schools, to ask him if he knew anyone who could do the job.

"What about me?" he replied.

Landrieu jumped at that.[698]

Vallas was well-suited for this role. An inveterate problem-solver, he always seemed to go where the action was ("Every single job I've held has been a government in crisis," he said[699]). In the early 1990s, as a certified teacher who then spent more than a decade working in finance for the State of Illinois, he'd caught the attention of Chicago Mayor Richard Daley, who brought him in to run his revenue department. When the city fell into political and financial crises in 1993, Daley shook up his cabinet and Vallas became city budget director. Vallas balanced the budget, secured bond rating upgrades, and helped Daley put 13,500 police officers on the street.[700]

In 1995, when Republican Governor Jim Edgar gave Daley control of the schools, Daley appointed Vallas as the Schools CEO. Before Vallas left in 2001, Chicago Public Schools saw six years of improved reading and five years of improved math scores, and the district had $1.2 billion in cash reserves, twelve bond rating upgrades, $3 billion in school construction, and a significant expansion of educational choices.[701] On his watch, the state opened its first charter schools and expanded the number of magnet schools, including a series of magnets within neighborhood schools. "The whole idea was to create choice within schools," he said.[702]

In 2001, he ran for Governor of Illinois (losing narrowly in the Democratic primary to Rod Blagojevich). A year later, he became CEO of the troubled School District of Philadelphia, and his work there also led to test score gains.[703]

Not long after Katrina hit, Vallas was invited by the Gates Foundation to travel to Houston to share some ideas, and he put together a presentation on what the transformation of New Orleans schools should look like.[704] He recalled:

> I advocated for the creating of a new system, a system of choice, where you would have 100 percent choice, traditional schools, non-traditional schools, etc.... I was agnostic. I didn't think we needed to charter everything; it's just that these schools should be independent schools. I also recommended there should be a mechanism set up so that the schools would have to perform, and if the schools did not perform you could go off and seek out new school models. The whole idea was to replicate the school models that were working and to phase out the models that were not.[705]

When Vallas was officially appointed in May 2007, he had 90 days to build 22 campuses and find 600-700 teachers. "I was so desperate for teachers that the state and the federal government were giving people $10,000 bonuses to come and teach," he recalled. "Returning teachers, too."[706] Teachers were able to reapply for their jobs, but about 30 percent failed a basic-skills test.[707]

Because the city of New Orleans was small enough for buses to get across town within 20 minutes, he instituted universal busing. He noted:

> Our goal was to create choice, but our attitude was to first of all open schools where they were needed, and when we transformed schools—when schools were converted from traditional public schools to charter schools—to do so without displacement of children. For example, when KIPP took over Douglas High School (because they now had enough feeder schools and they wanted to create their own high school), it was conditional that they keep the existing kids who were in the high school.... When we did school conversions, those conversions were all about the schools getting a better model, not coming in and simply displacing kids. The kids then get to be in a school that has a stronger school model.[708]

In this process of rebuilding and strengthening the schools, Vallas saw New Schools for New Orleans as a vital partner, yet he also believed that "what was important wasn't that the schools were chartered or not chartered; what was important was that schools be based on best practice models and that the obstacles be removed for the organizing and the structuring of schools." His role was "to identify the best models and to replicate them, and to remove the obstacles for the implementation of those models."[709]

Looking back, he said, "I essentially did what I recommended in that memo [in 2006]. It just so happened that the Recovery School District really gave me the power to do what I articulated … in that memo."[710] He added:

> One needs to ask oneself, why was New Orleans successful and why have efforts to replicate New Orleans… failed so abysmally? That might be well worth a few paragraphs, because everyone wants to create Recovery School Districts all over the country and I'm afraid that they're not going to

apply that model like we applied it in Louisiana, which is why we were successful.[711]

One likely factor in the successful growth of charters in New Orleans was that *they faced no significant opposition.* In typical school districts, when charters are opened and begin to absorb market share, districts lose enrollment and its attendant revenue, and some district schools become so under-enrolled that they must be closed, with the result that some adults lose their jobs and the union becomes more active in its opposition. Another source of tension is that parents whose children do not "win" the charter lottery often feel as though their children are not being offered the same choices as their peers; they feel that their children are missing opportunities and that the charter schools are draining resources from the district. In situations where district educators and some parents feel dis-enfranchised and actively oppose the growth of charters in their city, it is difficult to ensure that the entire school community is well served.

The RSD was no ordinary district, however. Post-Katrina New Orleans began with almost a blank slate. Charter schools met a crucial need: it was necessary to open new schools because so many had been destroyed by the floods. And of course enrollment grew as families returned to the city. Act 35, the law that enabled the RSD to scoop up all schools below the state average, gave the State tremendous latitude to re-launch schools without the normal limitations such as the governance structure and contracts, including the collective bargaining agreement. The RSD offered a fresh start.[712]

Somewhat similarly, in Chicago in the mid-late 1990s, when Paul Vallas oversaw the launch of charters there, enrollment in the city grew by 30,000. Although he didn't have all of the advantages of the RSD approach, growing enrollment meant growing revenues, so he had enough resources to not only open charter schools but also provide them with the facilities they needed.[713]

Along with enrollment increases or decreases, the perspective of whoever is leading a school improvement transition also makes a differ-ence. Reflecting on his experiences in New Orleans, Vallas noted, "I never viewed the charters as independent from the district. I viewed the charters as a part of the district and my responsibility was to support them [and] to provide them with all the supports that they needed, including the support from the facility side, and then to hold people accountable."[714]

On the issue of accountability, Greg Richmond credited the steadfast vigilance of BESE, the board governing the RSD. Composed largely of officials from outside New Orleans, the board resisted political pressure and refused to approve weak charter proposals. "They got that pressure in every single round and they would not yield," Greg observed.[715]

Cities interested in improving school options by expanding charter school market share need to determine how to balance the competing needs and interests of different stakeholders. Replicating the accomplishments of New Orleans will not be easy. Although you are not supposed to use the word "very" in front of the word "unique," in the case of New Orleans, that phrasing seems to apply.

CHAPTER 26

"DON'T STEAL POSSIBLE"

What happened in New York City illustrates why political support is necessary to keep a movement going.

Twelve years after New York City Mayor Michael Bloomberg gained control of the city's schools and hired Joel Klein to enact a dramatic set of educational reforms,[716] Bill de Blasio, a charter school critic, became the new mayor.

Although the charter school movement had gained steam in the city for more than a decade (and by 2014 had grown to 183 schools serving more than 70,000 students, about 6 percent of students citywide[717]), advocates were aware of how much Bloomberg's support had helped, and they dreaded losing it. While campaigning, de Blasio had shown his hand in various ways, perhaps most pointedly on May 11, 2013, when he proclaimed to a United Federation of Teachers (UFT) crowd that it was "time for Eva Moskowitz to stop having the run of the place. She has to stop being tolerated, enabled, supported."[718]

Bill and Eva had been on the City Council together for several years in the early 2000s, and as the Chair of the Education Committee, she'd held numerous hearings questioning the limitations of union contract rules. At one point, in a tone of exasperation, she asked UFT leader Randi Weingarten, "Is it the case that a principal, under any circumstance, could have to take a candidate *without ever having interviewed them?* Yes, or no?"

After initially dodging the question, Weingarten finally replied: "Yes."

When it was his turn to speak, de Blasio mocked those who complained about union rules. After several principals explained how the rules made it difficult to fire ineffective teachers, he remarked: "I served in the Clinton Administration, so I know what spin looks like when I see it, and this is spin."

You could say that Moskowitz lost the battle. Two years later, in 2005, when she ran for Manhattan Borough President, Weingarten and the UFT worked aggressively to defeat her.[719]

But then a funny thing happened. Seeing no path forward to transform the existing system, she decided to launch a charter school—not just one, in fact, but a network. And in short order, Success Academy Schools became some of the highest-performing schools in the city. By September 2014, the network served 9,500 predominantly minority and low-income students in 24 elementary schools, 7 middle schools, and a high school.[720] When the 2013-14 state test scores were released, the results were stunning: while only 35% of New York City students scored proficient in math, 94% of her students rated as proficient, and while only 29% of city students met English standards, 64% of her students met the standards.[721]

Though the accomplishments of Success Academy's students— along with those in other CMOs such as Achievement First, Democracy Prep, KIPP, and Uncommon Schools—were well documented, de Blasio had announced during his campaign that he planned to begin charging rent to charter schools that used district buildings. Charter advocates knew what that meant: without the ability to pay, some would be forced to close.[722]

Organizers put their heads together and agreed: it was time to make some noise.

A month before the election, on October 8, 2013, thousands of New York City charter school parents, children, and educators in fluorescent green T-shirts that proclaimed "MY CHILD, MY CHOICE" and "CHARTER SCHOOLS ARE PUBLIC SCHOOLS" marched across the Brooklyn Bridge, chanting in protest, "Don't charge us rent! We're the 99 percent!"[723]

Candidate de Blasio acted as though he had heard nothing. Then he won the election.

In early February, more than 1,000 charter supporters traveled to Albany to court lawmakers. As they stood out in the cold, Lieutenant Governor Robert Duffy emerged to express his support. Then word reached the organizers: Governor Andrew Cuomo wanted to meet with them.[724]

A small team met privately with the governor for 45 minutes. He told them he was concerned about Mayor de Blasio's "ambivalence" towards charter schools, and he wanted to help. He encouraged them to plan a larger rally.[725]

Over the next few weeks, Governor Cuomo worked to strengthen support for charters among state lawmakers, while charter advocates launched an aggressive public relations and lobbying effort that was, according to the New York Times, "financed by a group of charter school backers from the worlds of hedge funds and Wall Street, some of whom [had] also poured substantial sums into Mr. Cuomo's [fall re-election] campaign."[726] This well-funded, well-coordinated political operation was very different from the early grassroots days when advocates spent most of their time in small, community-based meetings trying to explain what a "charter school" was.

On Feb. 27, 2014, Mayor de Blasio announced that he would reverse Mayor Bloomberg's decision to provide three Success Academy schools with free space in the city's public schools. The schools had already hired principals and teachers and were in the midst of recruiting students. This announcement meant they would probably not be able to open in the fall. Many parents were upset.[727]

Charter activists urged them to channel their energy into political action.

The following Tuesday, another frigid day in Albany, hundreds of busloads arrived at the State Capitol, releasing an army of 11,000 parents, children, and educators from all across the state—all wearing oversized bright yellow T-shirts that said "#charterswork" over their winter coats. For hours, the crowd stood on the steps of the Capitol, stamping their feet and chanting, "Save our schools! Save our schools!" Their breath emerged in little clouds, over and over.

A few blocks away, inside a 19th century armory, de Blasio was speaking to a much smaller audience about the need to fund universal pre-K and after-school programs.[728] He was looking forward to his chance to convince the governor that a tax increase for that purpose was a good idea.

Governor Cuomo would meet with de Blasio later that day. But first he had something else to do.

He put on his overcoat, invited other state legislators to join him, and walked outside to speak to the charter school crowd. "We are here today to tell you that we stand with you!" he shouted. "You are not alone! We *will* save charter schools!"[729]

Maybe the governor can help, people in the crowd thought. *Maybe things will change.*

Over the next few months, the group that had organized the rally, Families for Excellent Schools,[730] launched a relentless TV ad campaign with the tagline "#DontStealPossible."[731] The governor and his staff worked with Republicans in the State Senate and others to create legislation that would reverse Mr. de Blasio's decisions on school space and require the city to provide public classrooms to new and expanding charter schools or contribute to the cost of renting private buildings. When it passed in April, the law also increased per-pupil funding for charter schools and allowed them to operate prekindergarten programs.[732]

Things had changed.

PART III

ROOTS TAKING HOLD

CHAPTER 27

THE PROMISE OF "R & D" LABS VS. THE REALITY

In the early days, when people speculated about how charters might influence district schools, they were perhaps overly optimistic. One of the stated objectives (often appearing in legislation) was that charters should function as "R & D" labs, developing innovative practices that could be replicated in the mainstream.[733] It seemed so simple at the time: like scientists, charter educators would invent things and district educators would immediately see their value and begin employing them.

The reality is that innovations don't work that way. As Ted Kolderie has pointed out (in *The Split-Screen Strategy*), what tends to happen is that early adopters try out ideas while everyone else keeps using the old approach. He explained:

> Usually the disruptive innovation is not quality when it first appears. (Think about "the first" anything.) Even so, early adopters pick it up quickly. Adoption is voluntary: The idea is not to make all their users give up their land-line phones or their petroleum-powered automobiles, for example. Those who prefer the traditional may stay with the traditional....

> Existing organizations usually continue to improve the cost and quality of the traditional model. But the new and disruptive innovations also improve, sometimes rapidly. Over time,

as the different gets better and as its price comes down, more people shift. At some point the curves cross. Ultimately the old might be closed out. The world's last typewriter factory has shut down; analog TV has gone dark. The incandescent light bulb might be dimming out....[734]

When charters began to appear, district educators did not adopt charter school best practices with as much enthusiasm as some idealists anticipated. As Kolderie noted in his 1990 "Withdrawing the Exclusive Franchise" paper, districts possess an exclusive franchise and feel no obligation to change.[735] Many districts, in fact, avidly opposed the creation of charters, which they viewed as competitors for funding. Taking this stance made it virtually impossible for district educators to see what was going on in charters.

It took a while for effective practices in charters to become visible. First the schools had to establish themselves as going concerns. Then work very hard to achieve some measure of success. Then host visitors and reporters, repeatedly. Early on, even if you were actively searching for evidence of innovation, the Internet was still in its infancy, so you had to look in newspapers or magazines, or on TV. You couldn't find videos on the Web (YouTube did not exist until 2005[736]). It was logistically hard to lay eyes on what was happening. This is why the *60 Minutes* episode that featured KIPP in 1999[737] was such a game-changer both for KIPP (which received millions of dollars to expand nationally after Scott Hamilton showed Donald Fisher the clip) and for many educators in the field, who suddenly saw an example of what was possible.

While the KIPP piece drew lots of attention and made a powerful impression, it was still only one segment about one type of school in a one-hour TV show on a random Sunday night. It couldn't capture the full array of best practices being developed in charters around the country. Those of us trying to get the word out about good things happening in various schools were forced to compete for attention with controversial or negative stories; "good news" often doesn't make the news. Though we wrote op-ed pieces, invited prominent politicians in, participated in research studies, and presented at conferences, it was difficult to reach a wider audience.

Over time, some of the more-publicized schools—such as KIPP, North Star, and Amistad Academy—became known for building intentional, college-prep-focused cultures and achieving extraordinary results with low-income students. Key features included extended instructional time (through longer school days and years), school uniforms (to minimize distractions and help students focus on learning), and a conscious effort to guide the behavior and values of their students.[738] One of their favorite slogans was "No Excuses." Walking through the halls, you might overhear classes chanting, "Excuses are the tools of the incompetent. They are used to build monuments to nothing.... And therefore we will have no excuses!"

The phrase "No Excuses" began to catch on. In 2001, the Heritage Foundation profiled the KIPP schools (along with 19 others) in a book called *No Excuses: Lessons From 21 High-Performing, High-Poverty Schools*, noting that "the failure of most public schools to teach poor children is a national tragedy and a national disgrace." The message of the book was that "there is no excuse for this tragedy. All children can learn." It went on to label the schools that had overcome the bureaucratic and cultural obstacles that keep low-income children behind as "No Excuses schools."[739]

Two years later, Abigail and Stephan Thernstrom borrowed that title for their own book, *No Excuses: Closing the Racial Gap in Learning*, and used the success of Amistad, North Star, and KIPP to highlight the failings of the public-school system in serving poor children.[740]

The term "No Excuses schools" became more widely used as these schools were replicated through Charter Management Organizations (CMOs). Linda Brown's nonprofit, Building Excellent Schools (launched in 2003), became another incubator for such schools.

These schools have garnered significant attention and are among an expanding list of schools that provide "proof points" that children from low-income communities can perform at high academic levels.

In addition to serving students directly, charter schools have also planted seeds for change and improvement in the wider field of K-12 public education. In the next few chapters, we'll explore how charter school leaders have developed and nurtured other important innovations that have begun to take hold.

CHAPTER 28

USING DATA DIFFERENTLY

If you give us autonomy, we'll be happy to be held accountable for our results: that was the "radical" premise of charter schools. Inherent in that premise is the need to study, reflect on, and adapt to data. Perhaps that explains why, to a large degree, charters have led the way in developing tools for this purpose. The need to hold schools accountable raised questions such as, "How can we tell if a school is succeeding or failing?" and "How can we measure students' performance?" and "How can we use data to improve instruction?" Over the years, key players involved in charters developed tools and resources to address these questions.

One major result is that in the decades since charters first appeared, the general public has increasingly come to expect that *all* schools, not just charter schools, should be held accountable for results.

Richard Wenning was a key figure in shaping that expectation because he was instrumental in developing the Colorado Growth Model (also known as the Student Growth Percentile model), which measures not just student (and school) performance but also growth. In the late 1980s, working at the General Accounting Office (GAO[741]) while he pursued graduate studies, Wenning's main focus was the Title I program, a source of funding to "improve the academic achievement of the disadvantaged."[742] Specifically, he needed to be able to respond intelligently when legislators asked, "How do you know this program is working?" At that point, only Title I students were tested annually. There *was* a growth model back then, but it was a rather blunt instrument. "It was just a normative growth measure," Wenning noted. "All we could tell was whether a kid was making more or less than a year's growth in a year's time, but we had no way of knowing whether that growth was good enough for anything."[743] He and others began looking for ways to improve upon that approach.

They knew they could do better. In 1966, the Coleman Study[744] had essentially blamed poor student performance on poverty and in that sense claimed that schools didn't matter. As statistical models became more advanced and researchers re-visited Coleman's data, it became apparent that Coleman's conclusions (while based on the best statistical models at the time) had been misguided. Coleman had used aggregate measures that failed to capture the student-level impact. In other words, the methodology was simply wrong for the task at hand. "We needed to use student-level models instead of aggregate-school models," Wenning explained. "And when we did, we found that *what you did in schools did matter.*"[745]

Wenning's work was guided by two key questions: *How do you break cycles of poverty?* and *What are the roles of schools in doing that?* He was particularly interested in the work of researchers such as Tony Bryk and others, who had found that "things like academic press, building expectations for kids, all of these things actually do matter." He became convinced that it was necessary to measure both achievement *and* growth in order to determine which schools were most effective.[746] Researchers could then study what those exemplary schools were doing to break the cycle of poverty.

When Wenning heard about the federal charter school legislation that Jon Schroeder (then Senator David Durenberger's director of policy development) was drafting, he became very intrigued by the notion that charter schools would have to be authorized and would have to prove that they had met their authorizers' standards in order to be renewed. From the Title I work, he'd been looking at the question "How do you properly hold schools accountable?" and the idea of chartering extended that question further. "This question of charter school authorization was really interesting to me," he said. "It wasn't just asking, 'Are they effective?' but 'Are they *so effective that they should be allowed to continue to operate?*'"[747] In 1994, he worked on the First National Charter Schools Study[748] and met, among others, Paul Hill (whose writing on contract schools and accountability influenced his thinking[749]) and Jim Griffin, the head of the Colorado League of Charter Schools, who would later become a vital partner in his work.

After leaving the GAO, Wenning served as professional staff at the Senate Appropriations Committee, where he helped shepherd the passage of charter school legislation in the District of Columbia, then he became the Senior Policy Advisor to General Julius Becton, the CEO of the DC Public Schools, and led the initial implementation of the charter law. He then launched a consulting firm, Choice Strategies Group, which provided accountability and special education services to charter schools and the DC Public Charter School Board as well as the Charter Friends National Network and later NACSA.[750] Choice Strategies was later acquired by New American Schools.

A breakthrough came in 2000, when Wenning secured a grant from the Carnegie Foundation while at New American Schools to study and compare the performance of different growth models.[751] He gave several teams of leading researchers the same set of data and asked them to apply their favorite models and to attempt to measure the adequacy of growth to reach a specific standard. The results confirmed that a variety of leading models produced similar information about student progress. More importantly, they could successfully measure the adequacy of growth to reaching a performance standard—and now that No Child Left Behind[752] (NCLB) had raised the accountability stakes for all schools, a growth model would be useful not just to charters but, in fact, to *all* schools. Wanting to run with this idea, Wenning moved his knowledge base from New American Schools to the Colorado League of Charter Schools, where Jim Griffin welcomed him with open arms.[753] In fact, the League had initiated steps to pilot cutting-edge performance measures, and Wenning was a perfect addition to the team.[754]

Because of his legislative background, Wenning knew it was important to establish a legislative foundation for what would become the Colorado Growth Model. Experience had taught him it was the best way to get things done "because it's harder for the bureaucrats to say no if there's a law that says you have to."[755] One of his board members, Keith King, a big fan of growth modeling, also happened to be the Senate Majority Leader.[756] They drafted a law to create a growth model. They also passed a law to require the State Department of Education to make the longitudinal database of record-level student data available to qualified researchers so they could work with the data sets.[757] In the end, Wenning (who had become the Associate Commissioner of Education) and Damian Betebenner led development of what became the final version with critical input from the Technical Advisory Committee.[758] Wenning then led the legislative overhaul of Colorado's education accountability system, making the Growth Model its cornerstone for understanding student progress and school effectiveness and ending use of the system established by NCLB.[759]

The Colorado Growth Model, or Student Growth Percentile (SGP) model, is designed to show how well students performed in relation to both other students who took the same test and an established passing score. What's more, it shows that information not as a snapshot but over the course of multiple years.

The model was first used for charter schools, then Denver Public Schools, then the State of Colorado when Wenning became the Associate Commissioner of Education. By 2016, it had spread across the country to 25 states and counting,[760] and was being used by the PARCC Consortium.[761] The growth model and its associated data visualizations enabled parents and educators to see the progress of individual students and how their schools compared to others in the neighborhood or in the whole state.[762] For example, it could identify a school that started with students on third base ("high achievement") but didn't push them ("low growth"), or a school that started with students on first base and brought them home ("high achievement and high growth")—in other words, a truly high-performing school.[763]

As the charter school movement spread, it became clear that Richard Wenning and his colleagues were not the only ones obsessed with school accountability. As the lead charter school authorizer in Chicago beginning in 1996, Greg Richmond shared this passion, and (as described in Chapter 16) he helped to launch the National Association of Charter School Authorizers to raise the quality of authorizing practices. On a related path, in 1999, Bob Bellafiore and Doug Lemov at the SUNY Charter School Institute in New York also worked on developing effective authorizer practices (See Chapter 20).

One challenge in those early years was the limited availability of data on student performance. Schools typically used low-stakes off-the-shelf standardized tests (such as the Iowa Test, the Stanford-9, or the Terra Nova) in combination with high-stakes state-mandated assessments. But the state tests were administered only intermittently. Federal policy at the time (stipulated by the Goals 2000 Act that President Bill Clinton signed in 1994[764]) required students to demonstrate competency by the end of grades 4, 8, and 12. In New Jersey, for instance, that meant students were only tested statewide in grades 4, 8, and 11. Although this policy was a step up from zero mandated testing (except for Title I students), it was impossible to measure student growth from year to year with any reliability or validity. Off-the-shelf tests were at best rough cuts. So educators did not spend a lot of time analyzing the results or acting on them. Nor did teachers devote much time to preparing their students to take them. Although the 1983 *Nation at Risk* report had made it clear that American schools were flagging,[765] and in fact many people on the street could name individual schools and entire districts that were particularly awful, there was not enough data to show precisely what the problems were.

In 2002, the bipartisan No Child Left Behind (NCLB) Act that President George W. Bush signed into law[766] changed that. Among other things, it required annual testing in reading and math for students in grades 3 through 8.[767] Having legitimate test results in these grades every year enabled charter and district schools to determine internal progress and compare their students' performance to those in other schools.

NCLB thus opened the door for "data-driven instruction." Although charter school educators did not invent the term, a noticeable handful of charter leaders championed the practice and contributed to its dissemination.

One day in 2002, Norman Atkins drove up from Newark to Amistad Academy in New Haven to observe Doug McCurry's "Curriculum-Based Measurements" in action. McCurry and his teachers had developed standards-aligned assessments that they administered every six weeks. On the day Atkins visited, McCurry met with each teacher individually to use the resulting data to diagnose, for example, which students were struggling to multiply fractions.[768] To Atkins, it seemed that McCurry had created the school equivalent of what data-driven leaders had done to revolutionize public service, business, politics, and sports. He was reminded of New York City Police Chief William Bratton's initiative to use fast data to fight crime and Oakland A's manager Billy Beane's metrics for finding productive, undervalued baseball players.[769]

He went back to North Star and told his colleagues what he had seen. After that, Atkins brought co-leader Jamey Verrilli to Amistad, to see what he thought. Verrilli looked at the tests and forms they were using at Amistad and thought, *We could do this. We could write our own tests.*[770]

What really sold Verrilli was watching Doug McCurry meet with one of his English teachers. It was unlike any principal-teacher meeting he'd ever seen. He recalled, "Most conversations I'd seen were: 'How did you teach this? What methods were used? Could you have done this, or tried this technique?'"

Instead, this discussion was all about outcomes.

McCurry asked questions such as, "Well, what happened here? Why did the kids do well on this? Okay, why did they struggle on this? What do you think happened to your instruction that helped cause this? What do you think you could do differently?"

Verrilli saw this focus on student outcomes as "a whole new level of consciousness."[771]

Atkins and Verrilli returned to North Star determined to start implementing this new approach, and they shared their enthusiasm with their new colleague Paul Bambrick-Santoyo.

Bambrick-Santoyo, a Duke graduate who'd spent two years in Jesuit Community Service as a campus minister in Mobile, Alabama and six years teaching AP English and coaching basketball at an International Baccalaureate high school in Mexico City, had been sent to North Star as a New Leaders for New Schools Fellow, and he was in training to step into Atkins's shoes.[772] He recognized the potential of this new approach and convinced his colleagues that instead of rolling it out for a subject or two, they should go big. He and Verrilli began working with teachers on changing the culture so that leaders and teachers used data more pro-actively to drive student learning.[773] The work spread quickly to other schools. As McCurry shared his tests and templates and materials, Verrilli and Bambrick-Santoyo in turn designed tests, spreadsheets, and systems for analysis, and they trained school leaders in how to use them.

Bambrick-Santoyo was invited by New Leaders for New Schools to give presentations on data-driven instruction. Initially he targeted New Leaders Fellows, who would then go into schools armed with a philosophy and the tools to implement it.[774] Before long, he was traveling all around the country. By 2010, when he published his first book, *Driven by Data*, he had trained more than a thousand principals serving a half million students in cities all over the country.[775] Bambrick-Santoyo would go on to continue his focus on systems, writing books on teacher coaching, school leadership, and elementary school literacy systems.[776]

As years passed and the concept of data-driven instruction spread more widely, NCLB shed light on something that had been largely hidden by the intermittent Federal testing regime: namely, the racial achievement gap. Because schools were now required to disaggregate student test scores and other performance data by student characteristics to enable better comparisons between groups,[777] the disparities became more apparent. A 2009 analysis by McKinsey and Company found that black and Latino students were, on average, roughly two to three years of learning behind white students of the same age[778] and asserted that the achievement gap in the U.S. had imposed "the economic equivalent of a permanent national recession."[779] Many education reformers began referring to the achievement gap as "the civil rights issue of our time," and the media focused increasingly on the extent to which schools were closing the gap or not.

Before charter schools arrived on the scene and before NCLB provided the data needed to determine how well a school was performing, when district schools were failing, they were rarely (if ever) closed; in fact, they were often given more money. By shining a brighter light on student performance in all schools, NCLB drew more attention to the "chartering" idea of school-wide accountability. The notion that a failing charter school should be closed became a more mainstream idea, and district leaders such as New York City Schools Chancellor Joel Klein,[780] Michelle Rhee[781] and Kaya Henderson in DC,[782] and Cami Anderson in Newark[783] began to close failing district schools, as well.

CHAPTER 29

CHANGING HOW TEACHERS
AND LEADERS ARE PREPARED, PART I

On the late afternoon of April 25, 2005, two potential rivals walked into Olives Restaurant in Union Square for a drink.

Though others in the field might have assumed Norman Atkins and Dave Levin were competitors, they had bonded over their shared sense of urgency to provide a college-prep education for children who typically would not have had access to one. From their earliest encounters at conferences and visits to each other's schools in Newark and the Bronx, they had become friends. "Instead of whacking each other, competing and fighting over talent and resources and ideas," Atkins remarked, "we were open book with each other and really shared." He considered Levin to be "the single most generous person in the education community, who shared everything about what he was doing and learning."[784] Levin, in turn, described Atkins as "the center of the education reform wheel" and "one of the most remarkable developers of leaders I have ever met."[785]

As the waiter delivered their beers, they talked about how they wanted their school networks to grow, and what the challenges were. It had quickly become apparent to them how right Jim Collins was about the importance of getting "the right people on the bus."[786] As small start-ups with tiny staffs, charter schools had no room for incompetence or divergence from the mission. Atkins and Levin knew that their success hinged on finding great people. But recruits they were finding—particularly as the charter movement expanded and competition grew—were often poorly prepared. They frequently had to retrain teachers who came from schools of education, which both agreed was a waste of time and energy. In order to scale their work, they needed to solve this problem: they needed to improve the quality of the pool.

Atkins pulled out a pen, scrawled on a napkin, and passed the note over to Levin. It said: "Your Name Here Teacher Training Institute."[787]

Levin nodded. By running separate teacher training programs, they had been trying to replicate each other's training. It would be better to collaborate.

And Atkins had another idea. That morning, the *New York Times* Metro section had featured an article about how Governors Island, which New York State and New York City had purchased in 2003 from the federal government for $1, was still in search of a purpose.[788] Maybe they could try to put their Teacher Training Institute on that island.[789]

They kept talking. They needed a Principal Training Academy, too. And maybe they should build a boarding school for students going into their last year of high school, as a bridge to college? Maybe they should create a youth hostel for kids from all over the country to come to Governors Island?[790]

The waiter delivered another round. They kept talking. Eventually they ordered dinner.

The next day, they went to work.

While both already had more than enough to do, they were determined to expand the pool of well-trained teachers. They reached out to their friend Dacia Toll, whose Achievement First schools recruited from the same pool, and she was excited to help.

The trio spent the next 12-18 months trying to figure out how to develop an education complex on Governors Island.[791] Although that impulse did not pan out, they ended up creating something else that would have an even wider impact on the field.

While strategizing about how to launch "Your Name Here Teacher Training Institute," they initially considered two scenarios. One was to take a flagging institution and remake it; another was to go to one of the best-known schools of education like Columbia Teachers College and try to build a program there.

Their first meeting was with Arthur Levine, the president of Columbia Teachers College. "We sat in his office," Atkins recalled, "and he said, 'It's a great idea. I hear what you want to do. Your idea doesn't really fit here. Our faculty won't let you. Our tuition is too high. Faculty won't let you develop a program along the lines of what you want to do. You should either try to buy or get under the wing of another university or ed school.'"[792]

Levine's advice inspired them to meet with presidents of other institutions of higher education, both those with and without schools of education. They met with leaders at ten different institutions.

A breakthrough came when Selma Botman, CUNY Executive Vice-Chancellor, and Jennifer Raab, the president of Hunter College, arranged for Dave Levin to meet with David Steiner, the dean of Hunter's School of Education. Steiner had recently arrived, and his research on ed schools had stirred up some controversy. Critical of existing ed school practices, he wanted to do new and innovative things to create more of a bridge between the academy and K-12 schools, and he had a positive impression about KIPP and charter schools. When Levin explained what he and his friends were hoping to accomplish, Steiner knew the devil was in the details, but he was intrigued. Definitely intrigued.[793]

Immediately after that meeting, Levin called Atkins. "I think I got our guy," he said.[794]

Atkins went and met with Steiner, and before long, they'd agreed to collaborate.

Among the many things they had to figure out was how to design an innovative program within the constraints of New York State laws and regulations.

"The first question that came up was, *Is this a new program, or is it a variation of a program that is already listed and approved by the State of New York?*" Steiner said. If it was a new program, then it would have to go through numerous review cycles at the departmental level at Hunter, at the school of education level at Hunter, at the Hunter College senate level, at CUNY and at the State, which would take at least a year. The alternative was to take existing course descriptions and work with them. If they left the three-sentence descriptors in the course catalog alone, they could change the readings and the assignments and they wouldn't have to go through a re-approval process.[795]

Next: *Who would teach the courses?*

They decided on a combination of faculty from Hunter and adjuncts identified by Atkins, Levin, and Toll.[796] Ultimately, the teachers had to be approved by Steiner and Hunter's chair of curriculum and teaching.

When it came to gaining Hunter's staff's approval, Steiner remarked, "obviously we couldn't just have this as a stealth program." At its height, the program would involve hundreds of students. He and Atkins ran an open question-and-answer session at the college, and Steiner reminded the staff that no one was *required* to be involved. "It was one hundred percent voluntary," he said. "And we already had a number of faculty who were interested."[797]

Steiner also pointed out to the staff that they could all learn something from this. Looking back, he noted, "What I still think of as the most innovative feature of the thinking that came from Norman and his folks was the idea that you *walk the walk*. That is, if you're going to tell teachers that they have to think about every ten minutes or twelve minutes of their own instruction, then when you design a university program to teach these teachers, you have to do the same thing."[798]

The next big hurdle was fundraising. While having a lower tuition would make the program more affordable for participants, private funding was needed to design and build it. Hedge fund manager Larry Robbins put up the initial $10 million,[799] and at the 2007 Robin Hood Foundation Annual Benefit, in about ninety seconds, twenty attendees raised their neon auction paddles and raised another $20 million.[800]

At that point, Atkins recalled, "We said, 'Oh my God, it's really happening. One of us needs to go and lead this.' I think I had the combination of the greatest interest and connection to the work along with the recognition that I had a bench; I had a team at Uncommon who was ready to step up and take over the leadership."[801]

Atkins and his colleagues met with Steiner and his colleagues and took the headings that were approved by the state for the Hunter College curriculum and worked together to build out new content underneath each one of those courses. As they began to think about building the leadership team, Atkins turned to Levin and said, "We've got to find somebody amazing to go do this." Levin recommended Mayme Hostetter, who'd most recently taught at KIPP in the South Bronx for three years and was one of the best teachers he'd ever seen.[802] She also had an interest in the science of learning and was at the time pursuing research at MIT about reading development.[803] They had also heard about Brent Maddin, who (as Atkins later described) was viewed as "a hero" in Teach For America in rural Louisiana and had been one of the founding teachers at IDEA Charter Network in Rio Grande Valley. He was doing his doctoral work at Harvard and had become well known on the professional development circuit. Atkins, Levin, and Steiner interviewed both candidates and liked both.[804]

"We called them up," Atkins recalled, "and said, 'We think we want to hire you and this other person. You guys should go get beer together. You guys should go meet with each other and figure out whether there's any chemistry.' They went and got beer in Cambridge and I think they fell in love with each other. They became great friends, really close friends, and did the work together." In February 2008, Hostetter and Maddin were hired as the founding deans.[805]

By July 2008, Atkins became the chair of the Board and CEO of Uncommon Schools and started working with Steiner to create TeacherU at Hunter College. A very small cohort participated in a partial version of the program in 2007, and the first full cohort came in the fall of 2008.[806]

By 2010, they knew they needed to make some changes. Steiner had left Hunter to become NYS Commissioner of Education. Beyond the loss of his partnership, "we realized that if we continued to operate TeacherU at Hunter College, we were going to run out of money," Atkins said, "because Hunter College collected all the tuition and we had all the expenses. And we were never going to be able to innovate in the way that we wanted to because we were inside of these approvals of the existing Hunter curriculum."[807] They had also come to feel that their long-term destiny was tethered more to the will of Hunter's faculty senate than the authority of the dean or even the president, and they wanted more control.

Beginning in February 2010, they petitioned the State of New York for permission to become the new institution of higher education. A year later, they were approved as the Relay Graduate School of Education, the first new graduate school of education in New York since Bank Street College of Education was approved in 1950.[808] They had wanted to keep the name TeacherU, but designation as a university required a tenure track, a doctorate program, and a brick and mortar library. Levin later joked, "As a Prince fan, I wanted it to be 'the organization formally known as TeacherU' with some random symbol. But calmer heads prevailed, and the 'Relay Graduate School of Education' was formed."[809] The new name was a reference to research that found that if you took an average student at the 50th percentile and gave that student four A-plus teachers—a *relay* of four great teachers in a row—that student would be on the path to college.[810]

As Relay was being developed, an important contributor to the course-work was Doug Lemov.

In 2004, not long after he'd graduated from business school, Doug was living near Albany and consulting with various schools. One day, a principal at a charter school told him that he and his staff had taken Doug's advice to visit Dave Levin's KIPP Academy in the Bronx, "and now we get it."[811]

Doug was thrilled. "What was the most powerful thing you took away?" he asked.

The response stunned him. He later recalled:

I don't remember what was on his list, but metaphorically it was something like, "The bulletin boards were so incredible." It was like they had been to Mecca, and what they had seen had nothing to do with what it took to run a great school. I couldn't believe that this was all that they had taken away. If you had the eyes to know what you were looking for, you would have pages of notes about what it took to be great. But if you rank-ordered from 1 to 50 the most important take-aways from spending a day at KIPP, they had seen numbers 37, 39, and 42. They didn't know how to see numbers 1 to 10.[812]

Driving home from Syracuse with his colleague Karen Cichon (a former Catholic school teacher),[813] he thought, *What is it that they don't get? They don't get high academic expectations. Well, what is "high academic expectations"? If you're at a school like Dave's, what would you see people doing?*[814]

He knew it was fruitless to tell people they should "have high expectations." He recalled some useful advice he'd received as a young teacher: a colleague had said, "When you want students to follow your directions, stand still. If you're walking around passing out papers, it looks like the directions are no more important than all of the other things you're doing. Show that your directions matter. Stand still. They'll respond."[815] Concrete, specific, actionable advice like that was what teachers needed. And they needed a common vocabulary. His soccer coaches—the good ones, anyway—had not said simply, "Defend better." They'd said specific things like, "Mark tighter" or "Close the space." Players knew what those terms meant. He and Karen agreed: they wanted the Syracuse principal to be able to sit in the back of a classroom, take notes, and at the end of class, pass the teacher a Post-it with a few key actionable phrases on it.[816]

But what would those key phrases be?

They began brainstorming a list.[817]

That day, he'd observed something that drove him crazy but also gave him an idea. A teacher stood up in front of her room, and when a boy gave her "the most egregiously vacuous answer," she replied, "Right! Good!" And then she put words in his mouth. Gave an answer that she said he'd said. But he hadn't. Doug thought, *You just lied to that kid out of your own best intentions.* It was the unprepared Indiana football player he'd met all over again: not wanting to hurt the kid's feelings, she'd pretended he'd understood things that he hadn't. *She was going to get her paycheck, and the only person who was going to pay the price for that lie was the kids.*[818]

He and Karen talked about that. You couldn't let students slide or pretend they were right. You had to hold them accountable for providing accurate responses, not just "close-enough" ones.[819] They decided to call this notion "Right Is Right."[820]

On the ride home, they continued to brainstorm and reflect on effective and ineffective practices they'd witnessed over the years. Gradually, a list of phrases—tied to concrete, specific tips—began to emerge.[821]

Doug pursued this idea relentlessly. He wanted to go see the best schools and the best classrooms he could find, and see what the teachers did.[822] Not only that: he wanted to videotape them, so he could study them like a football coach preparing for a game.[823]

One of the first schools he visited was North Star Academy. He went to Jamey Verrilli's history class and saw a technique that he later labeled "No Opt Out" (in which a teacher resists letting a student dodge a question and instead assists by providing cues or leveraging peer responses). Verrilli went back to a student who had gotten a question wrong and asked him to repeat the answer and also asked him to take a pen cap out of his mouth because he was garbling his words while he was speaking. Doug recalled, "It was so beautiful but so unheard of." A week later, he saw Darryl Williams, a teacher in Albany, 300 miles away, do the same thing. He thought, *OK, there are really granular-level, concrete things teachers do that seem powerful that these teachers have in common and I want to figure out what those things are.*[824]

He documented what he was learning with videotapes and a growing list of ideas and observations. Looking back, he said,

> In part, I started doing it for schools like this Syracuse school because I wanted to give them a list to tell their teachers what to do because their teachers were working so hard and they were wonderful people. And I think good people deserve to succeed, and it's the obligation of the organization to help them succeed. And the organization was not doing that.[825]

In retrospect, this was exactly the kind of work he had wanted to do when he was a frustrated graduate student in Indiana: to help design educational entities to make them work better.

Norman Atkins saw what he was doing and told him it should be a book. Doug said no, it was just a list. Norman insisted. It had to be a book. People needed it. Doug said no, really, it was just a 20-page document.

In 2005, Norman hired Doug to be a Managing Director at Uncommon Schools, and in the course of conducting school inspections across the network, Doug observed more and more effective practices. The document (which he called his "Taxonomy of Effective Teaching Practices"[826]) became 30 pages, then 50. He shared it with a few people, asked for their feedback, and kept adding to it.[827]

Teachers who got their hands on it called it "the Doug Lemov taxonomy."[828] Much like Ted Kolderie's photocopied memos, copies were passed from colleague to colleague more widely than he realized. Doug occasionally he received Emails from random strangers. One day, a guy in California wrote, "I lost my copy. Can you send me another?" Doug thought, *Who* are *you? And how do you have my taxonomy?*[829]

Norman kept insisting it needed to be a book. "People are going to love this far and wide. It's a really big factor in the way in which we train our teachers at Uncommon, and people will want this."[830] Doug demurred. He kept adding to it. But he really didn't think it would be a book.

Then Norman connected him with a publisher.

One day, journalist Elizabeth Green called Norman up to see if she could write an article about TeacherU for the *New York Times Magazine*. Norman said that he didn't think TeacherU was quite ready, but that she should write about Doug and what he was doing, and that his book was about to come out.[831]

When *Teach Like a Champion* came out in 2010, Doug wrote in his Acknowledgments, "In the end I knew it would be easier to write the thing than to battle Norman's will."[832] By this point, the ideas and materials in the book had become integral to the coursework at TeacherU and then Relay. The amazing timing of that *Times Magazine* story with the publication of the book led to a viral release, and it took hold.[833] Within five years, more than a million copies sold, and it was translated into nine languages.[834] By 2016, Doug had written four more books on instruction, adding to his taxonomy and further exploring the power of teacher practice and reading instruction.[835]

For Norman, Dave, Dacia, and their colleagues, the work to expand Relay Graduate School of Education from its launch with 400 students in 2011-12 continued apace. Over the decade since starting TeacherU, Norman had once again built a strong leadership bench, and in 2018, Dr. Mayme Hostetter was named President of Relay. By 2019, Relay had spread from New York City to Atlanta, Baton Rouge, Camden, Chicago, Connecticut, Dallas-Fort Worth, Delaware, Denver, Houston, Memphis, Nashville,

New Orleans, Newark, Philadelphia, San Antonio, and Washington, DC, and was serving not just teachers but also college students and principals.[836] On 18 campuses, Relay was serving 5,000 current and aspiring teachers and 1,200 school leaders, impacting an estimated 400,000 PK-12 students.[837]

CHAPTER 30

CHANGING HOW TEACHERS AND LEADERS ARE PREPARED, PART II

Mike Goldstein's story is one of curiosity, humility, and persistence. It's also a story—again—about how starting one school can lead to other innovations. And how innovators attract other innovators. And how innovations can spread farther than you might initially imagine—in this case, from one school to a network, to a graduate school, and to Web-based resources supporting educators around the globe.

Not unlike Norman Atkins, Goldstein was a journalist before he became interested in charter schools. After majoring in public policy at Duke, he worked for several years as a Broadway and Off-Broadway theater producer, then wrote for various publications such as *Business Week, New York Magazine,* the *Los Angeles Times Magazine,* and *Boston Globe.* Like many others who've tried tutoring—in his case, in a New York City middle school, where he was nominally charged with helping students put out a school newspaper—he found that the experience changed his life. The students were barely literate. He recalled, "You'd find out what they were doing in school, and it couldn't possibly add up to being educated."[838] He decided he wanted to solve this problem, somehow.

He applied to the Harvard Kennedy School, and in the fall of 1996 he went there to study education policy and figure out his next steps. His sense was that education policy "had not really worked very well to change things for the better," so he was "less and less excited about trying to work for a Department of Education or a governor or anything like that." The first Massachusetts charters had opened in 1995. The idea that "you could have your own little public school, put together a little team, and not deal with a ton of red tape" appealed to him.

That spring (1997), he took a class on charter schools at the Harvard Graduate School of Education with professor Katherine Merseth. Unlike most of his classmates, who included Evan Rudall (who founded Roxbury Prep), Jay Altman (who founded First Line Schools in New Orleans), and Emily Lawson (who founded DC Prep),[839] he had no education background. Except for the school where he'd tutored, he had never set foot in a school that didn't look like the suburban Pennsylvania high school he'd attended. But he was determined to do something meaningful for students like those he'd met in New York City, to change the trajectories of their lives.

His first ideas for MATCH, the Media and Technology Charter High School, were scrawled on a napkin in a Dunkin Donuts. Classes at Harvard had influenced his early thinking. "My instincts were towards 'do-the-traditional-stuff-very-well,'" he said, "but everybody seemed to love project-based learning so much." As a result, the original design of MATCH featured "a really good traditional school till about 3:00, then a whole bunch of projects till 7:00, with dinner included." He and classmate Jason Seda wrote a 3-4 page paper describing the idea, then the next year, he used his thesis project at the Kennedy School to write the complete charter application.[840] On Saturdays, he started going to Linda Brown's classes on "How to Start a Charter." He recalled with a chuckle,

> Of course Linda sized me up: scrawny grad student, ate her bagels, wasn't shaving, possibly late to some of these Saturday things…. She sized me up somewhat skeptically, looked at the proposal, saw there was a mention of projects, thought that was stupid, told me so, and off we went. I became a disciple of Linda.

While he was not entirely sure about the project-based approach, he was clear on the mission: to prepare children to be the first in their family for college. "The technology piece, the project stuff, that was supposed to be a means," he said, "but it was really supposed to be a rigorous college-prep high school." In retrospect, he admitted, "I think I had the end idea solid, but the means to get there, I didn't have a freaking clue what I was doing."

It turned out, however, that he knew plenty about start-ups. "Every Broadway and Off-Broadway show is a start-up and you'd be amazed at how well it aligns with starting a charter school," he said. "You need a concept, which is usually a script; and you need a director instead of a principal; and you need actors instead of teachers; and you need to rent a theatre, which in New York City is very tricky, not unlike trying to find a building for a charter school, so there's a lot of overlap." That said, he was painfully aware of his limitations: "*Writing proposals?* In my wheelhouse. *Actually knowing anything?* Not in my wheelhouse."

He was therefore not too surprised when his first application was rejected. He recalled going before the Board of Education: "Scott Hamilton and Ed Kirby [the Massachusetts authorizers at the time] said, 'Hey, look, you seem like a smart grad student. Are you really committed to this?'"

Although he had put a lot of work into the proposal, he hadn't assembled a true board of directors. He noted:

> I remember the meeting where they were supposed to interview your board and I'd managed to hustle some people together, but none of them had any idea what the proposal was. I had to answer every question. It was pretty transparently *just me*. And when it got rejected, I guess I had mixed feelings for a while because I felt like, *Well, I hate to get rejected. I put in all this work, but on the other hand, am I really remotely competent to open a school for actual children?*

Years later, Goldstein reflected on his mindset at the time: "In a way that infuriates a lot of veteran people...there's that thing in K-12 where to some extent, if you look at the actual unbelievably low achievement of kids, you almost can't help but think, *It'd be hard for me to do worse. I could probably do something better.*"

This was admittedly how he felt, and it motivated him to go back to the drawing board. He pulled together a real board of directors and strengthened the proposal. MATCH got approved in 1999.

As part of his start-up work, Goldstein enlisted Bob Flaherty, a retired principal of Framingham High School, to vet potential principal candidates.

One day in April of 2000, Flaherty told him, "I have this guy: he's an unbelievable teacher in Framingham. You two should have a cup of coffee." Charlie Sposato had taught in Framingham Public Schools for 32 years and had been a Massachusetts Teacher of the Year. He was not technically an administrator. He had his own small program for at-risk kids within the high school, but he only managed one other person. He was a front-line teacher.

Goldstein's approach to reference checking was admittedly a bit unorthodox: "I walked up to all the kids smoking in the parking lot of Framingham High School, and I said, 'Do you know this guy Charlie Sposato?' and the kids would put out their cigarettes and they talked glowingly about this guy. So I thought, *Those are the qualities that I care about.*"

Sposato turned out to be the perfect person for the job, and that fall (2000), MATCH opened with 80 9th-graders.[841]

Within two years, the school was being touted for its performance. In a case study he wrote about the school,[842] Goldstein noted:

Demand was high: eleven eighth-grade Bostonians applied for every slot in the random admission lottery.... MATCH had funding from many of the local blue-chip charitable foundations and had been written up in the *New York Times* and *Wall Street Journal.* A Washington think tank, the Progressive Policy Institute, had cited us as "Educational Innovators of 2002." In June 2003, Hewlett Packard would choose MATCH as one of 15 "High Achieving, High Poverty" schools nationwide for a $100,000 equipment grant. We were being approached for "replication".... On state math and English tests, our kids were tops of the 22 open-admissions high schools in Boston. We were the top predominantly African-American high school in the state on MCAS, the high-stakes standardized tests.

Even better, no one could argue that we'd creamed off the "good kids." We aggressively recruited in Boston's worst middle schools – most of which were technically designated as "failing" according to President Bush's 2001 No Child Left Behind Act. Not only did we have higher poverty levels than Boston as a whole, but only 20% of our incoming 9th graders had passed their math and English exams as 8th graders in their various middle schools; two years later, the pass rate was 82% -- and after the retest opportunity, 100%. In academic circles, MATCH was starting to be mentioned with other elite high-poverty high schools – the Met in Providence, Fenway High in Boston, High Tech High in San Diego – and invited to conferences and grad school classes to tell our success story.[843]

But for several months leading up to an important conference call with his trustees in February 2003, Goldstein was feeling anxious. He did not believe they were on track to achieve their mission. Although the rising seniors were dramatically outperforming their former peers in BPS, they seemed nowhere close to their suburban peers in skills, knowledge, and work habits.[844] The school's overall MCAS proficiency rates on English and math were 54% and 33%, respectively—roughly the same as the two other highest-regarded open-admissions public high schools in Boston—and obviously much higher than the "regular" Boston public schools, which were at 12% and 8%. But in middle and upper-class Brookline, just a few blocks away, proficiency was 75% and 70%.[845]

He was also worried about the number of students who left MATCH each year. And the boys were lagging behind the girls by every measure. "The level of remediation needed was just massively overwhelming to teachers even when they worked 70 hours a week," he said.[846] Teachers were burning out.

But what worried him the most was, as he put it, "a data question":

According to Census data, only 6% of low-income children ever earn a four-year college degree, with a slightly lower figure for African-Americans and Hispanics. If one realized that the top low-income minority children in Boston were already attending elite, highly selective "exam" schools – like Boston Latin – then the college chances of teenagers in an open-admissions public school like ours seemed even lower.

Yet many of the worst inner-city high schools… claimed to have upwards of 90% of their graduates going on to college. Some pretty unexceptional public schools were claiming 100%.

How could those numbers be reconciled?

The truth was that legions of inner-city high school grads were enrolling in colleges. A big chunk never made it to the first day. A sizable cohort dropped out in the first semester, and still more after the first year. Another group ended up in community colleges. Precious few made it to the four-year college finish line of cap and gown. There was a conspiracy of silence. Universities had no interest in publicizing the high failure rate of low-income minority students. Urban high schools didn't track the data at all, partly because it was labor-intensive, partly because it wasn't flattering. Outside of a few scholars and policy wonks, few Americans were familiar with the depth of the problem.[847]

When Goldstein asked admissions officers at a number of colleges to explain the dramatic dropout rate, they acknowledged there were financial and social obstacles, but mostly, the inner-city kids were "getting crushed by the academics."[848] They faced tougher readings than they'd ever seen before and longer essays and term papers that required critical thinking. And they lacked study skills like time management, skimming, and note-taking.

Goldstein felt that MATCH should take responsibility not merely for grades 9 to 12, but for grades 9 to 16. The mission, after all, was "college *success* for all students," not just college *enrollment*.

But he wondered: *Was that a realistic mission? Could it ever be accomplished? What was the closest anyone had come?*

He asked Casey Carter, who'd written the book *No Excuses: Lessons from 21 High-Performing, High-Poverty Schools*.[849] Carter admitted his research *had not surfaced even one* open admissions high-poverty high school in the nation that met his criteria for "high-performing." The closest were schools that started with sixth graders and kept them through high school. "So if you can pull it off starting with 9th graders," Carter told him, "so far as I can tell, you'd be the first."[850]

Although MATCH would later add a middle school (in 2008[851]), Goldstein could not immediately start with 6th graders because his charter had expressed the need specifically for strong high schools, and MATCH was not eligible for a waiver or revision yet.

He and his trustees needed to figure out a way to truly achieve their mission.

During a February 2003 call with trustees to decide what to do with the unused third floor in their building, Goldstein proposed what he admitted was a crazy idea. "What if, instead of leasing the third floor or expanding into it," he said, "we would build it out as housing? ... We would then hire roughly 45 recent college grads to become full-time tutors in exchange for housing and a small stipend. It would be like Teach For America, except instead of teaching classes of 20, each tutor would work with four kids, each for two hours a day."[852]

As the trustees listened intently, he explained that while they had clear data showing that one-on-one tutoring was the most powerful intervention they offered, they did not currently have the capacity to deliver enough of it.

High-dosage tutoring could transform their organization. "For our top kids," he said, "they'd be pushed academically for the first time in their lives. For our low kids, the ones who arrive as 9th graders unable to write a complete sentence, we've already found that the tutoring dramatically vaults their performance, especially among boys. For all of our students, I really think they'd graduate ready for college."[853]

He also saw a benefit for teachers. "The new supply of dependable tutoring would allow them to raise academic standards: to assign harder homework, and tougher exams. They'd worry less about how to remediate.... I mean right now, what the hell is a 9th grade math teacher supposed to do? She's trying to teach algebra and a bunch of kids don't know 8 times 5...." The way he saw it, teaching at MATCH would become a lower-stress, higher-satisfaction job. And that would bolster teacher retention.[854]

He paused.

The trustees all started talking at once. They decided to go for it.

What they didn't anticipate, perhaps, was how this idea would lead to other innovations.

Four years later, in the fall of 2007, after the school had been running the Tutor Corps successfully for three years, Goldstein began to mull over how to advance MATCH's mission while continuing to improve the quality of the school. One option was to form a charter management organization (CMO) like KIPP, Uncommon, or Achievement First so that MATCH could serve more students.[855]

Another option was to do something about the quality of the teacher pool. Like Norman Atkins, Dave Levin, Dacia Toll, and other CMO leaders, he was very aware of this challenge. Too often, they were forced to settle for new teachers with no experience and limited training. "While these teachers generally worked very hard," Goldstein noted, "there was so much to learn in the first year that they were rarely effective. Ultimately, it was the students who were penalized by this as they learned less under the guidance of new teachers."[856]

He believed that with its Tutor Corps, MATCH was uniquely positioned to run a teacher training program that could produce a pipeline of *effective* first-year teachers. Ultimately, he wanted it to be a graduate school of education, but in a preliminary inquiry, he discovered that the regulations for higher education were very different from those for charter schools. Goldstein recalled:

> When we first spoke to the Higher Ed Board and told them we wanted to deliver a much better graduate—schoolteachers who are more effective with kids—and to do that we needed some freedoms, they threw us out. They said, "We don't look at results in that way. We have no freedoms. How many books will you have in the library?"[857]

Goldstein and Kenny Wang, who had served as a MATCH tutor himself, researched existing teacher prep programs ranging from university-based and alternative training (such as the NYC Teaching Fellows and Teach For America) to residency programs (such as Boston Teacher Residency) and other emerging school-based teacher education programs (such as TeacherU [which later became Relay Graduate School of Education]).[858]

In framing the goals for their program, they also looked at research on what new teachers need in order to be effective. Goldstein modified what Tony Bryk of the Carnegie Foundation for the Advancement of Teaching asked in 2007—"What do teachers need to know, and how can we be sure they know it?"—to "What do *first-year* teachers need to be able to *do*, and how can we train them so we are sure that they can do it?"[859] From there, the focus naturally fell on classroom management skills.

Goldstein hired Orin Gutlerner, who had joined the field in 1996 through TFA in rural North Carolina and had overseen the Alternative Teacher Recruitment and Training programs for the Massachusetts Department of Elementary and Secondary Education. In an interesting twist, he had spent the previous five years directing Harvard's Undergraduate Teacher Education Program.[860]

As they designed this new program, Gutlerner and his colleagues focused on four key questions:

- How would the program best serve its trainees while also being an asset to this well-functioning charter school and its students?

- What strategies and structures would the program employ to ensure that all trainees would reach "unusually effective" status at the completion of the program?

- How would the progress of trainees be assessed and how would their progress be communicated in order to best promote their ongoing growth and development?

- How would the program know if it were successful?[861]

They began recruiting tutors in July 2008[862] and launched the MATCH Teacher Training program's first phase in November[863] with 24 tutors.[864] The program consisted of three phases.

In Phase One, for 15 days over the course of nine weeks, participants (who tutored all week at MATCH high school) received training on Friday afternoons and Saturdays and were given opportunities to practice teaching (role-plays with peers) and receive feedback from both skilled teachers and the students themselves.[865] Goldstein later noted that "Healthy Exit" was a big feature. "We tried to create a structure that was honest," he said. "Many new educators realize in several weeks that it's not for them. We wanted a beautiful way for them to speak up, with no shame, stay as tutors for the year, withdraw from teacher training, and then work with them to help them figure out what they DID want to do."[866]

Another unusual feature: The Gateway—a simulation, modeled on Top Gun type simulations, that actively sought to "knock out" some of the trainees who struggled even after lots of practice. "Either teaching is hard or it's not," Goldstein said. "I wish people wouldn't try to keep both narratives. I believe: hard. So then why wouldn't any sort of teacher prep say to some people, in the nicest but firmest way possible, we're not going to sign off on the idea that you're on track to be good at this very hard thing."[867]

In Phase Two, participants engaged in student teaching with heavy scaffolding: co-teaching SAT prep classes at MATCH high school on Friday afternoons and remedial 6th-grade language arts and math on Saturday mornings[868] (in the fall of 2008, MATCH Middle School opened with 6th-graders[869]). Goldstein recalled: "The focus here was to eliminate the niceties, to get away from pleasant conversation, and instead have very directive 'Do this, not that' type feedback from skilled, experienced teachers to the novices."[870]

In Phase Three, even after they'd all been hired, they taught their own classes in MATCH's July Academy and again, were given feedback and coaching support. Again, the goal was not quantity of feedback, but urgency and specificity.[871]

On July 31, 2009, 24 out of 36 of the trainees completed the program (The rest were Healthy Exits or failed the Gateway).[872] Those who completed the program all found teaching jobs: several at MATCH, the rest at other charter schools around the country.[873]

Three years later, when Mike Goldstein and his colleagues were finally able to turn the MATCH Teacher Residency into a full-blown graduate school of education, Goldstein felt it would be a fitting honor to name the school after Charlie Sposato, who had died on December 16, 2007 after a tough battle with cancer.[874] He noted:

> Charlie did not consider himself a superstar. He thought of himself as a grinder—someone who loved to try to build relationships with kids and their parents, often succeeding but sometimes failing (even after many attempts). Those relationships, to him, often allowed him to "hook" a student into a love of English literature and language.
>
> In naming our graduate school in memory of Mr. Sposato, we want him to serve as a symbol: a stand-in for all the amazing

schoolteachers who shaped the MATCH team (we are grateful), and for all the future teachers we develop, in hopes that they will go on to have the sort of influence on kids that Charlie did.[875]

In 2016, four years after the Charles Sposato Graduate School of Education opened, schools across the country were paying $7,000 to hire its graduates, and every single one of them had found a teaching job.[876]

As MATCH continued to expand its reach, Goldstein increasingly shared his dreams and plans with entrepreneur Stig Leschly. Leschly had founded Exchange.com, an early competitor to eBAY.com, and sold the company to Amazon in 1999. He'd worked for Amazon CEO Jeff Bezos for two years, then taught at Harvard Business School, where his teaching and research focused on entrepreneurship and education reform. When his wife (who'd gone to the Kennedy School with Goldstein) introduced the two men, Leschly was already serving on the board of KIPP in Lynn, Massachusetts.[877]

Leschly joined the MATCH board in 2001 and stayed on for a decade. In 2007 (with a tiny bit of consulting support from Goldstein[878]), he launched the Newark Charter School Fund[879] to help expand and strengthen the charter sector in New Jersey's largest city. In 2010, when he returned to Boston, he and Goldstein continued their conversation about the inner workings of MATCH and how the organization might evolve, except this time it was with an eye towards the possibility that Leschly would join the leadership team as an employee. Brainstorming about what a "Big MATCH" might look like, they came up with an array of plans. They would grow a bit in the schools, expand the Ed School, find ways to export some ideas, and keep an innovation focus instead of trying to become a large CMO.[880]

Leschly had little interest in replication. Like Goldstein, he was an innovator at heart. Not long after he'd become CEO at MATCH, he explained:

> We [at MATCH] think that we need to take on problems we don't know how to solve. I think actually a great loss is the sideways replication of all these "No Excuses" charters. I think it'd be better if they took risks in their designs. So, we're taking on ELL kids, we're going to run a hybrid school, we're going to keep doing things we don't know how to do. MATCH is going to do that. Because colonizing more seats, while beautiful in and of itself, leaves on the table something we could do, which is continue to invent.[881]

Mike Goldstein's life took another interesting turn one day in 2012, when Norman Atkins introduced him to Jay Kimmelman, the CEO of Bridge International Academies. Kimmelman (who'd co-founded EduSoft, an assessment platform provider used by hundreds of school districts) was launching private schools in Africa, trying to scale up rapidly, and he was looking for a Chief Academic Officer to be based in Kenya. Goldstein was intrigued. He loved puzzles and problems, and this work was nothing if not both. But his family couldn't leave Boston. So he thanked Kimmelman and used his blog ("Starting an Ed School") to advertise the position.[882]

A few months later, Kimmelman contacted him again. He said he was open to finding a CAO who could be based elsewhere.

The more Goldstein learned about Bridge, the more it appealed to him. He began to wonder if he could split time between MATCH and Bridge. Stig Leschly was doing a great job; maybe he could carry more of the load? Leschly agreed to help him convince the MATCH board to split the work, and after six weeks, they had all finally agreed, and it seemed like a done deal. "But then," Goldstein said, "the last guy whose approval I needed, a board member, said, 'I'll sign on but you're crazy. You should go all-in on one thing.' And, while others had said that, it kind of stuck and I hung up and called [my wife] and said, 'I think I should take the plunge, and go all-in on Bridge.'"[883]

At the time, Bridge had 134 schools operating in Kenya. "So the question was," he recalled, "could I recruit a small team that raised the day-to-day academic experience of all those kids? And if we could, the scale meant we could help a lot of kids. It felt like a 50-50 chance that once I had a team, that we could help." The idea of taking what he'd learned from people like Charlie Sposato and many others in ed reform to help hundreds of thousands of children in Africa felt like a great new puzzle.[884]

Three years later, Mike Goldstein was still at it. Bridge was up to 414 academies in Kenya, Uganda, and Nigeria.[885]

Meanwhile, Stig Leschly led Match Education, an "engine of discovery and applied innovation" comprised of Match Charter Public Schools, the Match Foundation, and the Charles Sposato Graduate School of Education.[886] This nonprofit expanded its reach with two ever-growing sets of online resources: "Match Minis," a series of animated videos for teachers and coaches to support effective instructional practices, and "Match Fishtank," the standards-based K-12 curriculum developed and refined over 15 years at Match Charter School[887]--both free and available to anyone in the world with Internet access.

CONCLUSION

WHY CHARTERS HAVE NOT FADED

There should probably be a sequel to this book that explores in more depth how charter school educators have developed ideas, resources, and programs that are having an impact on the broader field. In Part III, we examined several charter-seeded roots that have taken hold, but there are many more stories to tell.

To wrap up *this* book, I want to reflect on the endurance of the charter school movement. A couple of decades in, although challenges persist, charters show no signs of disappearing. In fact, in the 2016-17 school year, 58 districts (including major cities such as Denver, Houston, and Los Angeles, to name just a few) had a charter school enrollment share of 20 percent or higher, and those numbers continue to grow.[888] In education, so many ideas have come and gone. Why hasn't the idea of chartering schools been a passing fad?

I raised this question with the individuals I interviewed, and a few key themes emerged. Several people noted that as a practical matter, chartering is more a governance reform than an education reform. As Richard Wenning put it, charters are "a fundamental governance reform—a *democratic* governance reform, also—in the interests of liberty, autonomy, and competition. All of those values are captured within the charter movement and make it hard to go away...." Moreover, he added: "They are now one approach to creating a supply of schools that is available to a smart authorizer, superintendent, or commissioner. On the accountability side, charters are becoming very influential in how *all* schools are held accountable."[889] Indeed, the concept that schools should be held accountable for their performance and failing schools should be closed has definitely taken hold in the mainstream. We've seen failing and under-populated district schools replaced by charters in various cities—for example, in New York City, Washington, DC, and Newark, where the percentage of students attending charters increased from year to year and by 2016-17 was at 10 percent, 46 percent, and 31 percent, respectively.[890]

This growing fondness for accountability is also reflected in how educators use data: school districts and charter management organizations increasingly use data not simply to measure performance but also to inform instruction, both to identify and share best practices across campuses and to uncover ineffective practices and change them. One could argue that the standards movement also contributed to these data-related habits: people trying to meet standards must, after all, measure the extent to which they succeed. That said, the chartering concept of "autonomy in exchange for accountability," which arrived in 1991, planted the seeds for these habits to sprout—a full decade before No Child Left Behind (in 2002) established yearly testing in grades 3-8 and 11 and nearly two decades before the Common Core Standards (in 2010) established year-to-year K-12 standards in English Language Arts and Math from coast to coast.[891]

Beyond their function as an influential governance reform, charters have also tapped into three things that Jim Griffin described as "inherently American and lasting": choice, decentralization, and entrepreneurship.

"Our appetite for choice in our society and our country: that's not going to change," he said. "We're accustomed to it, we expect it, we believe that to a degree we're entitled to choices and options in our lives and in most everything we do."[892] The thousands of citizens who marched in New York City and Albany in support of their children's right to attend charter schools made it clear that parents—especially those whose options were previously limited by their income and zip code—have come to expect public school choices for their children. Those choices didn't exist in many cities before charter schools appeared.

As for decentralization, charters have pressed us to bring the management of the public good down to a "much more local, much more manageable, much more personal" level. Griffin remarked: "I don't believe anybody looks at Los Angeles Unified School District and says, 'Gosh, if we had it all to do over again as a state, when we're organizing the state of California, we're going to organize our public school system around a million-student school district.'"

While it remains to be seen what size is optimal for effective governance of schools, charters have raised that question and are experimenting with the numbers.

Lastly, and perhaps most importantly, as Griffin and many others also asserted, charters have tapped into the American entrepreneurial spirit. "Whether it's starting schools, or starting support organizations, or starting leadership programs, or whatever it is," he said, "charter schooling has brought opportunity—brought people into K-12 public education— that would never have gotten into this field otherwise." Numerous school incubators, CMOs, EMOs, and different companies and consulting opportunities have emerged and created space for substantial entrepreneurial, creative activity and a talent pipeline that did not exist before.

Where will these entrepreneurs take us next? Stay tuned.

ACKNOWLEDGMENTS

This book would not have been possible without the generous assistance of dozens of very busy people who took the time—over the past seven years—to share their remarkable experiences and insights. I'm sure some wondered if I was ever going to finish this thing. Some—especially those who launched new organizations, wrote new books, or took on new roles or responsibilities—spoke with me on multiple occasions. All were gracious, patient, and more helpful than I could have hoped, all the way through this process of trying to understand The Big Picture and get the details right. To everyone who participated, thanks more than I can say for your thoughtful, engaging storytelling: Jeanne Allen, Seth Andrew, Norman Atkins, John Ayers, Chris Barbic, Linda Brown, Ken Campbell, Matt Candler, Yvonne Chan, Jonas Chartock, Lisa Daggs, Mike Feinberg, Sy Fliegel, Jim Ford, Howard Fuller, Scott Given, Jim Goenner, Mike Goldstein, Jim Griffin, Steve Gunderson, Bryan Hassel, Leslie Jacobs, Lisa Graham Keegan, Neerav Kingsland, Ted Kolderie, Robin Lake, Doug Lemov, Stig Leschly, Dave Levin, Margaret Lin, Bruno Manno, Doug McCurry, Scott McVay, Alex Medler, Katherine Merseth, Shirley Monastra, Joe Nathan, Barbara O'Brien, Tom O'Neill, Jack Osander, Brett Peiser, Jim Peyser, Eric Premack, Ted Rebarber, Jeremy Resnick, Greg Richmond, Andy Rotherham, Evan Rudall, Jon Schnur, Jon Schroeder, Don Shalvey, Nelson Smith, Robin Steans, David Steiner, Dacia Toll, Sarah Usdin, Paul Vallas, Jamey Verrilli, and Richard Wenning.

Nearly everyone mentioned also reviewed the manuscript for accuracy; I am deeply thankful for their passion for precision; any errors are my responsibility. I am particularly grateful to the following people, who provided detailed, actionable feedback: Jeanne Allen, Norman Atkins, John Ayers, Linda Brown, Kenneth Campbell, Steve Chiger, Jim Ford, Sandy Gingras, Jim Griffin, Leslie Jacobs, Ted Kolderie, Doug Lemov, Margaret Lin, Katherine Merseth, Shirley Monastra, Joe Nathan, Thomas Peele, Ted Rebarber, Greg Richmond, Jon Schnur, Jon Schroeder, Nelson Smith, David Steiner, Sarah Usdin, Richard Wenning, and my father, Charles Tantillo.

Friends and family—especially my parents, who have always urged me to pursue my dreams: thank you for your relentless encouragement.

A few more shout-outs: Rick Hess, thanks for your timely input on the challenges of policy implementation. Mike Scotto, thanks for teaching me how to spell the drum sound. Susan Carter and Sandy Gingras, thank you for your advice on the front cover. Susan Leon and Jane Rosenman: thank you for pointing me to Mike Levine, whose editing suggestions helped me bring this project to the finish line (Thanks, Mike!).

Last but definitely not least, I would like to extend my gratitude to anyone and everyone who has played a role in trying to improve education in this country, whether you are mentioned in this book or not. Your work matters.

NOTE ON METHODOLOGY

The details recounted in this book are drawn primarily from interviews and public documents. Some are based on my personal experiences. In cases where I was directly involved in the actions described, I consulted notes or journal entries whenever possible, but in some instances had to rely on memory. Being human, I did the best I could. As much as possible, I checked the facts with those involved. Any errors or omissions—albeit unintended—are solely my responsibility.

ABOUT THE AUTHOR

SARAH TANTILLO founded and led the New Jersey Charter School Resource Center and the New Jersey Charter Public Schools Association. She also taught high school English in both suburban and urban public schools for 14 years, including seven at the high-performing North Star Academy Charter School of Newark. She consults with schools on literacy instruction, curriculum development, data-driven instruction, and school culture-building. She is the author of *The Literacy Cookbook: A Practical Guide to Effective Reading, Writing, Speaking, and Listening Instruction* (2012); *Literacy and the Common Core: Recipes for Action* (2014); and *Using Grammar to Improve Writing: Recipes for Action* (2018). For more information, see her Website, The Literacy Cookbook (www.literacycookbook.com).

NOTES

1   National Alliance for Public Charter Schools: Data Explorer: https://data.
publiccharters.org/

2   Sarah Tantillo, "Culture Formation in Charter Schools: Two Case Studies" (Ed.D.
diss., Rutgers University, 2001), 83.

3   National Commission on Excellence in Education, *A Nation at Risk: The Imperative
for Educational Reform* (Report to the Nation and the Secretary of Education, United
States Department of Education, April, 1983: http://reagan.procon.org/sourcefiles/a-
nation-at-risk-reagan-april-1983.pdf), 9.

4   *A Nation at Risk* Recommendations: http://www2.ed.gov/pubs/NatAtRisk/recomm.
html

5   In 1967, Kenneth B. Clark presented a paper at the National Conference on Equal
Educational Opportunity in America's Cities, sponsored by the U.S. Commission on Civil
Rights, in which he asserted that American public education suffered from "pervasive
and persistent" inefficiency, particularly in urban schools. He criticized the monopoly
of the educational system and proposed solutions that included an array of school
choice options. See Kenneth B. Clark, "Alternative Public School Systems," *Harvard
Educational Review*, 38: no.1 (Winter, 1968), 100-113. I am grateful to Joe Nathan for
pointing out this important work.

6   Sara Mosle, "The Answer is National Standards," *The New York Times*, October 27,
1996: http://www.nytimes.com/1996/10/27/magazine/the-answer-is-national-standards.
html?pagewanted=all&src=pm. Also cited in Kahlenberg, *Tough Liberal*, 275.

7   Richard Kahlenberg, *Tough Liberal: Albert Shanker and the Battles over Schools,
Unions, Race, and Democracy* (New York: Columbia University Press, 2007), 278.

8   Edward B. Fiske, "A Nation at a Loss," *The New York Times*, April 25, 2008: http://www.nytimes.com/2008/04/25/opinion/25fiske.html?pagewanted=all

9   Kahlenberg, *Tough Liberal*, 278.

10   *Time for Results: The Governors' 1991 Report on Education*, Gov. Lamar Alexander, Chairman, and Govs. Bill Clinton and Thomas H. Kean, Co-Chairmen, National Governors' Association Center for Policy Research and Analysis, August 1986.

11   Lamar Alexander, "Chairman's Summary," *Time for Results: The Governors' 1991 Report on Education*, National Governors' Association Center for Policy Research and Analysis, August 1986, 1.

12   National Center for Alternative Certification, "Alternative Teacher Certification: A State-by-State Analysis" http://www.teach-now.org/intro.cfm (page viewed on 4-16-12).

13   Jack Osander, Email message to the author, April 11, 2012.

14   U.S. 1 Staff, "About the Author: John Osander," U.S. 1 Princeton Info, May 26, 2010: https://princetoninfo.com/about-the-author-john-osander/

15   A2139- New Jersey Legislature: ftp://www.njleg.state.nj.us/20042005/A2500/2139_11.HTM (page viewed on 5-30-12).

16   Ernest Boyer, *High School: A Report on Secondary Education in America* (New York: Harper & Row, 1983).

17   Scott McVay, interview by author, Princeton, NJ, July 23, 2012.

18   Betty Sue Zellner, NJ Dept. of Education, "Cumulative Employment of New Teachers (1985-2012), data provided to the author on Sept. 26, 2012.

19   National Center for Alternative Certification, "Alternative Teacher Certification: A State-by-State Analysis" http://www.teach-now.org/intro.cfm (page viewed on 4-16-12).

20   C. Emily Feistritzer, "The Impact of Alternate Routes to Teaching," *Education Week*, published online 11-13-2009: http://www.edweek.org/ew/articles/2009/11/18/12feistritzer.h29.html?tkn=UMOFkXoizCTGJajRsETi4z%2FPuWY3j8ZYuu2c&intc=es (page viewed on 5-28-12).

21   National Center for Alternative Certification, "Alternative Teacher Certification: A State-by-State Analysis": http://www.teach-now.org/intro.cfm (page viewed on 4-16-12).

22   "Alternative Teacher Certification- A State-by-State Analysis 2010," C. Emily Feistritzer, National Center for Education Information, "Table 1: Number of Certificates Issued to Persons Entering Teaching Through Alternative Routes, by State: 1985-2009": http://www.teach-now.org/Table1_Stat.pdf (page viewed on 5-30-12).

23   Wendy Kopp, *One Day, All Children...* (New York: PublicAffairs, 2001), 15.

24   Jack Schneider, *Excellence for All: How a New Breed of Reformers Is Transforming America's Public Schools* (Nashville: Vanderbilt University Press, 2011), 86.

25   "Our Organization/History: Teach for America": http://www.teachforamerica.org/our-organization/history (page viewed on 4-16-12).

26   "Life as an Alum: Teach for America": https://www.teachforamerica.org/life-as-an-alum (page viewed on 2-23-19).

27   Kahlenberg, *Tough Liberal*, 384.

28   When asked by Joe Nathan and Ted Kolderie to testify before the Minnesota legislature on behalf of charter legislation, Shanker declined. According to Nathan, Shanker did not support Kolderie's notion of "withdrawing the exclusive franchise." Source: Joe Nathan, Email message to the author, December 6, 2014.

29   Kahlenberg, *Tough Liberal*, 310.

30   Ray Budde, *Education by Charter: Restructuring School Districts* (Andover, MA: Regional Laboratory for Educational Improvement of the Northeast and Islands, 1988).

31   Joe Nathan, *Charter Schools: Creating Hope and Opportunity for American Education* (San Francisco: Jossey-Bass, 1999), 62.

32   Nathan, *Charter Schools*, 63.

33   Casey Banas, "4% Raise Brings Tentative Pact to End School Strike," *Chicago Tribune*, October 4, 1987: http://articles.chicagotribune.com/1987-10-04/news/8703140884_1_end-school-strike-public-school-teacher-chicago-teachers-union

34   Casey Banas and Devonda Byers, "Education Chief: City Schools Worst," *Chicago Tribune*, November 8, 1987: http://articles.chicagotribune.com/1987-11-08/news/8703230953_1_dropout-rate-public-schools-mayor-harold-washington

35   Joseph Loftus, "Charter Schools: A Potential Solution to the Riddle of Reform," Urban Child Welfare Project: Center for Research, Planning and Advocacy, March 1989.

36   Albert Shanker, National Press Club Speech, Washington, DC, March 31, 1988, 4.

37   Shanker, National Press Club Speech, 6.

38   Ibid.

39   Ibid., 7.

40   Ibid., 10.

41   Ibid., 11.

42   Ibid., 12.

43   Albert Shanker, "Convention Plots New Course—A Charter for Change," *New York Times* (paid advertisement), July 10, 1988, E7.

44   John Merrow bio: http://learningmatters.tv/images/blog/JM.pdf

45   Ted Kolderie, phone interview with the author, December 29, 2014.

46   Nathan, *Charter Schools*, 63.

47   Joe Nathan, *Charter Schools: Creating Hope and Opportunity for American Education* (San Francisco: Jossey-Bass, 1996).

48   In fact, Governor Lamar Alexander had picked Nathan to coordinate the NGA report in part because he had urged that teachers be allowed to create new public schools in his 1983 book, *Free to Teach: Achieving Equity and Excellence in Public Education* (New York: Pilgrim Press). Source: Joe Nathan, Email message to the author, February 21, 2019.

49   Ember Reichgott Junge, *Zero Chance of Passage: The Pioneering Charter School Story* (Edina, MN: Beaver's Pond Press, 2012), 43. Also: Joe Nathan, Email message to the author, February 21, 2019.

50   Lamar Alexander, "Chairman's Summary," *Time for Results: The Governors' 1991 Report on Education*, National Governors' Association Center for Policy Research and Analysis, August 1986, 4, italics mine.

51   Reichgott Junge, *Zero Chance of Passage*, 43-44.

52   Nathan, *Charter Schools*, 64.

53   Seymour Fliegel, phone interview with the author, December 17, 2013.

54   Seymour Fliegel with James MacGuire, *Miracle in East Harlem: The Fight for Choice in Public Education* (New York: The Manhattan Institute, 1993), 3.

55   Fliegel with MacGuire, *Miracle in East Harlem*, 4.

56   "About Me: Deborah Meier on Education" found at https://deborahmeier.com/about/

57   Fliegel with MacGuire, *Miracle in East Harlem*, 3.

58   Reichgott Junge, *Zero Chance of Passage*, 52.

59   Ibid., 54.

60   Ted Kolderie, phone interview with the author, December 29, 2014.

61   For more details on how Minnesota's law got passed, see: Ember Reichgott Junge, *Zero Chance of Passage: The Pioneering Charter School Story* (Edina, MN: Beaver's Pond Press, 2012). See also: Joe Nathan, *Charter Schools: Creating Hope and Opportunity for American Education* (San Francisco: Jossey-Bass, 1996).

62   Seymour Fliegel, phone interview with the author, December 17, 2013.

63   Kahlenberg, *Tough Liberal*, 313. John E. Chubb and Terry M. Moe, *Politics, Markets, and America's Schools* (Washington, DC: Brookings Institution Press, 1990).

64   Reichgott Junge, *Zero Chance of Passage*, 75.

65   Joe Nathan, Email message to the author, March 16, 2019.

66   Reichgott Junge, *Zero Chance of Passage*, 76.

67   Joe Nathan, Email message to the author, December 6, 2014.

68   Another important seed was that "in 1985, the Minnesota legislature adopted the Post Secondary Enrollment Options (PSEO) law. This allowed high school juniors and seniors to attend colleges or universities, with state funds following them, paying ALL tuition, lab, and book fees. This helped lead to chartering. Just as with charters, the decision to participate in PSEO was up to the students/families. A high school could not block a student from participating." Source: Joe Nathan, Email message to the author, February 21, 2019.

69   Ted Kolderie, "The States Will Have to Withdraw the Exclusive," Public Services Redesign Project, July 1990: http://www.educationevolving.org/pdf/StatesWillHavetoWithdrawtheExclusive.pdf

70   While others used the term "monopoly," Kolderie himself studiously avoided it, preferring "exclusive franchise." Source: Ted Kolderie, Email message to the author, March 10, 2019.

71   Kolderie, "The States Will Have to Withdraw the Exclusive," 13.

72   Reichgott Junge, *Zero Chance of Passage*, 76-77.

73   Ted Kolderie, "Beyond Choice to New Public Schools: Withdrawing the Exclusive Franchise in Public Education" (Progressive Policy Institute, November 1990): http://files.eric.ed.gov/fulltext/ED327914.pdf Note: Marshall incorporated this as the "education" chapter into the policy book *Mandate for Change* (January 1993) that the DLC created for Bill Clinton. Source: Ted Kolderie, Email message to the author, March 10, 2019.

74   Reichgott Junge, *Zero Chance of Passage*, 185.

75   Joe Nathan, Email message to the author, December 6, 2014.

76   Ibid.

77   Ted Kolderie, phone interview with the author, May 31, 2012.

78   Ted Kolderie, phone interview with the author, December 29, 2014.

79   Ted Kolderie, phone interview with the author, May 31, 2012.

80   Ted Kolderie, phone interview with the author, December 29, 2014.

81   Ted Kolderie, phone interview with the author, May 31, 2012.

82   Ted Kolderie, phone interview with the author, December 29, 2014.

83   According to Joe Nathan, the late Senator Paul Wellstone also played a vital role: "He strongly supported chartering and reassured a lot of liberals that this was a good thing." Source: Joe Nathan, Email message to the author, December 6, 2014.

84   *Time for Results: The Governors' 1991 Report on Education*, Gov. Lamar Alexander, Chairman, and Govs. Bill Clinton and Thomas H. Kean, Co-Chairmen, National Governors' Association Center for Policy Research and Analysis, August 1986. Joe Nathan was one of the leading policy analysts involved in writing the report and functioned as the coordinator.

85   Joe Nathan, Email message to the author, June 3, 2014.

86   Joe Nathan, phone interview with the author, June 27, 2014.

87   Nathan, *Charter Schools.*

88   Joe Nathan, Email message to the author, March 16, 2019.

89   Reichgott Junge, *Zero Chance of Passage*, 269.

90   Ibid., 192.

91   Jon Schroeder, phone interview with the author, June 14, 2012.

92   Jon Schroeder, Email message to the author, March 5, 2019.

93   Ibid.

94   One other critical factor in passage of the original bill was the role played by Sen. Ted Kennedy (D-MA), lead Democrat on the House-Senate conference committee that resolved final differences in the legislation. Perhaps the most important of those differences was over what public agencies could grant charters eligible for federal grant funds. The House version of the bill limited chartering authority to state and local boards of education. The Senate bill – consistent with the original Durenberger bill -- let states determine who could grant and oversee charters. Kennedy and Durenberger both represented states with alternative authorizers and, with Clinton Administration support, prevailed in the House-Senate conference committee -- deferring to the states on what public chartering authorities could grant and oversee charters. This allowed charters to receive grants that were authorized by colleges and universities, cities, independent chartering boards and, in Minnesota, existing and newly created non-profit organizations. Source: Jon Schroeder, Email message to the author, March 5, 2019.

95   Reichgott Junge, *Zero Chance of Passage*, 240.

96   Eric Premack, phone interview with the author, June 19, 1996.

97   Eric Premack, phone interview with the author, December 20, 2013. All subsequent quotes from Eric Premack are from this interview unless otherwise noted.

98   Frank Premack, obituary, *New York Times*, April 7, 1975: http://timesmachine. nytimes.com/timesmachine/1975/04/08/76551326.html?pageNumber=40

99   Ted Kolderie, phone interview with the author, December 29, 2014. Note: Jerry Hume later helped Jeanne Allen launch the Center for Education Reform. See Chapter 6 for more information.

100   Jim McGee, Tom Fiedler, and James Savage, "The Gary Hart Story: How It Happened," originally printed in *The Miami Herald* on May 10, 1987, reprinted online with permission at: http://www.unc.edu/~pmeyer/Hart/hartarticle.html

101   Reichgott Junge, *Zero Chance of Passage*, 240.

102   Ibid., 242.

103   Ibid., 245.

104   Specifically, he overheard overheard Senator Hart's staff assistant, Sue Burr, and her boss, education committee chief of staff Bill Whiteneck, complaining about this broken deal.

105   Reichgott Junge, *Zero Chance of Passage*, 246.

106   Ibid., 246-7.

107   Ibid., 241.

108   James Goenner, "The Origination of Michigan's Charter School Policy: An Historical Analysis" (Ph.D. diss., Michigan State University, 2011).

109   "Honey, I Blew Up the Kids" (1993, Sept. 1). [Editorial] *Washington Post*, p. A22 (cited in Goenner, 62).

110   John M. Engler, "Our Kids Deserve Better! New Schools for a New Century," Special Message to a Joint Session of the Michigan Legislature: On Education (Oct. 15, 1993), p. 4. [Cited in Goenner, 71].

111   Joe Nathan, Email message to the author, December 6, 2014.

112   John M. Engler, "Our Kids Deserve Better! New Schools for a New Century," Special Message to a Joint Session of the Michigan Legislature: On Education (Oct. 15, 1993), p. 10. [Cited in Goenner, 71].

113   Goenner, "The Origination of Michigan's Charter School Policy," 69.

114   Joe Nathan, Email message to the author, December 6, 2014.

115   Goenner, "The Origination of Michigan's Charter School Policy," 164.

116   Reichgott Junge, *Zero Chance of Passage*, 337.

117   Goenner, "The Origination of Michigan's Charter School Policy," 165.

118   Linda Brown, in-person interview with the author, June 26, 2012.

119   Steven Baratte, "California's Charter Schools Grow, Over 1300 New and Expanded Charter Schools in 2018," California Charter Schools Association, Nov. 8, 2018: http://www.ccsa.org/blog/2018/11/californias-charter-schools-grow-over-1300-new-and-expanded-charter-schools-open-in-2018.html

120   Joseph V. Doria, "The Function of Political Capital in the New Jersey Legislature's Traditional Role in the Formulation of Educational Policy: A Participant Observation Illustrated by the Charter School Program Act of 1995" (Ed.D. diss., Teachers College, Columbia University, 2000). In his dissertation about how the New Jersey charter legislation was passed, Assemblyman Joseph V. Doria, a co-sponsor of that legislation, writes: "Throughout the charter school debate, some key players in the process defined the concept more in terms of its viability as an alternative to educational vouchers and less in terms of its intrinsic merits or shortcomings" (11). He cites similar experiences in California and Arizona.

121   Howard Fuller with Lisa Frazier Page, *No Struggle, No Progress: A Warrior's Life from Black Power to Education Reform* (Milwaukee: Marquette University Press, 2014).

122   Fuller with Page, *No Struggle, No Progress*, 16-18.

123   Ibid.

124   Ibid., 197.

125   Howard Fuller, phone interview with the author, June 5, 2012.

126   Ibid.

127   Howard Fuller, phone interview with the author, May 8, 2014.

128   Howard Fuller, phone interview with the author, June 5, 2012.

129   Howard Fuller, phone interview with the author, May 8, 2014.

130   Ibid.

131   Fuller with Page, *No Struggle, No Progress*, 249.

132   Ted Kolderie, "Beyond Choice to New Public Schools: Withdrawing the Exclusive Franchise in Public Education" (Progressive Policy Institute, November 1990), 2: http://files.eric.ed.gov/fulltext/ED327914.pdf

133   Howard Fuller, phone interview with the author, June 5, 2012.

134   Ibid.

135   Howard Fuller bio on BAEO (Black Alliance for Educational Options) Website found at http://activistcash.com/biography.cfm/b/3736-howard-fuller

136   Frederick Douglass, "West India Emancipation Speech," August 3, 1857, found at: http://www.blackpast.org/1857-frederick-douglass-if-there-no-struggle-there-no-progress

137   Jeanne Allen, Email message to the author, March 20, 2019.

138   Ibid.

139   Ibid.

140   Jeanne Allen, phone interview with the author, October 2, 2014. All subsequent quotes from Jeanne Allen are from this interview unless otherwise noted.

141   One of the earliest collaborative efforts was an American Online (AOL) forum led by Frank Dooling. Source: Joe Nathan, Email message to the author, December 6, 2014.

142   John E. Chubb and Terry M. Moe, *Politics, Markets, and America's Schools* (Washington, DC: Brookings Institution Press, 1990).

143   Jeanne Allen, Email message to the author, March 20, 2019.

144   Jeanne Allen, phone interview with the author, February 6, 2015.

145   Linda Brown, phone interview with the author, April 25, 2015.

146   Linda Brown, in-person interview with the author, June 26, 2012. All subsequent quotes from Linda Brown in this chapter are from this interview unless otherwise noted.

147   Jim Peyser, phone interview with the author, December 20, 2012.

148   Baker became Governor of Massachusetts in January, 2015.

149   When Baker left Pioneer to join the Weld Administration, Wilson replaced him; then a couple years later, Wilson left for the Weld Administration, and he recruited Peyser to launch the Charter School Resource Center. Source: Jim Peyser, phone interview with the author, December 20, 2012.

150   J. M. Lawrence, "Lovett 'Pete' Peters, Founder of Pioneer Institute; at 97," *The Boston Globe,* November 19, 2010: http://www.boston.com/bostonglobe/obituaries/articles/2010/11/19/lovett_pete_peters_founder_of_pioneer_institute_at_97/

151   Linda Brown, in-person interview with the author, June 26, 2012.

152   Jim Peyser, phone interview with the author, December 20, 2012.

153   Ted Kolderie, "Beyond Choice to New Public Schools: Withdrawing the Exclusive Franchise in Public Education" (Progressive Policy Institute, November 1990), 2: http://files.eric.ed.gov/fulltext/ED327914.pdf

154   Ibid.

155   Ibid., 8-9.

156   Jon Schnur interviewed by Matt Weber on Harvard EdCast, "The Presidential Advisor," Feb. 6, 2013, accessed on Feb. 4, 2014: http://www.gse.harvard.edu/news-impact/2013/02/harvard-edcast-the-presidential-adviser/

157   Jeremy Resnick, phone interview with the author, May 9, 2012. For more information about the Propel Schools network, see: http://www.propelschools.org

158   Full disclosure: I later taught high school English at North Star for seven years and helped design coursework for TeacherU and Relay Graduate School of Education, two of Norman's other ventures, discussed in Part III.

159   Norman Atkins, Email message to the author, March 22, 2019.

160   Norman Atkins, presentation on March 11, 2013 at Harvard Graduate School of Education Askwith Forum, "Reforming Education Reform: Opportunities for the Next Generation," published on YouTube on April 29, 2013: https://www.youtube.com/watch?t=12&v=jMOryfKuyF8

161   Norman Atkins, Email message to the author, March 22, 2019.

162   For more on Geoffrey Canada's upbringing, see his excellent memoir, *Fist Stick Knife Gun: A Personal History of Violence* (Boston, Beacon Press, 1995).

163   "Geoffrey Canada: Harlem Children's Zone," found at: https://hcz.org/about-us/leadership/geoffrey-canada/

164   Norman Atkins, Email message to the author, March 22, 2019.

165   For more information on the history of Rheedlen and Harlem Children's Zone, see: http://hcz.org/about-us/history/

166   For a book that explains Geoffrey Canada's story more fully, see Paul Tough, *Whatever It Takes: Geoffrey Canada's Quest to Change Harlem and America* (New York: Houghton Mifflin Harcourt, 2008).

167   Sarah Tantillo, "Culture Formation in Charter Schools: Two Case Studies" (Ed.D. diss., Rutgers University, 2001), 45.

168   Jamey Verrilli, Email message to the author, May 1, 2015.

169   Founded in 1969 by the Sisters of St. Dominic, Link eventually became a charter in 2014, though after Jamey Verrilli had left.

170   Jamey Verrilli, in-person interview with the author, June 3, 1999.

171   Ibid.

172   Ibid.

173   Tantillo, "Culture Formation in Charter Schools," 46.

174   Jamey Verrilli, in-person interview with the author, June 3, 1999.

175   Ibid.

176   Norman Atkins, Email message to the author, March 25, 2015.

177   For more information about De La Salle Academy, see: https://www.delasalleacademy.org/

178   Jamey Verrilli, Email message to the author, December 30, 1998.

179   Norman Atkins, in-person interview with the author, November 3, 1998.

180   Ibid.

181   Tantillo, "Culture Formation in Charter Schools," 277.

182   Although not the first national gathering of charter school supporters, it appears to have been the first supported by federal funding.

183   Joanne Jacobs, "Moving the Education Needle: A Conversation with Scott Hamilton," *Education Next*, Spring 2014, vol. 14, no. 2.

184   Ed Kirby, "Rethinking America's Schools: The Walton Family Foundation Responds," Excellence in Philanthropy/The Philanthropy Roundtable, *Philanthropy Magazine*, March-April 2005: http://www.philanthropyroundtable.org/topic/excellence_in_philanthropy/rethinking_americas_schools

185   Jay Mathews, *Work Hard. Be Nice: How Two Inspired Teachers Created the Most Promising Schools in America* (Chapel Hill, NC: Algonquin Books of Chapel Hill, 2009), 263-268. Scott would show the *60 Minutes* "KIPP" episode to Don Fisher, cofounder of the Gap Inc. clothing stores, and encourage him to invest millions in a national rollout of the KIPP Schools model.

186   Author's notes from National Charter School Conference, July 26, 1996. These three questions appear in many other sources, including: "The Massachusetts Charter School Initiative: Expanding the Possibilities of Education," 1998 Report, Massachusetts Department of Education, Boston, 4.

187   Greg Richmond, Email message to the author, May 12, 2014.

188   The Center for School Change, led by Joe Nathan, started in 1989 and began offering assistance to people who wanted to start charters immediately after the law passed in 1991. Source: Joe Nathan, Email message to the author, December 6, 2014.

189   "20th Annual California Charter Schools Conference Pays Tribute with Legacy Awards: Charter School Operators, Supporters, Funders and Elected Officials are Honored," California Charter Schools Association, Vicki Grenz, March 12, 2013 press release, accessed January 1, 2014: http://www.calcharters.org/blog/2013/03/20th-annual-california-charter-schools-conference-pays-tribute-with-legacy-awards-charter-school-ope.html

190   Yvonne Chan, in-person interview with the author, February 13, 2013.

191   Yvonne Chan, Email message to author, June 18, 2014.

192   Timothy Williams, "Poverty, Pride--and Power: In Line for Federal Help, Pacoima Hides Problems Below Neat Surface," *Los Angeles Times*, April 10, 1994, accessed on January 4, 2014: http://articles.latimes.com/1994-04-10/local/me-44400_1_pacoima-elementary

193   Beth Shuster, "Sunday Profile: A Special Educator: Yvonne Chan," *Los Angeles Times*, April 16, 1995, accessed on January 4, 2014: http://articles.latimes.com/1995-04-16/news/ls-55422_1_yvonne-chan

194   Yvonne Chan, in-person interview with the author, February 13, 2013. All subsequent quotes from Yvonne Chan are from this interview unless otherwise noted.

195   Eric Premack, Email message to the author, June 20, 2014. Note: Section 46711, in turn, merely specified that if a charter school opted to participate in the state teacher retirement system, then all of its eligible teachers were required to participate. Premack also added: "The mega-waiver remains on the books today, but has been substantially, though not wholly undermined by the imposition of myriad laws and restrictions over the years. Some of the 'biggies' included imposing laws governing: teacher credentialing, labor relations/collective bargaining, state standards and testing, minimum instructional time, and myriad accountability laws, including minimum test-based renewal thresholds."

196   Terrence E. Deal and Guilbert C. Hentschke [with Kendra Kecker, Christopher Lund, Scot Oschman, and Rebecca Shore], *Adventures of Charter School Creators: Leading from the Ground Up* (Lanham, MD: Scarecrow Press, 2004), 65.

197   Meal tickets are used to prove that the students claiming "free" or "reduced-price" meal status are legally entitled to that status. Yvonne learned that for schools with 95% or higher poverty rates, it was unnecessary for students to show that proof every day.

198   Leadership for Quality Education (LQE) was a reform organization under the wing of the Civic Committee, an organization of senior executives of the Chicago region's largest employers.

199 John Ayers, phone interview with the author, August 12, 2012. All subsequent quotes from John Ayers are from this interview unless otherwise noted.

200 Ibid.

201 Ibid.

202 Paul Vallas, phone interview with the author, September 3, 2015.

203 Ibid.

204 See *The Prize: Who Controls America's Schools* by Dale Russakoff (New York: Houghton Mifflin Harcourt, 2015) for some insights into the struggles of the Newark Public Schools.

205 Paul Vallas, phone interview with the author, September 3, 2015.

206 Margaret Lin, in-person interview with the author, March 23, 2014. All subsequent quotes from Margaret Lin are from this interview unless otherwise noted.

207 Margaret Lin, Email message to the author, June 28, 2014.

208 Greg Richmond, phone interview with the author, July 16, 2012. All subsequent quotes from Greg Richmond are from this interview unless otherwise noted.

209 Robin Steans, phone interview with the author, October 1, 2012.

210 For more information on Advance Illinois, see: http://www.advanceillinois.org/

211 Illinois State Charter School Commission staff bios (accessed July 1, 2014): http://www.isbe.state.il.us/scsc/pdf/staff_bios.pdf. For more information on the ISCSC, see: https://www.isbe.net/pages/illinois-state-charter-school-commission.aspx

212 Margaret Lin, Email message to the author, June 28, 2014.

213 Margaret Lin, in-person interview with the author, March 23, 2014.

214 Margaret Lin, Email message to the author, March 19, 2019.

215 Robin Steans, phone interview with the author, October 1, 2012.

216 John Ayers, phone interview with the author, August 12, 2012.

217 Margaret Lin, Email message to the author, June 28, 2014.

218 John Ayers, phone interview with the author, August 12, 2012.

219 Margaret Lin, Email message to the author, March 19, 2019.

220 Greg Richmond, Email message to the author, April 13, 2015.

221 Rebecca David, Kevin Hesla, and Susan Aud Pendergrass, "A Growing Movement: America's Largest Public Charter School Communities," National Alliance for Public Charter Schools, Oct. 2017, 12th Edition: https://www.publiccharters.org/sites/default/files/documents/2017-10/Enrollment_Share_Report_Web_0.pdf

222 Ibid.

223 Kenneth Campbell, phone interview with the author, July 31, 2012. All subsequent quotes from Kenneth Campbell are from this interview unless otherwise noted.

224 For more information, see: David A. Vise, "D.C. Control Board Takes Charge of Public Schools," *The Washington Post*, November 16, 1996, A01: http://www.washingtonpost.com/wp-srv/local/longterm/library/dc/control/schools.htm

225 Jim Ford, in-person interview with the author, July 2, 2014. All subsequent quotes from Jim Ford are from this interview unless otherwise noted.

226 Jim Ford, Email message to the author, October 19, 2014.

227 Jim Ford, in-person interview with the author, July 2, 2014.

228 Jim Ford, Email message to the author, March 20, 2019.

229 Kevin Chavous notes: "From 1970 to 1996, the Carlos Rosario Center graduated 50,000 'new Americans' who joined the workforce and established themselves as a new generation of naturalized citizens in the nation's capital." Source: Kevin P. Chavous, *Serving Our Children: Charter Schools and the Reform of American Public Education* (Herndon, VA: Capital Books, 2004), 107.

230 Jim Ford, in-person interview with the author, July 2, 2014.

231 Jim Ford, Email message to the author, March 20, 2019.

232 Ted Rebarber, Email message to the author, March 13, 2019; see also "DC Council Passes Charter Law" at https://focusdc.org/timeline

233 Jim Ford, in-person interview with the author, July 2, 2014.

234 Ted Rebarber, phone interview with the author, July 24, 2014. This section, unless otherwise noted, is based on this interview.

235 Chester E. Finn, Jr., Bruno V. Manno, and Gregg Vanourek, *Charter Schools in Action: Renewing Public Education* (Princeton: Princeton University Press, 2000).

236 Steve Gunderson, phone interview with the author, December 11, 2014.

237 Ibid.

238 Ibid.

239 Ted Rebarber, phone interview with the author, July 24, 2014.

240   Ibid. Note: Newt Gingrich declined to be interviewed for this book.

241   Steve Gunderson, phone interview with the author, December 11, 2014.

242   Ted Rebarber, phone interview with the author, July 24, 2014.

243   United States General Accounting Office, "Charter Schools: New Model for Public Schools Provides Opportunities and Challenges," GAO/HEHS-95-42, January 1995: http://www.gao.gov/assets/230/220825.pdf

244   Richard Wenning, phone interview with the author, January 27, 2015.

245   Richard Wenning, phone interview with the author, May 29, 2012. Additional information provided in phone interview with the author, January 27, 2015.

246   Richard Wenning, phone interview with the author, January 27, 2015. For more information on the SEED School, the longest-running residential charter in the country, which was founded by Rajiv Vinnakota and Eric Adler and has been in existence for more than 15 years, see: https://www.seedschooldc.org/ Note: The first residential charter in the country was the Samuel DeWitt Proctor Academy in Ewing, NJ, which opened in 1997; however, its charter was not renewed, and the school closed in 2001. For details about why that school failed—a primer on the challenges of running a residential charter school—see the NJ State Board of Education Decision, SB #14-01, "In the Matter of the Nonrenewal of the Samuel DeWitt Proctor Academy Charter School," May 1, 2001: http://www.nj.gov/education/legal/sboe/2001/aug/sb14-01.pdf

247   Richard Wenning, Email message to the author, January 20, 2015.

248   Ibid.

249   Ted Rebarber, phone interview with the author, July 24, 2014.

250   Ibid.

251   Ibid.

252   Shirley Monastra, Email message to the author, March 19, 2019.

253   District of Columbia Public Charter School Board, "DC's Public Charter Schools," Oct. 2018: https://www.dcpcsb.org/sites/default/files/report/PCSB%20background%20slides_current%2010.10.18.pdf

254   For more information, see: http://www.carlosrosario.org

255   Tom O'Neill, phone interview with the author, June 2, 2014. All subsequent quotes from Tom are from this interview unless otherwise noted.

256   "I Have a Dream Foundation" History: http://www.ihaveadreamfoundation.org/html/history.htm

257   "Our History in Depth: Google": http://www.google.com/about/company/history/

258   Pearl Rock Kane, Teachers College, Columbia University, "New Jersey Charter Schools: The First Year, 1997-1998," prepared for the New Jersey Institute for School Innovation. Kane also added charters to the syllabus of a leadership course that originally dealt with private schools.

259   Pennsylvania's charter school legislation: http://www.portal.state.pa.us/portal/server.pt/community/charter_school_regulations/7359 (accessed on January 20, 2015).

260   Author's notes from meeting on June 23, 1997.

261   Linda Brown, in-person interview with the author, June 26, 2012.

262   Kenneth Campbell, phone interview with the author, July 31, 2012.

263   Jeanne Allen, phone interview with the author, October 2, 2014, followed up on in-person meeting at 2014 National Charter Schools Conference.

264   Ted Kolderie, Email message to the author, October 26, 2014. Additional background on this meeting was provided by Jon Schroeder via a phone interview with the author on October 22, 2014.

265   William M. Steinbrook, Jr.'s bio is found at: http://teamcfa.org/who-we-are/teamcfa-foundation/boards-committees

266   Jeff Mapes, "Oregon's Two Big Super-pac Donors Come from Opposite Sides of Political Spectrum," *The Oregonian*, June 24, 2013, found at: http://www.oregonlive.com/mapes/index.ssf/2013/06/oregons_two_big_super-pac_dono.html

267   Cathy Nehf Lund later worked at the Walton Family Foundation. Cathy Nehf Lund, "The Walton Family Foundation: About Us": http://www.waltonfamilyfoundation.org/about/staff---special-initiatives (accessed on January 20, 2015).

268   Jon Schroeder, phone interview with the author, October 22, 2014.

269   Jon Schroeder's full bio: http://www.centerforpolicy.org/people/jon-schroeder/full-bio

270   The first round of start-up funding, released in 1995, was $6 million.

271   Jon Schroeder, phone interview with the author, October 22, 2014.

272   Jon Schroeder, Email message to the author, March 5, 2019.

273   Ibid.

274   Bryan C. Hassel, phone interview with the author, June 6, 2012. All quotes from Bryan Hassel are based on this interview unless otherwise noted.

275   Bryan C. Hassel, *The Charter School Challenge: Avoiding the Pitfalls, Fulfilling the Promise* (Washington, DC: Brookings Institution Press, 1999).

276   For more information on Opportunity Culture schools, go to: https://www.
opportunityculture.org/

277   Jim Griffin, phone interview with the author, July 24, 2012. All quotes from
Griffin are from this interview unless otherwise noted.

278   For a detailed history of the Colorado charter legislation, see "On the Road of
Innovation: Colorado's Charter School Law Turns 20," by Pamela Benigno and Kyle
Morin, Independence Institute, June 2013, accessed on December 14, 2013, found at:
http://www.i2i.org/files/file/IP-4-2013.pdf

279   Jim Griffin, National Charter Schools Hall of Fame Award speech, YouTube
video published July 25, 2012, accessed on January 4, 2014: http://www.youtube.com/
watch?v=3OKnf3VhUlg

280   "On the Road of Innovation: Colorado's Charter School Law Turns 20," by
Pamela Benigno and Kyle Morin, Independence Institute, June 2013: http://www.i2i.org/
files/file/IP-4-2013.pdf (accessed on December 14, 2013), page 31.

281   Two schools had opened the previous year, so this was the first big group. Source:
Jim Griffin, Email message to the author, February 27, 2019.

282   Bryan C. Hassel, *The Charter School Challenge: Avoiding the Pitfalls, Fulfilling
the Promise* (Washington, DC: Brookings Institution Press, 1999), 124.

283   Jim Griffin, National Charter Schools Hall of Fame Award speech.

284   Ibid.

285   National Alliance for Public Charter Schools Dashboard; 2012-2013 CO student
data accessed on December 14, 2013: http://dashboard.publiccharters.org/dashboard/
students/page/overview/state/CO/year/2013; 2012-2013 CO school data: http://
dashboard.publiccharters.org/dashboard/schools/page/overview/state/CO/year/2013

286   In that first year, the NJ Department of Education received 18 applications and
approved 16. Two charters were appealed and rescinded (then later re-approved); 13 opened
in 1997; three took a planning year and opened in 1998. Source: New Jersey Charter Public
Schools Association, "Facts About New Jersey's Charter Public Schools," February, 2003.

287   Larry Page and Sergey Brin had only just registered Google.com as a domain name.
"Google: About Company History": http://www.google.com/about/company/history/

288   "A Brief History of You Tube": https://sites.google.com/a/pressatgoogle.com/
youtube5year/home/short-story-of-youtube

289   Superior Court of New Jersey, Appellate Division, "In re: Charter School Appeal
of the Greater Brunswick Charter School," Decided: May 17, 1999: http://caselaw.
findlaw.com/nj-superior-court-appellate-division/1035396.html

290   Ken Schlager, "He's No Angel," *New Jersey Monthly*, October 13, 2009: http://njmonthly.com/articles/lifestyle/people/hes-no-angel.html

291   Bill Miller, "D.C. Charter School Principal Indicted in Clash with Reporter," *The Washington Post*, December 20, 1996, A1.

292   Rich Wenning, phone interview with the author, January 27, 2015.

293   Ibid.

294   Ibid.

295   "*60 Minutes* Highlights Failed Marcus Garvey Charter," Center for Education Reform Newsletter, Oct. 29, 1997: https://www.edreform.com/wp-content/uploads/2013/03/60-Minutes-Highlights-Failed-Marcus-Garvey-Charter-10-29-97.pdf

296   Valerie Strauss, "School Board Revokes Marcus Garvey Charter," *The Washington Post*, May 19, 1998, B1.

297   *A National Study of Charter Schools: Second-Year Report*, RPP International, Office of Educational Research and Improvement, U.S. Department of Education, July 1998, 11 (http://eric.ed.gov/?id=ED423612). Authors: Paul Berman, Beryl Nelson, John Ericson, Rebecca Perry, Debra Silverman.

298   William Jefferson Clinton, "State of the Union Address," February 4, 1997: http://www.let.rug.nl/usa/presidents/william-jefferson-clinton/state-of-the-union-1997.php

299   Sarah Tantillo, *Angels and Elbow Grease: A Handbook for Starting a Charter School in New Jersey*, New Jersey Institute for School Innovation: Charter School Resource Center, Second edition, June 1998, 1.

300   Charter school operating expenses are often a fraction of the district's per-pupil allotment. For a comprehensive analysis of facilities-related challenges, see Nelson Smith, "An Accident of History: Breaking the District Monopoly on Public School Facilities," National Alliance for Public Charter Schools, July 2012: http://www.publiccharters.org/publications/accident-history-breaking-district-monopoly-public-school-facilities/

301   Matt Candler, phone interview with the author, June 11, 2012.

302   Terrence E. Deal and Guilbert C. Hentschke [with Kendra Kecker, Christopher Lund, Scot Oschman, and Rebecca Shore], *Adventures of Charter School Creators: Leading from the Ground Up* (Lanham, MD: Scarecrow Press, 2004), 65.

303   Jim Ford, phone interview with the author, May 23, 2012.

304   Bryan C. Hassel and Michelle Godard Terrell, "The Rugged Frontier: A Decade of Public Charter Schools in Arizona," Washington, DC: Progressive Policy Institute, June 2004, 7.

305   Ibid.

306   Ibid, 13. Their sources included: Arizona State Board of Charter Schools (ASBCS), February 2004; Arizona Department of Education, Annual Financial Report, fiscal 2003: http://www.ade.state.az.us/annual report/annualreport2003/Summary/ FY2003AnnRptStateSummaryOfNumAndTypeOfPublicSchools.htm.

307   Ibid, 7. Their source was ASBCS, December 2003.

308   It is not known who first used this term to describe Arizona's charter school initiative, but here is one source: Bryan C. Hassel and Michelle Godard Terrell, "The Rugged Frontier: A Decade of Public Charter Schools in Arizona," Washington, DC: Progressive Policy Institute, June 2004, 6.

309   Jim Collins, *Good to Great: Why Some Companies Make the Leap...and Others Don't* (New York: HarperCollins, 2001).

310   Joanne Jacobs, "Disrupting the Education Monopoly: A Conversation with Reed Hastings," *Education Next*, Winter 2015, Vol. 15., No. 1: http://educationnext.org/ disrupting-the-education-monopoly-reed-hastings-interview/

311   "New York City Schools: A Retrospective with Joel Klein," CUNY Institute for Education Policy, event date: December 12, 2013, posting date: April 3, 2014; overview: http://ciep.hunter.cuny.edu/events/nyc-schools-retrospective-joel-klein/;

transcript: http://ciep.hunter.cuny.edu/new-york-city-schools-a-retrospective-with-joel-klein-transcript/

312   Sarah Childress, "After Michelle Rhee: What Happened Next in D.C.'s Schools," PBS *Frontline*, January 8, 2013: http://www.pbs.org/wgbh/pages/frontline/education/ education-of-michelle-rhee/after-michelle-rhee-what-happened-next-in-d-c-s-schools/

313   Emma Brown, "Judge Throws Out Lawsuit Challenging D.C. School Closures; Plaintiffs Plan Appeal," *The Washington Post,* July 21, 2014: http://www.washingtonpost.com/local/education/judge-throws-out-lawsuit-challenging-dc-school-closures-plaintiffs-plan-appeal/2014/07/21/3f4ad068-10e7-11e4-98ee-daea85133bc9_story.html

314   Peter Meyer, "Newark's Superintendent Rolls Up Her Sleeves and Gets to Work: A Conversation with Cami Anderson," *Education Next*, Winter 2013, Vol. 13, No. 1: http:// educationnext.org/newark's-superintendent-rolls-up-her-sleeves-and-gets-to-work/

315   "Top Ten Mistakes of Charter School Founding Boards," Marci Cornell-Feist: http://www.charterschooltools.org/tools/Top10Mistakes.pdf

316   James Goenner, phone interview with the author, May 1, 2014.

317   "School District Accountability Act," New Jersey School Boards Association: http://www.njsba.org/accountabilityact/

318   Ted Kolderie, phone interview with the author, December 29, 2014.

319   Randi Weingarten of the UFT and Steve Barr of Green Dot, a charter management organization, collaborated on the Green Dot New York Charter School. See "UFT and Green Dot Announce Tentative Contract Agreement for Bronx Charter," United Federation of Teachers press release, June 23, 2009: http://www.uft.org/press-releases/uft-and-green-dot-announce-tentative-contract-agreement-bronx-charter. For information on teacher-led charter schools in Minnesota, see the Education Evolving Website on "Teacher Leadership": http://www.educationevolving.org/tags/teacher-leadership

320   "Diane Ravitch Curriculum Vitae": http://www.dianeravitch.com/vita.html

321   Diane Ravitch and Joseph Viteritti, "A New Vision for City Schools," *National Affairs* (The Public Interest, Winter 1996), 5: http://www.nationalaffairs.com/public_interest/detail/a-new-vision-for-city-schools

322   Diane Ravitch and Joseph Viteritti, eds., *New Schools for a New Century* (New Haven: Yale University Press, 1997).

323   Joel Klein, *Lessons of Hope: How to Fix Our Schools* (New York: HarperCollins, 2014), 65.

324   Ibid., 74. For that op-ed, see: Diane Ravitch and Randi Weingarten, "Public Schools Minus the Public," *New York Times*, March 18, 2004: http://www.nytimes.com/2004/03/18/opinion/public-schools-minus-the-public.html

325   Diane Ravitch, *The Death and Life of the Great American School System: How Testing and Choice Are Undermining Education* (New York: Basic Books, 2010).

326   Debra Viadero, "In New Book, Ravitch Recants Long-Held Beliefs," *Education Week*, March 4, 2010: http://www.edweek.org/ew/articles/2010/03/04/24ravitch_ep.h29.html

327   In 2015, Ravitch was identified as the #1 university-based scholar contributing to public debates about education by the RHSU (Rick Hess Straight Up) Edu-Scholar Public Influence Rankings. SOURCE: Rick Hess, "The 2015 RHSU Edu-Scholar Public Influence Rankings," in "Rick Hess Straight Up" Blog, *Education Week*, January 7, 2015: http://blogs.edweek.org/edweek/rick_hess_straight_up/2015/01/2015_rhsu_edu-scholar_public_influence_rankings.html. Hess notes: "The metrics…recognize university-based scholars in the U.S. who are contributing most substantially to public debates about education. The rankings offer a useful, if imperfect, gauge of the public influence edu-scholars had in 2014. The rubric reflects both a scholar's body of academic work—encompassing the breadth and influence of their scholarship—and their footprint on the public discourse last year."

328   "NAACP Approves Resolution Calling for a Moratorium on Charter Schools," NewsOne, August 2, 2016: http://newsone.com/3497545/naacp-calls-for-charter-school-moratorium/

329   Howard Fuller, "NAACP's Call for K-12 Charter Moratorium Is Wrong," Commentary in *Education Week*, August 31, 2016: http://www.edweek.org/ew/articles/2016/08/31/naacps-call-for-k-12-charter-moratorium-is.html?cmp=eml-enl-eu-news2&mc_cid=97785e9ccd&mc_eid=3b1063d99e

330   Ibid.

331   Center for Research on Education Outcomes (2015), "Urban Charter School Study Report on 41 Regions," Stanford University: http://urbancharters.stanford.edu/download/Urban%20Charter%20School%20Study%20Report%20on%2041%20Regions.pdf

332   Frederick M. Hess, "The Missing Half of School Reform," *National Affairs*, Issue 17, Fall 2013, 19: http://www.nationalaffairs.com/publications/detail/the-missing-half-of-school-reform

333   Frederick M. Hess's bio: http://www.aei.org/author/frederick-m-hess/

334   The 1994 Arizona law also included a State Board for Charter Schools, in addition to the State Board of Education and districts as authorizers. Source: Lisa Graham Keegan, phone interview with the author, August 19, 2014.

335   David Osborne, "Improving Charter School Accountability: The Challenge of Closing Failing Schools," Progressive Policy Institute, June 2012, page 3: http://progressivepolicy.org/wp-content/uploads/2012/06/06.2012-Osborne_Improving-Charter-School-Accountability_The-Challenge-of-Closing-Failing-Schools.pdf

336   Jim Ford, phone interview with the author, May 23, 2012.

337   Hassel and Terrell, "The Rugged Frontier: A Decade of Public Charter Schools in Arizona," 6. Their source was ASBCS, December 2003.

338   Bob Bellafiore, comment to the author at 2013 National Charter Schools Conference, July 2, 2013.

339   Lisa Graham Keegan bio on National Association of Charter School Authorizers Website, accessed on January 28, 2015: http://www.qualitycharters.org/about-nacsa/board-of-directors/lisa-graham-keegan.html. Note: Her term on the NACSA Board was 2012-15, and as of January 28, 2015, she was Board Chair.

340   Lisa Graham Keegan, phone interview with the author, August 19, 2014.

341   Ibid.

342   Ibid.

343   A PPI study noted: "Far too many charter schools are not rated in the state's accountability system because of their small size; the resulting information vacuum makes it impossible to draw conclusions about performance in the charter sector." Bryan C. Hassel and Michelle Godard Terrell, "The Rugged Frontier: A Decade of Public Charter Schools in Arizona," Washington, DC: Progressive Policy Institute, June 2004, 7.

344   Lisa Graham Keegan, phone interview with the author, August 19, 2014.

345   Rachel Proctor May, "New Rules or New Roles for Charter Schools? TEA proposes a crackdown on failing charters, but can it be enforced?" *The Austin Chronicle*, January 14, 2005: http://www.austinchronicle.com/news/2005-01-14/247041/

346   Ibid.

347   Ibid.

348   Theola Labbe, "Board Seeks to Give Away Its Oversight of Charters," *The Washington Post*, November 9, 2006: http://www.washingtonpost.com/wp-dyn/content/article/2006/11/08/AR2006110802402.html

349   Keith L. Alexander, "35-Month Term in Schools Theft, and a Message," *The Washington Post*, November 20, 2007: http://www.washingtonpost.com/wp-dyn/content/article/2007/11/29/AR2007112901284.html

350   Greg Richmond, phone interview with the author, July 16, 2012.

351   Margaret Lin, in-person interview with the author, March 23, 2014, Part I.

352   "Jim Goenner Hall of Fame 2010" video: https://www.youtube.com/watch?v=wWpmja6KG2w

353   James Goenner, phone interview with the author, May 1, 2014, Part I.

354   Goenner ran MAPSA from August 1996 to February 1998, then hired Dan Quisenberry to lead that organization. Source: James Goenner, phone interview with the author, May 1, 2014, Part I.

355   James Goenner, phone interview with the author, May 1, 2014, Part I.

356   Margaret Lin, in-person interview with the author, March 23, 2014, Part I.

357   Alex Medler, phone interview with the author, September 18, 2012.

358   Alex Medler and Joe Nathan. *Charter Schools: What are they up to? A 1995 Survey*. Denver, CO, and Minneapolis, MN: Education Commission of the States and Center for School Change, 1995.

359   Alex Medler, phone interview with the author, September 18, 2012.

360   Margaret Lin, Email message to the author, May 3, 2015.

361   Margaret Lin, in-person interview with the author, November 6, 2016.

362   Greg Richmond, phone interview with the author, July 16, 2012.

363   Ibid.

364   Ibid.

365   Ibid.

366   Malcolm Gladwell, *The Tipping Point: How Little Things Can Make a Big Difference* (New York: Little, Brown, 2000).

367   Greg Richmond, phone interview with the author, July 16, 2012.

368   Ibid.

369   Ibid.

370   Ibid.

371   Charter Friends National Network: http://www.charterfriends.org

372   Margaret Lin, in-person interview with the author, November 6, 2016.

373   Greg Richmond, phone interview with the author, July 16, 2012.

374   Ibid.

375   Ibid.

376   Greg Richmond, letter to the editor, *New York Times*, July 30, 2012: http://www.nytimes.com/2012/07/31/opinion/charter-schools.html

377   Lisa Graham Keegan, Email message to the author, February 6, 2015.

378   See Chapter 5.

379   Don Shalvey, phone interview with the author, December 19, 2013.

380   Ibid.

381   Ibid.

382   "San Carlos Learning Center-History": http://scclc.net/san-carlos-charter-learning-center-history/

383   Don Shalvey, phone interview with the author, December 19, 2013.

384   William J. Clinton: "Remarks in a Roundtable Discussion on Charter Schools at the San Carlos Charter Learning Center in San Carlos, California," September 20, 1997. Online by Gerhard Peters and John T. Woolley, The American Presidency Project: https://www.presidency.ucsb.edu/documents/remarks-roundtable-discussion-charter-schools-the-san-carlos-charter-learning-center-san

385   Ibid.

386   Don Shalvey, phone interview with the author, December 19, 2013.

387   Ibid.

388   "Fellow Profile: Don Shalvey," Aspen Institute Global Leadership Network: http://agln.aspeninstitute.org/fellows/don-shalvey

389   Don Shalvey, phone interview with the author, December 19, 2013.

390   "How Netflix Got Started," Fortune Magazine/CNNMoney.com, January 28, 2009, accessed on August 22, 2016, found at: http://archive.fortune.com/2009/01/27/news/newsmakers/hastings_netflix.fortune/index.htm

391   Don Shalvey, phone interview with the author, December 19, 2013.

392   Steven Baratte, "California's Charter Schools Grow, Over 1300 New and Expanded Charter Schools in 2018," California Charter Schools Association, Nov. 8, 2018: http://www.ccsa.org/blog/2018/11/californias-charter-schools-grow-over-1300-new-and-expanded-charter-schools-open-in-2018.html

393   Don Shalvey, phone interview with the author, December 19, 2013.

394   KIPP National Report Card: https://www.kipp.org/results/national/#question-1:-who-are-our-students (accessed 2-18-19).

395   Jay Mathews, *Work Hard. Be Nice.: How Two Inspired Teachers Created the Most Promising Schools in America* (Chapel Hill, NC: Algonquin Books of Chapel Hill, 2009), 45.

396   Ibid., 49.

397   Ibid., 43-44.

398   Ibid., 46-47.

399   Ibid., 20-21.

400   Ibid., 25-27.

401   Ibid., 27.

402   Ibid., 27.

403   Ibid., 31-35.

404   Ibid., 57.

405   Ibid., 57-58.

406   Ibid., 58-59.

407   Ibid., 59-61.

408   *Making Schools Work with Hedrick Smith*, "School-by-School Reform: KIPP: Mike Feinberg Interview," PBS TV Hedrick Smith Productions, September 2005, transcript: http://www.pbs.org/makingschoolswork/sbs/kipp/feinberg.html

409   Mathews, *Work Hard. Be Nice.*, 61-62. The entire chant is: "You gotta read, baby read./ You gotta read, baby read./ The more you read, the more you know,/ 'Cause knowledge is power,/ Power is money, and/ I want it."

410   Ibid., 71.

411   Ibid., 76-78.

412   Ibid., 98-99.

413   Ibid., 143.

414   Ibid., 159.

415   For more on the Center for Educational Innovation, see: http://www.the-cei.org

416   Seymour Fliegel, phone interview with the author, December 17, 2013.

417   Mathews, *Work Hard. Be Nice.*, 121.

418   Chris Barbic, phone interview with the author, April 22, 2015. All subsequent quotes from Chris Barbic in this chapter are based on this interview unless otherwise noted.

419   Ibid.

420   Ibid.

421   Ibid.

422   Mike Feinberg, phone interview with the author, April 15, 2015.

423   Ibid.

424   Chris Barbic, phone interview with the author, April 22, 2015.

425   Ibid.

426   Ibid.

427   "Innovations in Education: Successful Charter Schools," U.S. Department of Education: https://www2.ed.gov/admins/comm/choice/charter/report_pg16.html

428   2012 Broad Prize for Public Charter Schools: http://www.broadprize.org/publiccharterschools/2012.html

429   "YES Prep Public Schools": http://www.yesprep.org/sites/default/files/downloads/2018-19_external_onepager.pdf (accessed on 2-20-19).

430   Jonas Chartock, "The Politics of Charter School Authorizing: The Case of New York State" (Ph.D. diss., University of Texas at Austin, 2012), 86.

431   Clifford J. Levy with Anemona Hartocollis, "Crew Assails Albany Accord On Opening Charter Schools," *New York Times*, December 19, 1998: http://www.nytimes.com/1998/12/19/nyregion/crew-assails-albany-accord-on-opening-charter-schools.html

432   Seymour Fliegel, phone interview with the author, December 17, 2013.

433   Dave Levin, phone interview with the author, July 29, 2015.

434   Ibid.

435   *60 Minutes* episode Sept. 19, 1999: http://www.imdb.com/title/tt2594894/ This episode was later rebroadcast on August 6, 2000: http://www.imdb.com/title/tt2596416/)

436   Mike Feinberg, phone interview with the author, April 15, 2015.

437   The Pisces Foundation was later renamed the Doris and Donald Fisher Fund.

438   Mathews, *Work Hard. Be Nice.*, 264.

439   Christopher Levenick, "Closing the Gap: The Philanthropic Legacy of Don Fisher," *Philanthropy*, Winter 2010: http://www.philanthropyroundtable.org/topic/excellence_in_philanthropy/closing_the_gap

440   "Mass-producing Excellence: Don Fisher's Strategies for Improving Public Schools Nationwide," *Philanthropy*, July/August 2005: http://www.philanthropyroundtable.org/topic/excellence_in_philanthropy/mass-producing_excellence

441   Mathews, *Work Hard. Be Nice.*, 264.

442   Ibid., 264-266.

443   Ibid., 266.

444   Ibid., 266-267.

445   Mike Feinberg, phone interview with the author, April 15, 2015.

446   Lisa Daggs, phone interview with the author, June 14, 2012.

447   Matt Candler, phone interview with the author, June 11, 2012.

448   Mike Feinberg, phone interview with the author, April 15, 2015.

449   Matt Candler, phone interview with the author, June 11, 2012.

450   Ibid.

451   Mike Feinberg, phone interview with the author, April 15, 2015.

452   "KIPP Houston Public Schools" (accessed on 2-20-19): https://www.kipp.org/wp-content/uploads/report-card-results/2017/region/kipp-houston-public-schools.pdf

453   Mike Feinberg, phone interview with the author, April 15, 2015.

454   Jim Collins, *Good to Great: Why Some Companies Make the Leap...and Others Don't* (New York: HarperCollins, 2001).

455   Mike Feinberg, phone interview with the author, April 15, 2015.

456   Ibid.

457   Ibid.

458   2014 Broad Prize for Public Charter Schools Winner: KIPP Schools: http://www.broadprize.org/publiccharterschools/2014.html

459   "KIPP: National Report Card 2018" (accessed on 2-20-19): https://www.kipp.org/results/national/#question-1:-who-are-our-students

460   Elizabeth Greene, "Building a Better Teacher," *New York Times*, March 2, 2010 (accessed on 8-21-12): http://www.nytimes.com/2010/03/07/magazine/07Teachers-t.html

461   Doug Lemov, *Teach Like a Champion: 49 Techniques That Put Students on the Path to College* (San Francisco: Jossey-Bass, 2010).

462   Doug Lemov, phone interview with the author, November 21, 2012.

463   Ibid. Note: A slightly different version of this story also appears in *Building a Better Teacher* by Elizabeth Green (New York: W.W. Norton, 2014, 151-154).

464   Doug Lemov, phone interview with the author, November 21, 2012.

465   Ibid..

466   Doug later added: "In retrospect, I also now see the unhealthy aspects of the culture I was building by trying to outwork everyone.... There were so many lessons from that school. I think a lot of my career is about taking the learnings from the early mistakes--the school was good but we still made a lot of mistakes--and trying to make sure they happened in the service of longterm good in the world...." Source: Doug Lemov, Email message to the author, February 26, 2019.

467   Doug Lemov, phone interview with the author, November 21, 2012.

468   Ibid.

469   For more information on KIPP Bayview Academy, see: http://www.kippbayarea.org/schools/bayview

470   Scott McCue went on to become Dean at the Charles Sposato Graduate School of Education, which was launched by another Boston charter school founder, Michael Goldstein. See more on Goldstein and Sposato in Chapter 30. McCue's bio (accessed on 2-20-19): http://www.sposatogse.org/people/faculty/

471   Doug Lemov, phone interview with the author, November 21, 2012.

472   Ibid.

473   "No Child Left Behind," *Education Week*, published August 4, 2004; updated September 19, 2011: http://www.edweek.org/ew/issues/no-child-left-behind/

474   Norman Atkins, Email message to the author, May 3, 2015.

475   Norman would do this 14 years later, convincing Jamey to become Newark's Dean for the Relay Graduate School of Education. Source: Jamey Verrilli, Email message to the author, March 3, 2019.

476   For more information on Horace Mann and the Common School, see "Only a Teacher: Schoolhouse Pioneers—Horace Mann," PBS Online: http://www.pbs.org/onlyateacher/horace.html

477   Norman Atkins, phone interview with the author, June 12, 2012.

478   Ibid. Full disclosure: I started teaching English at North Star when they opened the high school. I designed the English curriculum, and I stayed there for seven years.

479   For more on Paul Tudor Jones, see "Inside Philanthropy: Paul Tudor Jones": http://www.insidephilanthropy.com/wall-street-donors/paul-tudor-jones.html

480   At the time, New Jersey did not permit single-sex schools, but New York did.

481   Norman Atkins, phone interview with the author, June 12, 2012.

482   Ibid.

483   For more information on Excellence Boys Charter School, see: http://excellenceboys.uncommonschools.org/excellence-boys/our-school

484   Norman Atkins, phone interview with the author, June 12, 2012.

485   Jim Collins, *Good to Great* (New York: HarperCollins, 2001), chapter 3.

486   Brett Peiser, phone interview with the author, March 27, 2014.

487   Ibid.

488   Ibid.

489   "By the end of the epidemic, there had been six hanging deaths, all young white males, along with forty-eight serious but nonlethal suicide attempts, including five nearly fatal hanging attempts resulting in medical intensive care- unit hospitalizations (all young white males aged fifteen to seventeen), eight intentional overdoses serious enough to require medical hospitalization in addition to psychiatric care, at least thirty-five other hanging, overdose, and other self-injury attempts, and seventy-eight other crisis evaluations resulting in psychiatric hospitalizations among adolescents primarily aged

fifteen to seventeen in this community." For more information on this suicide epidemic in South Boston, which resulted in 6 deaths and more than 200 suicide attempts, see: David M. Cutler, Edward L. Glaeser, and Karen E. Norberg, "Explaining the Rise in Youth Suicide" in *Risky Behavior among Youths: An Economic Analysis*, Jonathan Gruber, ed. Chicago, IL: University of Chicago Press, January 2001, pp. 219-270: http://www.nber.org/chapters/c10690

490   Linda Brown, phone interview with the author, April 25, 2015.

491   Ibid.

492   Ibid.

493   Brett Peiser, phone interview with the author, March 27, 2014.

494   Ibid.

495   Ibid.

496   Ibid.

497   Aine Cryts, "Public Service Innovators -- Brett Peiser (MPP '96) A Hundred Little One Percent Solutions Add Up to a Better Education for South Boston Youth," Harvard Kennedy School, April 5, 2002: http://www.hks.harvard.edu/news-events/news/alumni/public-service-innovators-brett-peiser-mpp-%2296-a-hundred-little-one-percent-solutions-add-up-to-a-better-education-for-south-boston-youth

498   Brett Peiser, phone interview with the author, March 27, 2014.

499   Ibid.

500   Evan Rudall, phone interview with the author, October 13, 2015.

501   Ibid.

502   Ibid.

503   David M. Herszenhorn, "Boston School Shows Cities a Way," *New York Times*, January 31, 1996: http://www.nytimes.com/1996/01/31/us/boston-school-shows-cities-another-wa.html

504   Sarah Kass, "Boston's City on a Hill," *National Affairs*, 125 (Fall 1996): 27-37: http://www.nationalaffairs.com/public_interest/detail/bostons-city-on-a-hill

505   Ibid., 34.

506   Ibid., 27.

507   Evan Rudall, phone interview with the author, October 13, 2015.

508   "John B. King, Jr., Secretary of Education Biography (Archived Information)," U.S. Department of Education, modified March 18, 2016: http://www2.ed.gov/news/staff/bios/king.html?src=hp

509   John King, "Education: The Difference Between Hope And Despair," *The HuffingtonPost.com*, originally posted Jan. 7, 2009, updated Nov. 17, 2011: http://www.huffingtonpost.com/john-king/education-the-difference_b_148855.html

510   Ibid.

511   Ibid.

512   Linda Brown, phone interview with the author, April 25, 2015.

513   Evan Rudall, phone interview with the author, October 13, 2015.

514   Ibid.

515   Ibid.

516   Doug Lemov, phone interview with the author, November 21, 2012.

517   Brett Peiser, phone interview with the author, March 27, 2014.

518   Ibid.

519   Evan Rudall, phone interview with the author, October 13, 2015.

520   John King, "Education: The Difference Between Hope And Despair."

521   Jamey Verrilli, phone interview with the author, March 22, 2019. All other quotes from Verrilli in this chapter are from this interview unless otherwise noted.

522   Norman Atkins, Email message to the author, March 22, 2019.

523   Norman Atkins, phone interview with the author, June 12, 2012.

524   Doug Lemov, phone interview with the author, November 21, 2012.

525   Ibid.

526   Norman Atkins, phone interview with the author, June 12, 2012.

527   Doug Lemov, phone interview with the author, November 21, 2012.

528   Brett Peiser, phone interview with the author, March 27, 2014. Also, Norman Atkins, phone interview with the author, June 12, 2012.

529   Brett Peiser, phone interview with the author, March 27, 2014.

530   Norman Atkins, phone interview with the author, June 12, 2012.

531   Brett Peiser, phone interview with the author, March 27, 2014.

532   "Uncommon Schools Wins 2013 Broad Prize for Public Charter Schools": https://broadfoundation.org/uncommon-schools-wins-2013-broad-prize-public-charter-schools/

533   For more information on Uncommon Schools: http://www.uncommonschools.org/our-schools/all-charter-schools-by-city

534   "Uncommon Schools Academic Results": http://www.uncommonschools.org/results-for-charter-schools

535   Brett Peiser, Email message to the author, March 18, 2019.

536   Progressive Policy Institute, *From Margins to Mainstream: Building a Stronger Charter School Movement* (Washington, D.C.: Progressive Policy Institute, 2003).

537   Tantillo, "Culture Formation in Charter Schools."

538   For more information on New Leaders (which shortened its original name), see: http://www.newleaders.org/about/

539   Linda Brown, phone interview with the author, April 25, 2015.

540   For more information on Lorraine Monroe, see her book *Nothing's Impossible: Leadership Lessons from Inside and Outside the Classroom* (New York: PublicAffairs, 1997).

541   Linda Brown, phone interview with the author, April 25, 2015.

542   Ibid.

543   The Birth of the Building Excellent Schools Fellowship from Conception to the Present: The Real Story," Massachusetts Charter School Resource Center at Pioneer Institute, Nov. 1999-May 2001, internal document provided by Linda Brown.

544   "About Building Excellent Schools: Our Impact": https://buildingexcellentschools.org/about/

545   According to the conference transcript, the conference was funded largely by the Annie E. Casey Foundation, with additional support from the NewSchools Venture Fund, Standard & Poors, and Connections Academy.

546   Andy Rotherham, in-person interview with the author, September 26, 2012.

547   From 1986 to 1993, Bruno Manno worked in the United States Department of Education, holding several senior positions—including Special Assistant to U.S. Secretary of Education Lamar Alexander and Assistant Secretary for Policy and Planning. Bruno V. Manno's bio: http://educationnext.org/author/bmanno/

548   Chester E. Finn, Jr., Bruno V. Manno, and Gregg Vanourek, *Charter Schools in Action: Renewing Public Education* (Princeton: Princeton University Press, 2000). Manno went on to write *Charter Schools at the Crossroads: Predicaments, Paradoxes, and Possibilities* with Chester E. Finn, Jr., and Brandon L. Wright (Cambridge: Harvard Education Press, 2016).

549   Progressive Policy Institute, *From Margins to Mainstream: Building a Stronger Charter School Movement* (Washington, D.C.: Progressive Policy Institute, 2003), Ted Kolderie, 6.

550   Common Core State Standards Initiative, "Development Process": http://www.corestandards.org/about-the-standards/development-process/

551   http://www.corestandards.org/standards-in-your-state/

552   A number of states later withdrew their support for the Common Core Standards, primarily for political reasons. Republican Governors wanted to stand in opposition to Democratic President Barack Obama, whose administration supported the standards. But many withdrew support in name only. Typically they made very minor changes and rebranded the standards with a different name. For examples and more information, see "States Ditch Common Core Name But Keep Common Core Ideas" at ThinkProgress blog, April 29, 2015: https://thinkprogress.org/states-ditch-common-core-name-but-keep-common-core-ideas-1ca02c959218#.1fjzhkyad

553   Progressive Policy Institute, *From Margins to Mainstream: Building a Stronger Charter School Movement* (Washington, D.C.: Progressive Policy Institute, 2003), Eva Moskowitz, 9.

554   Ibid., James A. Peyser, 10-11.

555   Ibid., Wendy Kopp and Abigail Smith, 24-25.

556   Ibid., Jonathan Schnur, Monique Burns, Doug Lemov, and Stefanie Cyr, 26-27.

557   Jon Schnur, Email message to the author, March 21, 2019.

558   Progressive Policy Institute, *From Margins to Mainstream: Building a Stronger Charter School Movement* (Washington, D.C.: Progressive Policy Institute, 2003), Margaret Lin, 43-45.

559   Andy Rotherham, in-person interview with the author, September 26, 2012.

560   Ibid.

561   Ibid.

562   Ibid.

563   Ibid.

564   Ibid.

565   Ibid.

566   Joel Klein, *Lessons of Hope: How to Fix Our Schools* (New York: HarperCollins, 2014), 25.

567   This would create a bit of awkwardness later, when Klein had to ask the Gates Foundation to support his small-school efforts, but apparently Bill Gates forgave him because the Foundation's first gift was $51 million. See: Joel Klein, *Lessons of Hope: How to Fix Our Schools* (New York: HarperCollins, 2014), 104-106.

568   "Paige Joins President Bush for Signing of Historic No Child Left Behind Act of 2001: Bold New Federal Law to Improve Student Achievement," January 8, 2002 USDOE Press Release (Lindsey Kozberg): http://www2.ed.gov/news/pressreleases/2002/01/01082002.html

569   Klein, *Lessons of Hope*, 46-47.

570   Ibid., 48.

571   Ibid., 64.

572   Ibid., 107.

573   Ibid., 104-105.

574   Ibid., 105.

575   Ibid., 113.

576   Ibid., 114.

577   Ibid.

578   David M. Herszenhorn, "City Misses State's Deadline for Replacing School Boards," *New York Times*, October 31, 2003: http://www.nytimes.com/2003/10/31/nyregion/city-misses-state-s-deadline-for-replacing-school-boards.html

579   Klein, *Lessons of Hope*, 115.

580   Ibid., 112.

581   Ibid.

582   Dave Levin, phone interview with the author, July 29, 2015.

583   Dacia Toll, phone interview with the author, August 13, 2012.

584   Ibid.

585   Ibid.

586   Ibid.

587   Stefan Pryor, Commissioner of Education for the State of Connecticut, bio: http://www.sde.ct.gov/sde/lib/sde/pdf/pressroom/commissioner_pryor.pdf

588   Robin Finn, "Go West, Young Man, to the Other Side of the Hudson," *New York Times*, August 4, 2006: http://www.nytimes.com/2006/08/04/nyregion/04lives.html

589   Dacia Toll, phone interview with the author, August 13, 2012.

590   Ibid.

591   Ibid.

592   Ibid.

593   Doug McCurry, phone interview with the author, September 18, 2012.

594   "Achievement First: About Us": https://www.achievementfirst.org/about-us/

595   Dacia Toll, phone interview with the author, August 13, 2012.

596   "Spotlight on Success: Closing the Achievement Gap at Amistad Academy, New Haven," *Connecticut State*

Board of Education, October 9, 2002: http://www.sde.ct.gov/sde/lib/sde/PDF/board/Oct02.pdf

597   Doug McCurry, phone interview with the author, September 18, 2012.

598   Ibid.

599   Dacia Toll, phone interview with the author, August 13, 2012.

600   Marc Michaelson is Regional Superintendent for Achievement First schools. He oversees a portfolio of schools and is responsible for coaching Achievement First principals in the development and implementation of academic programs and school culture initiatives. He previously served as principal of Elm City College Preparatory Middle School. He began his Achievement First career at Amistad Academy Middle School, where he taught reading and history and directed the school's MicroSociety and Encore! programs. While at Amistad Academy, Mr. Michaelson's students consistently showed two to three years of reading growth in one year on state and national assessments: http://www.achievementfirst.org/index.php?id=1315#MarcBio

601   Dacia Toll, phone interview with the author, August 13, 2012.

602   Ibid.

603   Ibid.

604   The description of this meeting is based on phone interviews with Dacia Toll (August 13, 2012) and Doug McCurry (September 18, 2012).

605 "Achievement First: Our Results: New York Results: https://www.achievementfirst.org/how-we-work/our-results/

606 Klein, *Lessons of Hope*, 117.

607 Jon Schroeder, Email message to the author, March 5, 2019.

608 Ibid.

609 Ibid.

610 Jim Ford, phone interview with the author, May 23, 2012. For more on for-profit involvement in Arizona charters, see Chapter 15.

611 Terrence E. Deal and Guilbert C. Hentschke [with Kendra Kecker, Christopher Lund, Scot Oschman, and Rebecca Shore], *Adventures of Charter School Creators: Leading from the Ground Up* (Lanham, MD: Scarecrow Press, 2004), 65.

612 David M. Herszenhorn, "Boston School Shows Cities Another Way," *New York Times*, January 31, 1996: http://www.nytimes.com/1996/01/31/us/boston-school-shows-cities-another-wa.html

613 Geraldine R. Dodge Foundation Annual Report, 1996.

614 Jon Schroeder, confidential memo provided to the author, June 22, 2012.

615 Ibid.

616 Jon Schroeder, Email message to the author, March 5, 2019

617 Jon Schroeder, confidential memo provided to the author, June 22, 2012.

618 Caroline Hendrie, "Alliance Hopes to Serve as Voice for Charter Schools," *Education Week*, November 13, 2002: http://www.edweek.org/ew/articles/2002/11/13/11charter.h22.html

619 Ted Kolderie, *The Split-Screen Strategy: Improvement + Innovation: How to Get Education Changing the Way Successful Systems Change* (Edina, MN: Beaver's Pond Press, 2014), 24.

620 Ibid., 24-25.

621 Caroline Hendrie, "Leaders May Disband New Charter School Organization," *Education Week*, November 5, 2003: http://www.edweek.org/ew/articles/2003/11/05/10charter.h23.html

622 Kolderie, *The Split-Screen Strategy*, 25. Also: Jeanne Allen, Email message to the author, March 20, 2019.

623 Nelson Smith, Email message to the author, March 20, 2019.

624 Nelson Smith, Email message to the author, January 15, 2015.

625   Nelson Smith, phone interview with the author, July 24, 2012.

626   Ibid.

627   Ibid.

628   Kolderie, *The Split-Screen Strategy*, 25-26.

629   National Alliance for Public Charter Schools. (2005). *Renewing the Compact: A Statement by the Task Force on Charter School Quality and Accountability* (p. 10). Washington, DC: Author. Retrieved from http://www.publiccharters.org/data/files/ Publication_docs/Renewing_the_Compact_2005_20110402T222337.pdf.

630   Kolderie, *The Split-Screen Strategy*, 24-25.

631   Jeffrey W. Snyder, "How Old Foundations Differ from New Foundations," *The New Education Philanthropy: Politics, Policy, and Reform*, ed. by Frederick M. Hess and Jeffrey R. Henig (Cambridge, MA: Harvard Education Press, 2015), 40-41. Note: These percentages capture "new foundation" grants; Snyder identifies those "new" foundations as "The Eli and Edythe Broad Foundation, the Michael and Susan Dell Foundation, Bill and Melinda Gates Foundation, Robertson Foundation, and Walton Family Foundation" (34).

632   Walton Family Foundation, January 7, 2016 press release: http://bigstory.ap.org/article/ c882b45fe6a647bfaa03f1f862d02e28/walton-foundation-puts-1-billion-boost-charters

633   Leslie Brody, "Charter Schools Get $250 Million Boost," *Wall Street Journal*, June 28, 2016: http://www.wsj.com/articles/charter-schools-get-250-million-boost-1467086401

634   "From Margins to Mainstream: Building a Stronger Charter School Movement" Abridged Transcripts from the Progressive Policy Institute Charter School Forum, July 17-18, 2003, page 7: http://www.dlc.org/ndol_ ci.cfm?contentid=252250&kaid=110&subid=134

635   Douglas N. Harris, "Good News for New Orleans," *Education Next*, Fall 2015, page 11: http://educationnext.org/files/ednext_XV_4_harris.pdf

636   Leslie Jacobs, phone interview with the author, October 12, 2015.

637   Ibid.

638   Ibid.

639   Ibid.

640   "Paige Joins President Bush for Signing of Historic No Child Left Behind Act of 2001: Bold New Federal Law to Improve Student Achievement," January 8, 2002 USDOE Press Release (Lindsey Kozberg): http://www2.ed.gov/news/ pressreleases/2002/01/01082002.html

641   Leslie Jacobs, phone interview with the author, October 12, 2015.

642   Ibid.

643   "Federal Judge Sentences Two Major Orleans Parish School Board Probe Figures," press release from U.S. Attorney's Office, March 5, 2009: https://www.fbi.gov/neworleans/press-releases/2009/no030509a.htm

644   Leslie Jacobs, Email message to the author, February 15, 2016.

645   Leslie Jacobs, phone interview with the author, October 12, 2015.

646   Ibid.

647   Jed Horne, "New Schools in New Orleans," *Education Next* (Spring 2011), 15-24: http://educationnext.org/files/ednext_20112_Horne.pdf

648   Thomas Toch, "The Big Easy's Grand Experiment," *U.S. News & World Report*, August 18, 2015: http://www.usnews.com/opinion/knowledge-bank/2015/08/18/lessons-from-new-orleans-post-katrina-charter-school-experiment

649   New Orleans Public School Employees Justice update, May 18, 2015: http://www.nopsejustice.com/current_status.htm

650   According to Leslie Jacobs, "academic crisis" was defined by the percentage of failing schools or the percentage of students in failing schools.

651   Leslie Jacobs, phone interview with the author, October 12, 2015.

652   "Recovery School District," Tulane University Cowen Institute for Public Education Initiatives, April 2011, page 2: http://www.coweninstitute.com/wp-content/uploads/2011/04/SPELA-2011-4.pdf

653   Leslie Jacobs, Email message to the author, February 15, 2016.

654   Ibid.

655   Ibid.

656   Jeanne Allen, "The Untold Story of Post-Katrina Ed Reform Informs Progress": http://www.jeanneallen.net/edreform101/the-plight-of-katrinas-children/

657   Letter from Cecil J. Pickard to Margaret Spellings, September 14, 2005: http://www.nopsejustice.com/Letter%20from%20Cecil%20Picard%20to%20Margaret%20Spellings%20Sept%2014%202005.pdf

658   Secretary of Education Margaret Spellings, "Key Policy Letters Signed by the Education Secretary or Deputy Secretary," December 30, 2005: http://www2.ed.gov/policy/elsec/guid/secletter/051230.html

659   Gary Rivlin, *Katrina: After the Flood* (New York: Simon & Schuster, 2015).

660   For more information on what happened in New Orleans after the flood, see Gary Rivlin's *Katrina: After the Flood* (New York: Simon & Schuster, 2015).

661   Sarah Usdin, phone interview with the author, October 6. 2015.

662   "History of FirstLine Schools": http://www.firstlineschools.org/history-of-firstline-schools.html

663   Sarah Usdin, phone interview with the author, October 6. 2015.

664   Nelson Smith, phone interview with the author, October 1, 2015.

665   Ibid.

666   Sarah Usdin, phone interview with the author, October 6. 2015.

667   Ibid.

668   Ibid.

669   Ibid.

670   Ibid.

671   It was later renamed "New Leaders." For more information: http://www.newleaders.org/about/

672   Jon Schnur, Email message to the author, April 18, 2016.

673   Jon Schnur, phone interview with the author, May 14, 2014.

674   Ibid.

675   Matt Candler, phone interview with the author, June 11, 2012.

676   Ibid.

677   Allison Plyer, "Facts for Features: Katrina Impact," The Data Center, August 28, 2015: http://www.datacenterresearch.org/data-resources/katrina/facts-for-impact/

678   Neerav Kingsland, phone interview with the author, October 6, 2015.

679   Ibid.

680   "Sarah Usdin Wins Orleans Parish School Board 3rd District race," *Nola.com/The Times-Picayune*, November 7, 2012: http://www.nola.com/politics/index.ssf/2012/11/sarah_usdin_wins_orleans_paris.html

681   For more information on the work of NSNO, see *New Orleans Style Education Reform: A Guide for Other Cities—Lessons Learned 2004-2010*, by Dana Brinson, Lyria Boast, Bryan C. Hassel, and Neerav Kingsland (Public Impact, January 2012: http://eric.ed.gov/?id=ED539572)

682   Neerav Kingsland, phone interview with the author, October 6, 2015.

683   Ibid.

684   Dana Brinson, Lyria Boast, Bryan C. Hassel, and Neerav Kingsland, *New Orleans Style Education Reform: A Guide for Other Cities—Lessons Learned 2004-2010*, Public Impact, January 2012, page 11: http://eric.ed.gov/?id=ED539572

685   The 93 percent figure was for 2014-15. National Alliance for Public Charter Schools, *A Growing Movement: America's Largest Charter School Communities,* Tenth Annual Edition, November 2015, page 3: http://www.publiccharters.org/publications/enrollment-share-10/

686   National Association of Charter School Authorizers, "NACSA Case Study: Great Expectations in New Orleans," July 2014, page 9: http://conference.publiccharters.org/uploads/NCSC2015/HANDOUTS/KEY_16161367/NewOrleansCaseStudyFINAL0814.pdf

687   Greg Richmond, phone interview with the author, July 16, 2012.

688   Prior to becoming U.S. Secretary of Education in January 2009, Arne Duncan served as the chief executive officer of the Chicago Public Schools (CPS) from June 2001 through December 2008. For more information, see "Arne Duncan, U.S. Secretary of Education--Biography: Archived Information," U.S. Department of Education: http://www2.ed.gov/news/staff/bios/duncan.html

689   Greg Richmond, phone interview with the author, July 16, 2012.

690   Ibid.

691   Ibid.

692   Ibid.

693   National Association of Charter School Authorizers, "NACSA Case Study: Great Expectations in New Orleans," July 2014, page 8: http://conference.publiccharters.org/uploads/NCSC2015/HANDOUTS/KEY_16161367/NewOrleansCaseStudyFINAL0814.pdf

694   Ibid., 14.

695   Ibid.

696   "Recovery School District," Tulane University Cowen Institute for Public Education Initiatives, April 2011, page 2: http://www.coweninstitute.com/wp-content/uploads/2011/04/SPELA-2011-4.pdf

697   Greg Richmond, phone interview with the author, July 16, 2012.

698   Paul Vallas, phone interview with the author, September 3, 2015.

699   Ibid.

700   Ibid.

701   Ibid.

702   Ibid.

703   Adam Nossiter, "Prominent Education Reformer to Lead New Orleans Schools," *The New York Times*, May 5, 2007: http://www.nytimes.com/2007/05/05/us/05orleans.html

704   Paul Vallas, phone interview with the author, September 3, 2015.

705   Ibid.

706   Ibid.

707   Eric W. Robelen, "Desperately Seeking Educators: New Orleans Struggles to Recruit Teachers, Principals," *Education Week*, February 20, 2007: https://www.edweek.org/ew/articles/2007/02/21/24orleans.h26.html

708   Paul Vallas, phone interview with the author, September 3, 2015.

709   Ibid.

710   Ibid.

711   Ibid.

712   Leslie Jacobs, phone interview with the author, October 12, 2015.

713   Paul Vallas, phone interview with the author, September 3, 2015.

714   Ibid.

715   Greg Richmond, Email message to the author, March 3, 2016.

716   Joel Klein, *Lessons of Hope: How to Fix Our Schools* (New York: HarperCollins, 2014), 117.

717   Javier C. Hernandez, "De Blasio Seeks to Halt 3 Charter Schools from Moving into Public Spaces," *New York Times*, Feb. 27, 2014: http://www.nytimes.com/2014/02/28/nyregion/de-blasio-seeks-to-halt-3-charter-schools-from-moving-into-public-spaces.html

718   Daniel Bergner, "The Battle for New York Schools: Eva Moskowitz vs. Mayor Bill de Blasio," *New York Times*, Sept. 3, 2014: http://www.nytimes.com/2014/09/07/magazine/the-battle-for-new-york-schools-eva-moskowitz-vs-mayor-bill-de-blasio.html

719   Jim Epstein, "Sick: NYC's de Blasio Puts Politics Before Poor Kids," ReasonTV, March 6, 2014: https://www.youtube.com/watch?v=KFMmSVbRQN4

720   Daniel Bergner, "The Battle for New York Schools: Eva Moskowitz vs. Mayor Bill de Blasio," *New York Times*, Sept. 3, 2014: http://www.nytimes.com/2014/09/07/magazine/the-battle-for-new-york-schools-eva-moskowitz-vs-mayor-bill-de-blasio.html

721   Richard Whitmire, "Eva Moskowitz Just Got More Toxic," NY Daily News, Aug. 18, 2014: http://www.nydailynews.com/opinion/eva-moskowitz-toxic-article-1.1905381

722   Javier C. Hernandez, "City's Charter Schools Fear Having de Blasio for a Landlord," *New York Times*, Oct. 8, 2013: http://www.nytimes.com/2013/10/09/nyregion/charter-schools-fear-having-de-blasio-for-a-landlord.html

723   Ibid. See also embedded video: Stephen Farrell, "March in Support of Charter Schools," *New York Times*, Oct. 9, 2013: http://nyti.ms/1a96zCj

724   Aaron Short and Carl Campanile, "Cuomo Expresses Support for Charter Schools," *New York Post*, February 5, 2014: http://nypost.com/2014/02/05/cuomo-expresses-support-for-charter-schools/

725   Javier C. Hernandez and Susanne Craig, "Cuomo Played Pivotal Role in Charter School Push," *New York Times*, April 3, 2014: http://www.nytimes.com/2014/04/03/nyregion/cuomo-put-his-weight-behind-charter-school-protections.html

726   Ibid.

727   Javier C. Hernandez, "De Blasio Seeks to Halt 3 Charter Schools from Moving into Public Spaces," *New York Times*, Feb. 27, 2014: http://www.nytimes.com/2014/02/28/nyregion/de-blasio-seeks-to-halt-3-charter-schools-from-moving-into-public-spaces.html

728   Thomas Kaplan, Susanne Craig, and Michael M. Grynbaum, "Cuomo Burnishes His Political Brand, Using de Blasio as His Foil," *New York Times*, March 6, 2014: http://www.nytimes.com/2014/03/06/nyregion/cuomo-burnishes-his-political-brand-using-de-blasio-as-his-foil.html

729   Jim Epstein, "Sick: NYC's de Blasio Puts Politics Before Poor Kids," ReasonTV, March 6, 2014: https://www.youtube.com/watch?v=KFMmSVbRQN4

730   Al Baker and Javier C. Hernandez, "De Blasio and Operator of Charter School Empire Do Battle," *New York Times*, March 4, 2014: http://www.nytimes.com/2014/03/05/nyregion/de-blasio-and-builder-of-charter-school-empire-do-battle.html

731   One of these "Don't Steal Possible" ads can be found at: https://www.youtube.com/channel/UCqnXHa-8PupYXnpJvncohYw

732   Javier C. Hernandez and Susanne Craig, "Cuomo Played Pivotal Role in Charter School Push," *New York Times*, April 3, 2014: http://www.nytimes.com/2014/04/03/nyregion/cuomo-put-his-weight-behind-charter-school-protections.html

733   The New Jersey charter school law, for example, stated: "The Legislature finds and declares that the establishment of charter schools as part of this State's program of public education can assist in promoting comprehensive educational reform by *providing a mechanism for the implementation of a variety of educational approaches which may not be available in the traditional public school classroom.* Specifically, charter schools offer the potential to improve pupil learning; increase for students and parents the educational choices available when selecting the learning environment which they feel may be the most appropriate; *encourage the use of different and innovative learning methods*; establish a new form of accountability for schools; require the measurement of learning outcomes; make the school the unit for educational improvement; and establish new professional opportunities for teachers." [*Italics* mine] (New Jersey Charter School Program Act of 1995, N.J.S.A. 18A:36A, Effective January 1996, Amended November 2000 , Amended August 2011; section cited: 18A:36A-2: http://www.nj.gov/education/chartsch/cspa.htm

734   Ted Kolderie, *The Split-Screen Strategy: Improvement + Innovation: How to Get Education Changing the Way Successful Systems Change* (Edina, MN: Beaver's Pond Press, 2014), 11.

735   Ted Kolderie, "The States Will Have to Withdraw the Exclusive," Public Services Redesign Project, July 1990: http://www.educationevolving.org/pdf/StatesWillHavetoWithdrawtheExclusive.pdf

736   "A Brief History of You Tube": https://sites.google.com/a/pressatgoogle.com/youtube5year/home/short-story-of-youtube

737   *60 Minutes* episode Sept. 19, 1999: http://www.imdb.com/title/tt2594894/ This episode was later rebroadcast on August 6, 2000: http://www.imdb.com/title/tt2596416/)

738   Paul Tough, "What It Takes to Make a Student," *New York Times Magazine*, November 26, 2006: http://www.nytimes.com/2006/11/26/magazine/26tough.html

739   Samuel Casey Carter, *No Excuses: Lessons from 21 High-Performing, High-Poverty Schools* (Washington, DC: The Heritage Foundation, 2000), 1. Note: Foreword by Adam Meyerson cited here: http://files.eric.ed.gov/fulltext/ED440170.pdf

740   Tough, "What It Takes to Make a Student." Note: Abigail and Stephan Thernstrom, *No Excuses: Closing the Racial Gap in Learning* (New York: Simon & Schuster, 2003).

741   Effective July 7, 2004, the name was changed to Government Accountability Office. For more information: http://www.gao.gov/about/history/goodgov.html

742   Title I program is part of the 1965 Elementary and Secondary Education Act. For more information on Title I: http://www2.ed.gov/policy/elsec/leg/esea02/pg1.html

743   Richard Wenning, phone interview with the author, May 29, 2012.

744   "Equality of Educational Opportunity," James S. Coleman et al., U.S. Department of Health, Education, and Welfare, Washington, DC, 1966: http://files.eric.ed.gov/fulltext/ED012275.pdf

745   Richard Wenning, phone interview with the author, May 29, 2012.

746   Ibid.

747   Ibid.

748   United States General Accounting Office, "Charter Schools: New Model for Public Schools Provides Opportunities and Challenges," GAO/HEHS-95-42, January 1995: http://www.gao.gov/assets/230/220825.pdf

749   For more information, see *Reinventing Public Education: How Contracting Can Transform America's Schools* by Paul T. Hill, Lawrence C. Pierce, and James W. Guthrie (Chicago: RAND, 1997).

750   Richard Wenning, Email message to the author, June 12, 2016. (Incidentally, this group conducted the first national analysis of KIPP results for KIPP and incubated and helped launch E.L. Haynes Charter School with Jennie Niles, funding her to become the first charter school founder with New Leaders for New Schools.)

751   Ibid.

752   "Paige Joins President Bush for Signing of Historic No Child Left Behind Act of 2001: Bold New Federal Law to Improve Student Achievement," January 8, 2002 USDOE Press Release (Lindsey Kozberg): http://www2.ed.gov/news/pressreleases/2002/01/01082002.html

753   Richard Wenning, phone interview with the author, January 27, 2015.

754   Jim Griffin, Email message to the author, February 27, 2019.

755   Richard Wenning, phone interview with the author, January 27, 2015.

756   Richard Wenning, Email message to the author, June 12, 2016.

757   The statute established a Technical Advisory Committee comprised of a broad group of stakeholders to explore different growth models, involving key stakeholders in the process so that the tool would be as effective as possible.

758   Richard Wenning, phone interview with the author, January 27, 2015.

759   Richard Wenning, Email message to the author, June 12, 2016.

760   Ibid.

761   Damian Betebenner, Email message to the author, June 28, 2016. "PARCC" is the Partnership for the Assessment of Readiness for College and Careers. For more information: http://parcconline.org/about/states

762   The National Council on Measurement in Education recognized the model with its prestigious annual award for Outstanding Dissemination of Educational Measurement Concepts to the Public. Wenning and Betebenner received this award at the NCME Annual Conference in May 2010 in Denver. In addition, the SchoolView Colorado Growth Model data visualization software was recognized by Adobe Software as a Max Award Finalist at its 2009 Adobe Max convention for innovative uses of Adobe technology.

763   The Student Growth Percentile model, originally known as the Colorado Growth Model, is the most widely used statewide growth model. It yields a normative and criterion-referenced growth percentile and is capable of measuring growth across different assessments. It was developed by the Colorado Department of Education in partnership with the National Center for Improving Educational Assessment and is available to the public on GitHub under a Creative Commons license. Student Growth Percentiles are based on annual statewide assessments of reading, mathematics, and college and career readiness. The corresponding metrics are Median Growth Percentiles, with 50th percentile growth reflecting the normative concept of a year's growth in a year's time; and Adequate Growth Percentiles, which provide a student-level growth target constituting "good enough" growth, and which yield the percentage of students on track to proficiency or on track to college and career readiness.

For more information, see http://www.cde.state.co.us/schoolview.

764   H.R. 1804 Goals 2000: Education America Act, signed January 25, 1994: http://www2.ed.gov/legislation/GOALS2000/TheAct/index.html (Note: Section 102 lists the National Education Goals.)

765   National Commission on Excellence in Education, *A Nation at Risk: The Imperative for Educational Reform* (Report to the Nation and the Secretary of Education, United States Department of Education, April, 1983: http://reagan.procon.org/sourcefiles/a-nation-at-risk-reagan-april-1983.pdf).

766   "Paige Joins President Bush for Signing of Historic No Child Left Behind Act of 2001: Bold New Federal Law to Improve Student Achievement," January 8, 2002 United States Department of Education, Press Release (Lindsey Kozberg): http://www2.ed.gov/news/pressreleases/2002/01/01082002.html

767   For more information about the *No Child Left Behind Act of 2001*: http://www2.ed.gov/policy/elsec/leg/esea02/index.html

768   Paul Bambrick-Santoyo, with foreword by Norman Atkins. *Driven by Data: A Practical Guide to Improve Instruction* (San Francisco: Jossey-Bass, 2010), xvi.

769   Ibid.

770   Jamey Verrilli, phone interview with the author, May 30, 2016.

771   Ibid.

772   Paul Bambrick-Santoyo, with foreword by Norman Atkins. *Driven by Data: A Practical Guide to Improve Instruction* (San Francisco: Jossey-Bass, 2010), xiv-xv.

773   Ibid., xvi.

774   Jamey Verrilli, phone interview with the author, May 30, 2016.

775   Paul Bambrick-Santoyo, with foreword by Norman Atkins. *Driven by Data: A Practical Guide to Improve Instruction* (San Francisco: Jossey-Bass, 2010), xvii.

776   Bambrick-Santoyo's books include: *Leverage Leadership: A Practical Guide to Building Exceptional Schools*, with contributions from Brett Peiser and foreword by Doug Lemov (San Francisco: Jossey-Bass, 2012); *Great Habits, Great Readers: A Practical Guide for K-4 Reading in the Light of Common Core*, co-authored with Aja Settles and Juliana Worrell and foreword by Norman Atkins (San Francisco: Jossey-Bass, 2013); *Get Better Faster: A 90-Day Plan for Coaching New Teachers* with foreword by Jon Saphier (San Francisco: Jossey-Bass, 2016).

777   Editorial Projects in Education Research Center. (2011, July 7). Issues A-Z: Achievement Gap. *Education Week.* Retrieved May 10, 2016 from http://www.edweek. org/ew/issues/achievement-gap/

778   McKinsey & Company, *The Economic Impact of the Achievement Gap in America's Schools, Summary of Findings*, April 2009, page 9: http://mckinseyonsociety. com/the-economic-impact-of-the-achievement-gap-in-americas-schools/

779   Ibid., 5.

780   "New York City Schools: A Retrospective with Joel Klein," CUNY Institute for Education Policy, event date: December 12, 2013, posting date: April 3, 2014; overview found at: http://ciep.hunter.cuny.edu/events/nyc-schools-retrospective-joel-klein/;

transcript: http://ciep.hunter.cuny.edu/new-york-city-schools-a-retrospective-with-joel-klein-transcript/

781   Sarah Childress, "After Michelle Rhee: What Happened Next in D.C.'s Schools," PBS *Frontline*, January 8, 2013: http://www.pbs.org/wgbh/pages/frontline/education/ education-of-michelle-rhee/after-michelle-rhee-what-happened-next-in-d-c-s-schools/

782   Emma Brown, "Judge Throws Out Lawsuit Challenging D.C. School Closures; Plaintiffs Plan Appeal," *The Washington Post,* July 21, 2014: http://www.washingtonpost.com/local/education/judge-throws-out-lawsuit-challenging-dc-school-closures-plaintiffs-plan-appeal/2014/07/21/3f4ad068-10e7-11e4-98ee-daea85133bc9_story.html

783   Peter Meyer, "Newark's Superintendent Rolls Up Her Sleeves and Gets to Work: A Conversation with Cami Anderson," *Education Next*, Winter 2013, Vol. 13, No. 1: http://educationnext.org/newark's-superintendent-rolls-up-her-sleeves-and-gets-to-work/

784   Norman Atkins, phone interview with the author, May 3, 2016.

785   Dave Levin, Email message to the author, July 25, 2016.

786   Jim Collins, *Good to Great: Why Some Companies Make the Leap…and Others Don't* (New York: HarperCollins, 2001).

787   Norman Atkins, phone interview with the author, May 3, 2016.

788   Glenn Collins and Charles V. Bagli, "Out in the Harbor, Still Waiting," *New York Times*, April 25, 2005: http://www.nytimes.com/2005/04/25/nyregion/out-in-the-harbor-still-waiting.html

789   Norman Atkins, phone interview with the author, May 3, 2016.

790   Ibid.

791   Ibid.

792   Ibid.

793   David Steiner, phone interview with the author, March 27, 2015.

794   Norman Atkins, phone interview with the author, May 3, 2016.

795   David Steiner, phone interview with the author, March 27, 2015.

796   Full disclosure: I was one of those early adjuncts, and I helped to design coursework for TeacherU and its successor, Relay Graduate School of Education.

797   David Steiner, phone interview with the author, March 27, 2015.

798   Ibid.

799   Norman Atkins, phone interview with the author, May 3, 2016.

800   Jenny Anderson, "Big Names, Big Wallets, Big Cause" The New York Times, May 4, 2007: http://www.nytimes.com/2007/05/04/business/04insider.html

801   Norman Atkins, phone interview with the author, May 3, 2016.

802   Prior to her work at KIPP, after graduating from Harvard, Hostetter had taught high school English at Deerfield Academy in western Massachusetts and had earned an M.Ed. at Harvard, as well. Hostetter's bio found at: "Deans for Impact: Five Questions for Mayme Hostetter," at http://www.deansforimpact.org/post_Five_questions_for_mayme_hostetter.html

803   Anne McCarley, Email message to the author, March 22, 2019.

804   Norman Atkins, phone interview with the author, May 3, 2016.

805   Ibid.

806   Ibid.

807   Norman Atkins, phone interview with the author, May 3, 2016.

808   The organization that became Bank Street College of Education in 1950 was originally founded in 1916 as the Bureau of Educational Experiments by Lucy Sprague Mitchell and her colleagues. For more information on Bank Street College of Education: https://www.bankstreet.edu/about-bank-street/history/

809   Dave Levin, phone interview with the author, July 29, 2015.

810   Norman Atkins, presentation on March 11, 2013 at Harvard Graduate School of Education Askwith Forum, "Reforming Education Reform: Opportunities for the Next Generation," published on YouTube on April 29, 2013: https://www.youtube.com/watch?t=12&v=jMOryfKuyF8

811   Doug Lemov, phone interview with the author, November 21, 2012.

812   Ibid.

813   Elizabeth Green, *Building a Better Teacher: How Teaching Works (and How to Teach It to Everyone)* (New York: W.W. Norton, 2014), 174.

814   Doug Lemov, phone interview with the author, November 21, 2012.

815   Doug Lemov, *Teach Like a Champion: 49 Techniques That Put Students on the Path to College* (San Francisco: Jossey-Bass, 2010), 3.

816   Green, *Building a Better Teacher*, 173-5.

817   Ibid., 174-9. For more information, see 174-195.

818   Doug Lemov, phone interview with the author, November 21, 2012.

819   Green, *Building a Better Teacher*, 177.

820   Doug Lemov, phone interview with the author, November 21, 2012. Also mentioned in Green, 177.

821   Green, *Building a Better Teacher*, 174-7.

822   Doug Lemov, phone interview with the author, November 21, 2012.

823   Lemov, with foreword by Norman Atkins, *Teach Like a Champion*, xi.

824   Doug Lemov, phone interview with the author, November 21, 2012.

825   Ibid.

826   Green, *Building a Better Teacher*, 188. For more information, see 174-195.

827   Doug Lemov, phone interview with the author, November 21, 2012.

828   Green, *Building a Better Teacher*, 181. For more information, see 174-195.

829   Doug Lemov, phone interview with the author, November 21, 2012.

830   Norman Atkins, phone interview with the author, June 12, 2012.

831   Ibid.

832   Lemov, *Teach Like a Champion*, xv.

833   Norman Atkins, phone interview with the author, June 12, 2012.

834   Publication data provided by Kate Gagno, editor at Jossey-Bass, in an Email to the author, July 15, 2016.

835   *Teach Like a Champion Field Guide: A Practical Guide to Make the 49 Techniques Your Own* (San Francisco: Jossey-Bass, 2012); *Practice Perfect: 42 Rules for Getting Better at Getting Better*, with Erica Woolway and Katie Yezzi (San Francisco: Jossey-Bass, 2012); *Teach Like a Champion 2.0: 62 Techniques That Put Students on the Path to College* (San Francisco: Jossey-Bass, 2015); *Reading Reconsidered: A Practical Guide to Rigorous Literacy Instruction*, with Colleen Driggs and Erica Woolway (San Francisco: Jossey-Bass, 2016).

836   "Relay GSE: Campuses": http://www.relay.edu/campuses

837   "Relay GSE: Impact": https://relay.edu/about-us/impact

838   Mike Goldstein, phone interview with the author, June 26, 2012. The rest of this chapter is based on this interview except where otherwise noted.

839   Evan Rudall, phone interview with the author, October 13, 2015.

840   Michael Goldstein, Email message to the author, August 14, 2016.

841   Ibid.

842   Michael Goldstein, "The Third Floor: Planning the MATCH School's Future," Hauser Center for Nonprofit Organizations, Harvard University, Case Study, September 2003.

843   Ibid., 3-4.

844   Ibid., 4.

845   Ibid., 4-5.

846   Mike Goldstein, phone interview with the author, June 26, 2012.

847   Goldstein, "The Third Floor," 5-6.

848   Ibid., 6.

849   Samuel Casey Carter, *No Excuses: Lessons from 21 High-Performing, High-Poverty Schools* (Washington, DC: The Heritage Foundation, 2000): http://files.eric.ed.gov/fulltext/ED440170.pdf

850   Goldstein, "The Third Floor," 6.

851   For more information about Match Middle School: http://www.matchschool.org/campuses/mms/

852   Goldstein, "The Third Floor," 8.

853   Ibid., 9.

854   Ibid.

855   Joshua M. Beauregard (under the supervision of Katherine K. Merseth), "MATCH Teacher Training (MTT) Program: With the Goal of Producing 'Unusually Effective First-Year Teachers' through Coaching and Student Teaching," Harvard Graduate School of Education, April 2010, 5.

856   Ibid., 6.

857   Michael Goldstein, Email message to the author, August 14, 2016.

858   Beauregard, "MATCH Teacher Training (MTT) Program," 6-7.

859   Ibid., 7. NOTE: The 2007 Bryk reference in Beauregard's paper is not fully cited, but Bryk's draft (requiring permission) can be found at: http://cdn.carnegiefoundation.org/wp-content/uploads/2014/09/DED_paper.pdf

860   Orin Gutlerner's biographical information: http://www.matchschool.org/team/mco/

861   Beauregard, "MATCH Teacher Training (MTT) Program," 3-4.

862   Ibid., 11.

863   Ibid., 16.

864   Ibid., 13.

865   Ibid., 16-27.

866   Michael Goldstein, Email message to the author, March 3, 2019.

867   Ibid.

868   Beauregard, "MATCH Teacher Training (MTT) Program," 28-47.

869   For more on Match Middle School, see: http://www.matchschool.org/campuses/mms/

870   Michael Goldstein, Email message to the author, March 3, 2019.

871   Ibid.

872   Ibid.

873   Beauregard, "MATCH Teacher Training (MTT) Program," 53.

874   Charles Sposato's obituary in *The Westerly Sun*, December 18, 2007: http://www.legacy.com/obituaries/thewesterlysun/obituary.aspx?pid=99817300

875   Match Education/Sposato Graduate School of Education, "Who We Are: Charles Sposato": http://www.sposatogse.org/people/charles-sposato/

876   Match Education/Sposato Graduate School of Education, "A Different Kind of Graduate School: Job Placement and Support": http://www.sposatogse.org/about/job-placement-and-support/

877   Michael Goldstein, Email message to the author, July 23, 2016.

878   Michael Goldstein, Email message to the author, March 3, 2019.

879   For more on the Newark Charter School Fund: http://ncsfund.org/about

880   Michael Goldstein, Email message to the author, July 23, 2016.

881   Stig Leschly, in-person interview with the author, June 27, 2012.

882   Michael Goldstein, Email message to the author, August 26, 2016.

883   Michael Goldstein, Email message to the author, July 23, 2016.

884   Michael Goldstein, Email message to the author, August 26, 2016.

885   Bridge International Academies, "Who We Are: History" history: https://www.bridgeinternationalacademies.com/who-we-are/history/

886   For an overview of Match Education, see "Match Education: About Us": http://www.matcheducation.org/about/overview/

887   To see these resources: Match Minis: https://www.matchminis.org/ and Match Fishtank: https://www.matchfishtank.org/

888   Rebecca David, Kevin Hesla, and Susan Aud Pendergrass, "A Growing Movement: America's Largest Public Charter School Communities," National Alliance for Public Charter Schools, Oct. 2017, 12th Edition: https://www.publiccharters.org/sites/default/files/documents/2017-10/Enrollment_Share_Report_Web_0.pdf

889   Richard Wenning, phone interview with the author, May 29, 2012.

890   Rebecca David, Kevin Hesla, and Susan Aud Pendergrass, "A Growing Movement: America's Largest Public Charter School Communities."

891   Prior to the existence of the Common Core Standards, some states—including New Jersey—featured standards that skipped grades, using language like "By the end of second grade," or "By the end of eighth grade," leaving teachers to wonder what was expected in the grades that weren't mentioned.

892   Jim Griffin, phone interview with the author, July 24, 2012.